CULTURE, PLACE, AND NATURE
Studies in Anthropology and Environment
K. Sivaramakrishnan, Series Editor

Centered in anthropology, the Culture, Place, and Nature series encompasses new interdisciplinary social science research on environmental issues, focusing on the intersection of culture, ecology, and politics in global, national, and local contexts. Contributors to the series view environmental knowledge and issues from the multiple and often conflicting perspectives of various cultural systems.

The Snow Leopard and the Goat

POLITICS OF CONSERVATION
IN THE WESTERN HIMALAYAS

Shafqat Hussain

UNIVERSITY OF WASHINGTON PRESS

Seattle

The Snow Leopard and the Goat was made possible in part by grants from the Donald R. Ellegood International Publications Endowment and the Office of the Dean of the Faculty at Trinity College.

Copyright © 2019 by the University of Washington Press

Composed in Warnock Pro, typeface designed by Robert Slimbach

All rights reserved. No part of this publication may be reproduced or transmitted in any form or by any means, electronic or mechanical, including photocopy, recording, or any information storage or retrieval system, without permission in writing from the publisher.

UNIVERSITY OF WASHINGTON PRESS
uwapress.uw.edu

LIBRARY OF CONGRESS CATALOGING-IN-PUBLICATION DATA ON FILE
LC record available at https://lccn.loc.gov/2019018740
LC ebook record available at https://lccn.loc.gov/2019980120

Cover design by Amanda Weiss
Cover photographs: Snow leopard by Andyworks, iStock. Karakoram mountains panorama, Pakistan, by Patrick Poendl, Shutterstock. Balti herder at Skoyo broq (pasture), Baltistan, northern Pakistan, by Thierry Grobet/Rolex.
Maps by Chris Milan. Pen and ink drawings by Samirah Akhlaq.

The paper used in this publication is acid free and meets the minimum requirements of American National Standard for Information Sciences—Permanence of Paper for Printed Library Materials, ANSI Z39.48–1984.∞

For Musa and Askari

CONTENTS

Foreword by K. Sivaramakrishnan   ix

Preface   xiii

List of Abbreviations   xix

INTRODUCTION   3

CHAPTER ONE
The Snow Leopard and the Goat in Historical Perspective   14

CHAPTER TWO
Producing Wilderness Predators   40

CHAPTER THREE
Human-Wildlife Conflict   58

CHAPTER FOUR
Domesticating Landscapes   89

CHAPTER FIVE
Modernization and the Transactional Mode of Conservation   107

CHAPTER SIX
The Political Economy of the Snow Leopard   129

CONCLUSION   153

Notes   161

References   181

Index   201

FOREWORD

This unusual and important study draws on nearly twenty years of work by the author in snow leopard conservation in northern Pakistan. In 1999 Shafqat Hussain set up Project Snow Leopard, later named the Baltistan Wildlife Conservation and Development Organization (BWCDO). Since then, he also completed a PhD in environmental anthropology, and the subject of his dissertation became the substance of a fine book, *Remoteness and Modernity: Transformation and Continuity in Northern Pakistan* published in 2015. He has dedicated much of his life to snow leopard conservation in consonance with sustaining livelihoods of poor mountain farmers and herders in northern Pakistan.

Wildlife and endangered-species conservation has moved in the last two decades from what has been often characterized as "fortress conservation" (Brockington 2002) or "imposing wilderness" (Neumann 2002) to people-and-parks projects and community-based conservation. This has, in turn, meant that human conflict with wild animals targeted for protection in their prescribed natural habitat has been governed through a system of disciplining conduct and financial incentives. Such inculcation of coexistence as a modern avatar of rural development coupled with nature preservation has been described as a governmental technology (West 2006). This process emanates at times from the complex collaboration between national governments and international conservation organizations.

Nature conservationists make a business of species endangerment and extinction threat, mobilizing economic resources through spectacular accounts of imminent disappearance of charismatic megafauna. But as Hussain shows, local residents of places like the semiarid rangelands of the Baltistan intermountain regions also participate in these calculations and regimes of conduct by coming to rely on the infusions of funds, modern technology, and the care lavished on their lived landscape even if it comes at the price of being seen as human impediments to wildlife flourishing in that territory. He aptly describes this as the political economy of nature conservation as he documents how ordinary people in northern Pakistan experience and shape its contours.

Hussain has traveled annually to the Baltistan region to participate in snow leopard enumeration studies and to investigate programs to provide livestock insurance to farmers and herders in the area. These are programs that he helped devise, and their success has earned him awards and recognition from various organizations, including the National Geographic Society's Emerging Explorer award. A crucial part of this study is thus a fine ethnography of these community-based conservation initiatives, which, as he notes, received mixed reviews from some conservationists even as the snow leopard population stabilized and as the animal was moved from Endangered to the less ominous Vulnerable classification. It is this long-term engagement as both scholar and practitioner that brings hard-won insights to enrich this book and makes it useful to a wide range of readers.

Hussain offers up a careful examination of how categories of wildness and domestication, or threatened versus predatory, are constituted in the modern universe of nature conservation. Rarely do social-scientific studies pay close attention to the history of conservation thought and science with such flair. As other ecologists and historians have observed of elephants, lions, and tigers, the expansion of agriculture and plantations, as well as forest management policies, since the colonial period has created conditions for wild animals to adapt to new forms of proximity with human habitation and their domesticated companion species of animals. Migration patterns and diets changed, as ecologist Raman Sukumar (2011), for instance, strikingly illustrates for the Asian elephant or as Divyabhanusinh Chavda (2008) does for the Asiatic lion.

Hussain shows how changing ideas about ecology and the place of wilderness in desirable natural landscapes combined with patterns of adaptation in historical time. First was the spread of disturbance into habitats and then the introduction of management of those very habitats composed of intermingled wild and domesticated terrain. Snow leopards earned the disfavor of farmers and hunters as they interrupted the pursuit of pastoral livelihoods and game-hunting pastimes in the colonial period. Elusiveness, a biological trait that marked snow leopards as shifty and mysterious in earlier times, later came to be a sign of their scant presence in the landscape, meshing well with the rise of conservation ideologies that linked dispersal and hard-to-sight qualities of snow leopards to an estimate of their dwindling numbers.

The snow leopard, as an actor, is excellent to consider with many big questions that have to do with nature, social production of conservation discourse, and the geopolitics of managing frontier landscapes. This book provides a refreshing, jargon-free account of multispecies mutualism. It reminds us that such mutual relationships are constituted as much in conflict as in accommodation, and that they take shape in a wider politics and economy of global investments in development, conservation, nation-building, and discovering and managing frontiers.

K. SIVARAMAKRISHNAN
Yale University

PREFACE

This book is informed by my involvement with the community-based Project Snow Leopard in the Baltistan region in northern Pakistan. The goal of the project is to resolve farmers' conflicts with this charismatic predator. The research for this book is based on participant-observation work, during which I was engaged in the conservation of snow leopards while also studying those—like myself—who study and work on snow-leopard conservation. This dual role as researcher and practitioner led to some complications. First, although I participated in numerous discussions in person and by email with various people involved in conservation, I am not able to publicly disclose all of my sources. Some of the conversations were in confidence, and in others I was viewed as a fellow conservationist, not as someone writing a book on the subject. I have as far as possible relied on information in the public domain, supporting it with ethnographic data where necessary. Also, I have had to think carefully about the critiques I have made, and how I make them. As a conservationist myself, I am sympathetic to the concerns of others that critiques such as those I present in this book could threaten the support and funding that conservationists rely on. While I stand by those critiques, I recognize that despite our disagreements, we all share fundamentally similar goals.

The ethnographic process gives conservation researchers a sense of reality that supplements scientific knowledge gained through ecological modeling. The ethnographic method requires long-term residence or repeated shorter contacts over a long period of time. Doing ethnography about snow leopard conservation provides insight not only about the snow leopard and its prey but also about people's worldviews, values and belief systems, rituals, and practices related to wildlife and nature. As a practicing conservationist, doing ethnography gives me the opportunity to come face to face with people and develop a sense of empathy with their point of view. Of course, all of these positive aspects of the ethnographic process depend upon the researcher's initial intentions and motivations. This book provides a unique vantage point that combines scholarly insights with practitioner experiences from both an insider's and outsider's perspective.

I personally initiated Project Snow Leopard in 1999 and have been closely involved in its management since then. The initial goal was snow leopard conservation. As I had previously been employed in human development in the region with the Aga Khan Rural Support Program (AKRSP), I was perhaps more attuned to the concerns of local people than if I had arrived with just snow leopard conservation in mind. Initially, it was obvious to me that the local people had no interest in snow leopard conservation. This was an absurd idea to them, given their economic toll as a result of livestock killed by snow leopards.

The main intervention of Project Snow Leopard (now Baltistan Wildlife Conservation and Development Organization or BWCDO) is a community-based livestock insurance program whereby the farmers buy insurance for their livestock against snow leopard predation. Farmers pay a small premium per head of livestock, and when they lose livestock to snow leopard predation, they are compensated. This ongoing project is based on the simple assumption that farmers are not irrational beings who take pleasure in killing snow leopards, but rather that killing snow leopards is the most efficient and logical recourse farmers have for dealing with the threat snow leopards pose to their livelihoods.

The project's approach has aroused a considerable degree of debate within the snow leopard conservation community. Although the idea of compensation as a tool for management has been taken more seriously over time, there was and continues to be significant opposition to the idea. Insurance and compensation programs are now being tried out in the snow leopards' home range countries including India, Nepal, China, Bhutan, and Afghanistan, but even so, this compensation is generally not seen as a long-term solution. This book examines this opposition and analyzes the ideological content to reveal and challenge the assumption that wild and domesticated are two oppositional realms.

I have participated in various symposia, fora, and conferences convened to develop strategies, plans, and reports about snow leopard protection. At these gatherings, I have had the opportunity to interact with a small but vibrant community of snow leopard conservationists in the field with whom I have discussed factors contributing to the human-wildlife conflict and possible solutions to resolve it. Almost all of these conservationists are natural scientists with PhDs in conservation biology, wildlife biology/ecology, and wildlife management.

I have openly and sometimes awkwardly protested that despite the lip service paid by these conservation scientists to the social dimensions of conservation, in these fora I am always the only social scientist present. Because of this lack of input from social sciences, conservation policies fail to give serious thought to the social implications of conservation. A similar omission occurs in other contexts; for example, geographers Andreas Malm and Alf Hornborg (2014, 66) write about the lack of perspective by social scientists in study of the so-called Anthropocene: "Geologists, meteorologists and their colleagues are not necessarily well-equipped to study the sort of things that take place between humans (and perforce between them and the rest of nature), the composition of a rock or the pattern of a jet stream being rather different from such phenomena as world-views, property and power." The problem is not that conservation policies ignore the issue but rather that they address it poorly.[1] For example, conservation scientists generally acknowledge livestock predation and the antipathy of local people toward snow leopards due to this fact, but the solution they typically offer to overcome this antipathy is to develop projects that revive local cultural values that they believe support conversation. Such conventional solutions fail to fully take into account the deep structural factors that cause an unfair distribution of cost and benefits of snow leopard conservation. In some cases conservation organizations have started vaccination programs to decrease livestock losses due to disease so that farmers will be able to tolerate losses due to predation. This is illogical, as any behavioral economist will tell you. Subsistence and risk-averse farmers value gains and losses differently. In fact, making goats healthier via vaccination might actually decrease tolerance for predation because of goats' increased value!

This kind of research is often conducted to understand how conservation objectives can be achieved by tweaking local cultural practices rather than assessing the prospect of success for conservation intervention under current, altered social conditions.

This book would not have been possible without the support, hospitality, and love of the people of Baltistan. They provided me with their valuable time and spent endless hours answering my questions. I particularly cherish the time I spent in the company of Balti herders at high pastures, enjoying their company and learning from their experience of living in harsh mountain environments. I am thankful to the hunters, farmers, storytellers, and village conservation committee members for providing me a perspective about their relationship with the snow leopard, which forms the backbone of my argument in this book. In particular I would like to mention Shakoor Ali of Satpara Lake and Ali Mohammed, Mohammed Issa, and Kazim, who accompanied me on surveys, acting as my porters, guides, friends, and informants.

In Skardu I am thankful to the staff of the Aga Khan Rural Support Program–Baltistan for giving me logistical support during the early years of research. I am particularly indebted to Dr. Jawad Ali, Athar Ali, Dr. Mohammed Abbas, Akbar Raza, Wazir Shabbir, Fida Ali, and Mohammed Nazeer, who provided technical, logistical, and intellectual support to the project. I am also thankful to Khadim Abbas and Jibran Haider of the Gilgit-Baltistan Forest and Wildlife Department who were always willing to provide me with information on wildlife population and status in Baltistan. The local Pakistani army commander in Skardu, General Ehsan Mahmud Khan, provided me with all the logistical and bureaucratic support I needed to do my work.

The following people accompanied me to Baltistan over the past two decades and helped me conduct surveys and interviews, set camera traps, and collect scat samples: Khawar Javed Bhatti, Zille Mohammed, Shariat Hussain, Saadat Hassan, Shaffat Hussain, Ghulam Mehdi Sadpara, Amir Khalid, Qazi Saheb, and Hashim Raza. I am enormously grateful for all of their help over the years.

In New Haven and Hartford, I benefited immensely from the intellectual input of Michael Dove, K. Sivaramakrishnan (Shivi), Jim Scott, Jonathan Padwe, Alder Kelleman, Alark Saxena, Vikvamaditya Thakur, Todd Holmes, Eric Rutkow, Isiah Wilner, Sara Osterhoudt, Shaila Seshia, Vijay Prashad, and James Trostle. Thanks to Alark Saxena and Tim Gregoire, I am grateful to have had the opportunity to present my work at the Yale Himalayan Initiative on several occasions and receive valuable feedback. I am particularly grateful to my undergraduate students in the political ecology and cultural ecology classes that I taught at Trinity College and Lahore University of Management Sciences over the past decade. I have benefited from their enthusiasm and sometimes naïve but always challenging and penetrating questions about my work. I would like to thank the Trinity College Faculty Research Committee for providing research funding for this project. Cathy Shufro's wonderful, sensitive editorial expertise has been essential in helping me formulate a clear and coherent argument. I'd particularly like to thank Dan Brockington for his brutal and frank but extremely helpful comments on the first draft of this book. Lorri Hagman, executive editor at the University of Washington Press, gave brilliant comments on the structure and style of the writing.

I am more grateful than I can explain to Dr. Rodney Jackson of the Snow Leopard Conservancy in Seattle; his encyclopedic knowledge of the snow leopard and willingness to spend hours talking with me about my work has been central to the development of my knowledge and understanding of the issues I discuss in this book. We may not agree on everything, but I would think very differently had I not had the benefit of his wisdom.

Several organizations have provided funding to Project Snow Leopard and Baltistan Wildlife Conservation and Development Organization over the course of twenty years. The UK-based Whitley Fund for Nature provided the initial grant to set up an insurance program in Skoyo, as well as provided ongoing funding for the past ten years. In 2006 Project Snow Leopard won the Rolex Award for Enterprise, which allowed us to expand our work to ten communities. The National Geographic Society has also supported our work through its Emerging Explorer Award and the Big Cat Initiative. BWCDO won the United Nations Development Program Equator Prize in 2017, the first Pakistani community-based organization to win this award. Since 2006 the Snow Leopard Conservancy has been our most loyal supporter, through hard times and good, and all of us at BWCDO are so grateful.

BWCDO would not exist, and this book would not have been written, were it not for the dedication, hard work, and honesty of Ghulam Mohammed, the heart and soul of snow leopard conservation work in Baltistan. He does everything that needs to be done, including running the organization on a tight budget, without waste, and ensuring that every penny goes toward the work on the ground. I am indebted to him. In the end, I would like to thank my lovely wife, Annie Harper, who started this quest with me more than two decades ago when I started searching for the snow leopard. And to our children, Khadija, Musa, and Askari, who are everything to me.

Proceeds from the author's royalties will go toward supporting the mission of SSARA Foundation, a Pakistan-based charity dedicated to justice and peace on earth.

ABBREVIATIONS

AKRSP	Aga Khan Rural Support Program
BWCDO	Baltistan Wildlife Conservation and Development Organization (originally Project Snow Leopard)
GSLEP	Global Snow Leopard and Ecosystem Protection Program (and Plan)
IUCN	International Union for Conservation of Nature
KPK	Khyber-Pukhtunkhwa
SLIMS	Snow Leopard Information Management System
SLN	Snow Leopard Network
SLSS	Snow Leopard Survival Strategy
SLT	Snow Leopard Trust
WCS	Wildlife Conservation Society
WWF	World Wildlife Fund
WWF-PAKISTAN	World Wide Fund for Nature–Pakistan

THE SNOW LEOPARD
AND THE GOAT

Introduction

It was a cold and misty January morning in 2009 in the mountainous Baltistan region of northern Pakistan. I was conducting snow leopard surveys in the Sadpara Valley with my Balti assistant Ali, trying to figure out whether the cats ever travel close to Skardu, a city of sixty thousand people, with an airport, a radio station, and a large military garrison. We climbed up from the eastern end of Sadpara Lake. It started to snow, and the temperature rose a little. At thirteen thousand feet, the air was thin, and the dense silence of the western Himalayas was broken only by the occasional guttering of a *ram chakor*, or Himalayan snowcock. After six hours of placing trail cameras in suitable locations along the way, we reached the summer pasture huts of the local herders, now empty in winter, and stopped to make tea. Ali went to fetch wood, and I sat down to make a stone base for a fire in front of one of the huts. I heard a growl, and the crunch of Ali's footsteps in the snow instantly froze. This was a snow leopard growl: low-pitched and in short intervals. Another growl, and each of us quickly scanned the mountain face in front of us for any signs of movement. The growl was coming from the eastern end of the valley, which climbed to an eighteen-thousand-foot-high rampart obscured by clouds and covered with snow and glaciers. Instead of making tea, we sat silently, crouching in frigid air in front of the hut for the next two hours and focused binoculars intently on the broken ridges in front of us. Unable to sight the snow leopard, we eventually returned to town.

A month later we heard that a snow leopard had killed three goats where we had heard the growl, in Manthal, a village between Skardu and Sadpara Lake. Some villagers saw the attack, which took place in broad daylight. A couple of years before, in a similar attack, a resident of Sadpara Lake village had lost five goats to snow leopard predation. He ran after the snow leopard with his rifle, but he was unable to take a shot. Such attacks on domestic livestock raise an important question: what allows such an elusive and rare cat to live so close to human populations?

Conservation organizations portray snow leopards as an iconic wild species, elusive and ghostlike because of their stealthy nature, who survive on wild and natural prey, including various kinds of mountain goats and sheep, such as ibex, markhor, and blue sheep. But evidence from Pakistan and other parts of the snow leopard's home range shows that in areas where human population is relatively dense, snow leopards rely on human society and prey on domestic livestock. In Pakistan, Nepal, China, India, and Mongolia, between 20 and 70 percent of snow leopard scats contain remains of domestic livestock.[1] Snow leopards kill 2 to 5 percent of a village herd annually throughout its range in what is known as "depredation hotspots," areas of particularly high predation on domestic livestock (Hussain 2000; Oli 1994). The snow leopards' reliance on domestic livestock suggests that in some ways humans have kept snow leopard populations at an "artificially" higher level than the "natural" limit. Viewing human–snow leopard interactions in this way reverses the usual framings that see snow leopards as threatened by human incursions.

Since the 1980s many US-based and international conservation institutions, such as the World Wildlife Fund (WWF) US and International, the Seattle-based Snow Leopard Trust (SLT), the New York–based Wildlife Conservation Society (WCS) and Panthera, and the California-based Snow Leopard Conservancy (SLC) have led the campaign for snow leopard protection globally. Snow leopards have been protected worldwide since the 1970s under various international treaties and national wildlife regulations.[2] They are considered keystone, or indicator, species and play an important role in maintaining the functions of an ecosystem. Their conservation is imperative on ecological grounds, and farmers today are prohibited from killing them. Nonetheless, snow leopards frequently come under attack from local farmers across their range, including in Baltistan, where they are viewed as vermin (Oli, Taylor, and Rogers 1994; Hussain 2000, 2003).[3] Conservation organizations regard this as one of the biggest threats to the global snow leopard population, and while they acknowledge the economic burden of livestock losses borne by local farmers, they implicitly associate this problem with "disturbance" created by the subsistence practices of local farmers whose hunting and herding intrude on the "natural" ecosystem.[4]

Two main documents outline programs and initiatives to protect the snow leopard population globally: the Snow Leopard Survival Strategy (SLSS), which has been periodically revised, and the Global Snow Leopard and Ecosystem Protection Plan (GSLEP).⁵ Both are long documents that are similar in their scope and assessment of the ground conditions. In their classification of causes of threats to snow leopards, they directly implicate local farmers. For example, the SLSS 2003 (McCarthy and Chapron 2003, 29) states, "Perhaps the most commonly observed form of habitat alteration within snow leopard range is more subtle, yet still potentially destructive, and comes in the form of livestock grazing and disturbance by their human owners." The revised version of SLSS 2014 describes the problem: "Although relatively few humans live in snow leopard habitat, their use of the land is becoming increasingly pervasive, resulting in escalating conflicts between conservation and livestock production even within protected areas" (SLN 2014, 33).

The SLSS 2003 states, "Greatest [livestock] losses occur where native prey species (ibex, blue sheep, argali, and marmot) have been reduced, but are also more serious where herders employ poor guarding practices" (McCarthy and Chapron 2003, 30). The revised version of SLSS 2014 states, "Complacent guarding, poorly constructed night-time pens, favorable stalking cover and insufficient wild prey are cited as the primary factors contributing to livestock depredation" (SLN 2014, 40). This kind of discourse has a deep genealogy and to a certain extent tells us how little things have changed. It can be traced back to some of the earliest writings on the snow leopard. For example, Helen Freeman, founder of the International Snow Leopard Trust, wrote decades before the SLSS and GSLEP were published: "The numbers of snow leopards in the wild are decreasing at an alarming rate because of direct annihilation by humans, increased usage of fragile mountain meadows for the grazing of domestic stock, and the declining populations of wild ungulates" (1983, 2). In these documents local herders and their herding techniques are presented as the root cause of the most serious threats to snow leopards, so most efforts by conservation organizations have been targeted at creating boundaries between farmers and snow leopards.

The SLSS and GSLEP construct a particular narrative of the snow leopard–farmer conflict and the challenge that it poses. This narrative claims that snow leopards attack domestic livestock only when herders take them into snow leopard habitat or only when snow leopards' natural prey are depleted because of overhunting, mainly by farmers.⁶ As a consequence of this framing of the causes of livestock predation (that is, due to human-induced disturbances), conservation institutions advocate policies that limit those disturbances. They call for decreased access to snow leopard habitat by local herders and modifications and bans on local subsistence practices, including hunting, to keep snow leopards in a state of undisturbed nature. They call for the establishment of more protected areas and better management of existing ones.

Recommendations to establish protected areas reflect the core principles of modern conservation theory and practice, which have their origin in the nineteenth-century nature conservation movement in the United States.[7] In the 1970s this approach also became the dominant paradigm for conservation in Pakistan, Nepal, and India. Conservation today continues to carry the intellectual baggage of the earlier era, perpetuating the core idea that nature and culture are two separate and autonomous realms. This worldview privileges the idea of the wild and simultaneously denigrates the idea of the domesticated, seen as representing an inferior form of nature (Milton, 2000; Knight, 2000). The implicit logic behind most wildlife conservation policies is that the only part of nature worth protecting is that which is wild and untamed.[8] This conception of the wild implies that because nature is separate from human society natural species are (and should be) independent of human control, autonomous, and spontaneous in action.

In conservation literature on snow leopards, their wildness is sullied by contact with humans. But this image of snow leopards as completely wild, along with protective attitudes toward them, becomes difficult to maintain in light of evidence from the field. An often overlooked fact in literature on snow leopards is that they kill domestic livestock even when their natural prey is not depleted (Wegge, Shrestha, and Flagstad 2012; Suryawanshi et al. 2013). Evidence from studies on other carnivores suggests the same pattern (Odden et al. 1999; Knight, 2000, 6). It seems snow leopards like to hang around human populations.

In contrast with the conservationists' view that snow leopards are wild animals and farmers' own behavior and practices are responsible for predation of their livestock, Balti farmers see the snow leopard as a wild animal that is out of their control and whose agency is independent of theirs.[9] The Baltis do not consider their own behavior, such as lax herding techniques, to be responsible for snow leopard predation of their livestock. Rather they place that agency squarely on the natural world of wild animals.[10] In Balti culture, a snow leopard is considered, among other things, a quintessential predator, because of its prey on domestic livestock, and predatory human rulers are called "snow leopards" because of their mode of rule (Emerson 1983, 421).

Balti herders learn from their elders what to do with predators of their domestic livestock, based on their collective and intergenerational experience. Snow leopards feature in Balti daily discourse as a species of danger.

Snow leopard in the rocks

Paw prints that to a conservationist appear as indexical of snow leopard habitat and density represent something else to a Balti farmer—a lurking threat that disturbs the normal flow of everyday village life.

The Baltis, like the conservationists, see wildness as the essential agentive quality of snow leopards, but they do not see wildness as exclusively belonging to the realm of wild animals. Rather, it is a quality that can also be possessed by domesticated animals.[11] For example, many Balti herders told me about a rare but commonly believed phenomenon in which a timid domestic goat becomes *rashore*, that is, it runs away and becomes part of a wild ibex herd. Likewise, the snow leopard is a wild predator, but one that regularly crosses the line between wild/nature and domesticated/culture when it kills domestic goats. The Baltis see predation of their livestock by snow leopards as unwelcome and economically damaging, a kind of occupational hazard. While they don't see it as unnatural, Balti farmers do become enraged when snow leopards come down into their village and engage in "surplus killing."[12] In their view, it is the snow leopard that creates "disturbance" by crossing its natural boundary to enter society; hence the animal is in a sense "asking" for retaliation.[13]

POLITICAL ECONOMY OF SNOW LEOPARD CONSERVATION

Social scientists, as opposed to conservation scientists, generally see conservation as a clash of cultural values and struggles over meaning. They look at the ways in which human societies ascribe meanings and values to certain species of wildlife and how they go about defending those values (Herda-Rapp and Goedeke 2005).[14] Many social science critiques show that conservation is increasingly becoming a site of conflict between the ideologies and cultural views of international conservation organizations and their donors, and those of the people on whom conservation is imposed (Neumann 2002; West, Igoe, and Brockington 2006). Even within a country, this cultural divide can often be seen in divisions between different classes regarding the aesthetic and social value they attach to nature. For example, studies have shown that in the United States, rich, urban, and well-educated segments of society hold more romantic attitudes toward the environment, whereas rural, poorer, and less-educated segments show more utilitarian ones (Guha 2003; Kellert et al. 1996). Clashes occur when resources found in rural areas become the focus of care of the urban rich. This class-based cultural analysis also applies internationally in developing countries (Lowe, 2006).

A study of human-wildlife conflict found that "environmental conflicts implicate consciousness and social interaction, are intensely political, and are always linked to power relationships and values" and that modern conservation is largely based on Western cultural values, social perceptions, and scientific methods (Peterson et al. 2010, 76). This influence of ideology on conservation decisions and actions, and the accompanying conflict, is evident in the case of the protection of large carnivores and predators. Seen as threatened and as the last remaining icons of wild nature, predators are held in great awe and value by most Western conservationists, invoking sentimental, nostalgic, and symbolic value. But the same predators often are held in an almost totally opposite structure of feeling by people who live close to them. In her study of tiger conservation in the Sunderban region of Bengal, India, the anthropologist Annu Jalais (2011) describes how different visions of a single animal can prevail side by side—that of the conservationist and that of the villagers.[15] In Baltistan I have encountered numerous situations in which villagers openly demanded that since people in New York and London want to protect the snow leopards, they should take the animals away with them. Similar conflicts can be seen in the reintroduction efforts of the wolf, the iconic predator of the American West (Lopez [1978] 2004; Coleman, 2006).[16]

Based on an ethnographic study that spans more than fifteen years, in this book I argue that snow leopard conservation not only entails a struggle over whose vision of nature prevails but addresses the maintenance of positions of power through creation of scientific expertise and access to financial resources for wildlife conservation. There is a certain political economy of conservation that is at work here in which farmers are sustaining the snow leopards ecologically—by feeding them with their livestock. Through this, they are also sustaining the snow leopard conservation industry because ongoing livestock predation sustains the rhetoric and spectacle of conservation organizations that suggests that wild snow leopards are threatened by human activity. Conservation organizations are kept afloat by their misreading of the social ecology and because they are able to convince a concerned and wealthy Western public that they understand and can deal with the threats to wild snow leopards. Conservation rhetoric about the snow leopard's decline portrays the animal both as a particular natural object and as a commodity in the cultural and technical economy of international conservation, tied to the production and sustenance of institutional funding.

Viewing snow leopard conservation through a political economy lens shows that the production of scientific practice and knowledge is not as apolitical or objective as it is believed to be. Rather, it often involves value judgments informed by nonscientific goals. Production of knowledge about nature is not only about certain historical views of nature and its transformation but is tied to issues of control, influence, and, money, or political economy (Robbins 2012).[17]

In September 2017 the International Union for Conservation of Nature (IUCN) Red List of Threatened Species decided to down-list the snow leopard from Endangered to Vulnerable status. The decision, ostensibly a purely scientific exercise and based on scientific knowledge, sparked intense debate and political wrangling within snow leopard conservation institutions. Some snow leopard organizations and countries were concerned that if the status of the snow leopard fell below the Endangered status, less funding would be available for their work, especially after the launch of the new initiative, Global Snow Leopard and Ecosystem Protection Program (GSLEP), with World Bank funding. The group that opposed the down-listing challenged the decision, stating that there was not enough evidence to support this move. Others thought that the IUCN should follow the current state of scientific knowledge objectively and not become subservient to funding expediency.[18]

The political economy of snow leopard conservation presented here shows that the fates of institutions, farmers, snow leopards, goats, and conservationists are tied together in a complex but recognizable way: while conservation institutions need the snow leopard to survive in the wild so that they can generate funding, they also need it to remain "threatened."[19] The specter of a world without snow leopards also engenders political and cultural support that allows conservation organizations to implement a conservation approach (variously named as reserve or conservation landscape) in which local people are asked to modify their practices and/or curtail their access to their traditional lands. This specter is used in "spectacles" by conservation organizations that sustain the political economy of conservation and take many forms and shapes. Such a spectacle is not merely an assemblage of images and texts that people consume vicariously, but it is what mediates the relationship between people and nature.

Conservation NGOs engage in spectacular accumulation, through which images of panoramic landscapes and exotic people and animals are used to communicate urgent problems in desperate need of the timely solutions that these organizations claim to be uniquely qualified to offer. They present an audience of potential supporters with compelling virtual opportunities (problems that need to be solved) and the resources necessary to realize these opportunities, provided they make the necessary investment (a generous gift). These productions influence individuals to provide financial support for conservation interventions, while presenting the only reality of conservation interventions that most will ever know (Igoe 2010, 378).[20]

One example is a video advertisement sponsored by the Snow Leopard Trust that played on a giant screen at New York City's iconic Times Square in early 2017. Including dramatic images of the snow leopard, the ad read, "One snow leopard is killed every day"; it asked passersby to contact the Snow Leopard Trust to find out how to help—that is, to give money. Spectacles such as these turn the object of concern into a virtual commodity to be consumed, a type of commodification made possible by the condition of total alienation created by late capitalist modernity (Igoe 2010). The emergence of the spectacle of nature is a process that has gone hand in hand with the commodification of nature and natural areas and expanding ties between conservation and corporations (Brockington, Duffy, and Igoe 2008; Igoe and Brockington 2007).

People who are moved by the spectacle of snow leopards under threat enter into an exchange relationship when they give donations. What the donor gets in return is a feeling of satisfaction or fulfillment for doing something good for nature. Conservation organizations often arrange for donors to regularly receive photos, news, and social media messages about how their donation is being used, providing the donor with an opportunity to continue consuming the spectacle and to create an ongoing relationship with nature.

When I first became involved in snow leopard conservation two decades ago, the main focus of research was to assess how many snow leopards were left in the world. At that time the Snow Leopard Management Information System, or SLIMS, was developed, providing a standardized survey methodology for reporting and recording snow leopard density across its entire range. In 2016 snow leopard conservationists embarked on a new exercise known as PAWS, Population Assessment of World Snow Leopards. Different names, but the same goal: to count how many snow leopards are left. Despite years of research, snow leopard numbers remain as elusive as they were twenty years ago, and the tone and tenor of many research papers on snow leopards is also the same. One may ask what happened to the twenty years of efforts of all those scientists and how we can be sure that in 2040 we will not still be doing another counting exercise. But this, perhaps, is the wrong question. The real question is not why snow leopard conservation institutions have not been able to come up with a reliable estimate of the global snow leopard population, but rather, what purpose does the perpetual quest for reliable numbers serve for institutional funding and keeping the conservation industry alive?

The power of the snow leopard as commodity depends on its status of continually being under threat. The spectacle is not simply that of the snow leopard in the wild; it is that of the threatened snow leopard in the wild. At the heart of the spectacle, then, is a persistent specter of snow leopards becoming extinct; this specter has to be first conjured and imagined before the snow leopard can effectively become a commodity that generates money. The specter of the world without snow leopards is created through a persistent focus on the need to count how many are left (implying that there were more in the past, but those numbers have dwindled over time). This creates panic, guilt, and anxiety about the plight of the snow leopard, which can be resolved by consuming—making a purchase or donation. The constant need to count gives the anxious donor a sense of urgency, a sense that time is running out, and that more money must be spent to verify and stabilize the numbers.

Mystification or obfuscation occludes the relationship between the snow leopard and the farmer. The calls for more accurate counts and the appeals for better protection elide the fact that snow leopard conservation incurs economic, labor, and psychological costs to the farmers who actually sustain the snow leopards. As with conventional commodities, where the social conditions of production are hidden from consumers, the social relations of the production (continued existence) of the snow leopard are hidden from the donors. Donors do not know how local farmers are literally producing the snow leopard by feeding them their goats; these goats are the products of farmers' labor, which has now become part of the snow leopard. Donors continue to donate and consume the commodity, without understanding how that commodity is produced.

Throughout the home range of the snow leopard there is no official policy to address the negative impact of predation on farmers' livelihoods. Rather, farmers are expected to provide a kind of subsidy to the snow leopards directly by "feeding" them their domestic livestock. In this scenario, the benefit of this subsidy—that the farmers provide—goes to conservation NGOs, urban elites, and state agencies in the form of aesthetic and ethical satisfaction, professional achievement and funding, and social and political power and prestige. Based on this asymmetrical cost-benefit relationship, some scholars have argued that the human-wildlife conflict should be seen as a conflict between two human groups: farmers and conservationists (Knight 2000). In the case of the snow leopard, the latter tries to force its vision of snow leopards onto the local community without due consideration of the economic cost to the farmers of such an imposition (but perhaps intense consideration of the economic implications for their own institutions and profession).

THE STUDY AREA

Baltistan is a part of the specially administered area called Gilgit-Baltistan in the north and northeastern region of Pakistan. Baltistan is mentioned in the twelfth-century Sanskrit chronicle *Rajatarangini* and in sixteenth-century Muslim sources, such as *Tārīkh-e-Rāshidī* by Mirza Haider Tughalt, who described the region as Boloristan and as Tibet-e-Khurd, or "Little Tibet" because of its ethnic and cultural affiliation with Tibetan culture (Dani 1989; Jettmar 2002). The region came under the expanding Tibetan Empire in the eighth century after a series of attacks. As in Gilgit, the rulers of Baltistan at this time paid nominal allegiance to the Tang dynasty of China. Soon after their fall to the invading Tibetan army, the local Patola Shahi dynasty of Baltistan entered into an alliance with the Tibetans. The Balti state was to rule Gilgit again in the sixteenth and the seventeenth centuries under the local Maqpoon dynasty. In the sixteenth century, the ruler of Skardu, Ali Sher Anchan, established a large state bordering Afghanistan to the west and Tibet to the east.

An animistic religion called Bon prevailed here alongside Buddhism until the sixteenth century, when Islam spread to the area. In 1842 the region was conquered by one of the generals of Ranjeet Singh, the maharajah of Punjab at the time, and Skardu Tehsil became part of the Ladakh district of the state of Jammu, part of Punjab. In the British colonial period during the late nineteenth and the first half of the twentieth centuries, it became a playground for adventurers, sportsmen, and "great gamers," who went there looking for the unique trophies and the best thrill of big game hunting. Despite being geographically isolated, the region was a main conduit through which western Tibet connected with central Asia. The region has thus been an important crossroads of culture, empire, and history (Hussain 2015; Mock 2018). But today, due to the conflict between Pakistan and India stemming from Partition in 1947, the line of control between the two countries, which passes through the region, is a closed and hostile border. All traffic from the south via the valley of Kashmir over the Deosai Plains and through Kargil and Gultari is prohibited. There is no way to go beyond Baltistan if one is traveling east and south from Gilgit.

Geographically, Baltistan is one of the most spectacular regions in the world. Tucked between the Great Himalayan range to the south and west and the gigantic Karakoram to the north and west, this intermountain region has one of the highest concentrations of the loftiest mountains in the world. The upper Indus valleys, which are green, give way to more jagged and arid conditions, an "oases ecology" (Filippi 1915). In the immense barrenness of towering, rocky peaks are human settlements.

Baltistan is not far from Gilgit and Hunza, areas that have been more thoroughly studied by anthropologists and social scientists; but unlike those areas, which fall on the main road linking south and central Asia, Baltistan is a cul-de-sac.

Various conservation and development organizations have been working in Baltistan for the last thirty years. Under the project for which I worked, the government started a community-based trophy hunting program where the village received the equivalent of around US$3,000 for each ibex hunt that took place. These development and conservation organizations have brought about great transformations in the social and institutional landscape of Baltistan. Through their everyday interactions with the local farmers, conservation and development institutions have created a "political community" (Chatterjee 2004) that is able to make effective demands for rights and resources on various hard and soft powers. Because of the work of these institutions, local Balti farmers have developed a new form of rationality that is based on an ethics informed by market transactions: they see conservation and development institutions as sources of money and resources for the village.

CHAPTER ONE

The Snow Leopard and the Goat in Historical Perspective

WITH increased trade and colonization in the nineteenth century, the remote and isolated snow leopard country of central and south Asia was further integrated into the lowland valleys and the world economy. The demand grew for wild snow leopard specimens by many European zoos in the second half of the nineteenth century, catalyzing the systematic capture of wild snow leopards in Russia and China. Demand also grew for snow leopard pelts as collector's items among the affluent classes in Europe.

In the Baltistan region during the colonial era, British sportsmen shot snow leopards to "bag" perhaps the most elusive trophy of them all and to protect game species such as ibex and markhor. The representations of the snow leopard that emerged during the second half of the nineteenth and the first decade of the twentieth centuries are quite different from those today. This is despite the fact that there is similarity between the ecological conditions and experiences described by the British sportsmen and what a twenty-first-century snow leopard conservationist might experience in similar ecological habitats across Baltistan. Today, snow leopards are seen as a threatened species whose numbers are thought to be dwindling; back in the nineteenth century, they were seen as vermin to be killed. The sportsmen of the nineteenth century expressed their frustration at not obtaining the snow leopard trophy because of the animal's elusive nature. Today, this quality frustrates conservationists who express their difficulty in studying snow leopards in the wild and, in an era of increased environmental awareness, produces it as a species under threat.

This new interpretation of preexisting ecological reality is couched in what I call the standard conservation narrative.[1] According to that narrative, certain wildlife species, especially charismatic megafauna such as large carnivores, were once abundant but have become rare in the recent past. The main reason for this decline in wildlife population, according to this account, is purported increased human encroachment on wildlife habitats and systematic eradication of wildlife. Capsulated in a concrete form, this narrative would appear as the criteria for the categorization of wild species according to their level of threat of extinction. For example, the International Union for Conservation of Nature (IUCN) maintains the Red List of Threatened Species. This list categorizes wild animals according to their danger of going extinct in the wild. The criteria used for categorizing a species as Critically Endangered (the highest threat level) or Endangered, or Vulnerable is based on a set of indicators. These indicators collectively represent a story, a narrative, about the decline. For a species to be listed as Endangered, its population must have declined by 20 percent in the last decade or over two generations. The criteria impose its own narrative on the species' status as it is placed on a scale of threat of extinction. The snow leopard was listed as Endangered for four decades beginning in 1973. This means that according to the most respected scientific institution in the world, the global snow leopard population had been steadily declining. It is this trend of decline that becomes a spectacle that is consumed by society and generates exchange value. It is to arrest the decline of snow leopard population and fulfill our global responsibility to avert extinction, perhaps also out of guilt, that affluent people donate to conservation institutions.

This standard conservation narrative, simply put, is a story of perpetual decline and degradation of nature, especially since the Industrial Revolution.[2] It was in the second half of the twentieth century that this narrative became truly global and popular. The birth of international conservation institutions, organizations, treaties, and legislation further universalized this narrative. The most pertinent example of the standard conservation narrative is the Theory of Himalayan Degradation, a dubious prediction in the 1970s, according to which the rate of erosion of the central Himalayas due to deforestation was so severe that in a few years the entire soil of the country of Nepal might be washed away and into the Bay of Bengal (Eckholm 1976). A dispassionate analysis of the theory shows there was simply not enough data to support drastic environmental losses and a fair amount of uncertainty existed in terms of any definitive future trends.

Today, many conservation experts, institutions, and policy makers assert that the snow leopard population has been steadily declining due to encroachment by herders and their livestock in its habitat.[3] While this standard conservation narrative may accurately represent the trend in population and range of some other large megafauna in Asia, such as lions and cheetahs, it is my contention that it does not apply in the case of the snow leopard. The standard conservation narrative is guilty of what I call "ecological presentism" that is, uncritically accepting current dominant attitudes and values toward wildlife and applying them to past experiences and reality. Snow leopard population may have undergone serious decline in the former states of the USSR (Koshkarev 1994) after its disintegration, but there are indications that this trend has now stopped. There are no firm ecological bases upon which we can chart a trend in snow leopard population over the last century, yet snow leopards had been categorized as under threat of extinction.

Contemporary understanding of the snow leopard's population status and its historical trend and conflict with local farmers in Baltistan is questionable. Was the snow leopard once abundant, say, in the second half of the nineteenth century? Has its population now declined sharply, mainly due to human action?[4] Did the animal start killing livestock as a response to a decrease in its natural prey of wild goats and sheep, which had been hunted by farmers? Attention to the disturbance side of human interaction with the snow leopard has obfuscated the fact that the snow leopard population may be supported by human presence.

Information on definitive trends in snow leopard population over the last century in our region of focus is lacking, but an alternative interpretation or a competing narrative could be that the snow leopard's natural rareness and elusiveness renders it a species that has managed to survive with humans for some time. This counter-narrative also problematizes that reality of human encroachment on wild habit as a source of conflict.

DISTRIBUTION, STATUS, AND ECOLOGY OF SNOW LEOPARDS

Snow leopards (*Panthera uncia*; Schreber 1775) are widely but thinly distributed throughout the mountains of Central and South Asia. Here, snow leopards have coexisted with humans since the Pleistocene. This region, with its unique flora and human cultural diversity, includes the Altay, Tien Shan, Kun Lun, Pamir, Hindu Kush, Karakoram, and Himalaya mountain ranges and the countries of Afghanistan, Bhutan, China, India, Kyrgyzstan, Kazakhstan, Mongolia, Nepal, Pakistan, Tajikistan, and Uzbekistan. Snow leopards are also found in Russian Siberia.

Despite their rarity and elusive nature, snow leopards have always been entangled with human societies. Rock drawings of snow leopards dating back to the Neolithic and Bronze Age (Smirnov, Sokolov, and Zyryanov 1990, 10)

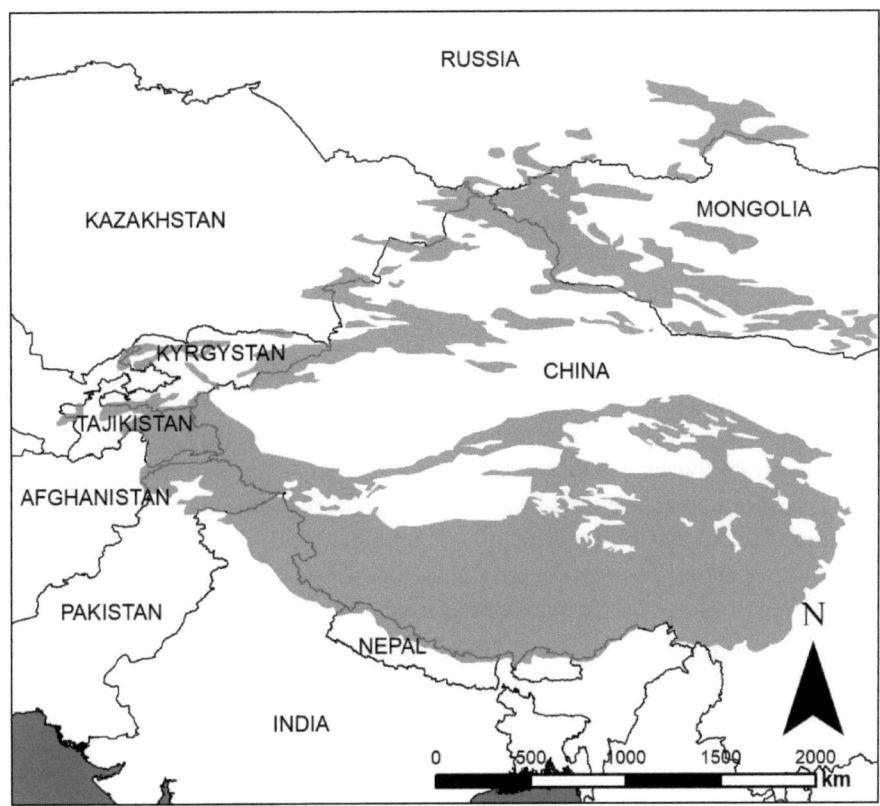

The shaded areas indicate global snow leopard habitat.

are found in southern Siberia. Rock drawings of snow leopard in western Tibet date back to the Iron Age, and in Kyrgyzstan there is a rock drawing of a tamed snow leopard used by nomads for hunting.[5] These carvings may reflect the ancient beliefs of the inhabitants of these mountain communities about the snow leopard as, perhaps, an archetypical hunter. Snow leopard pelts were not used as trade articles, but local Siberian people used them to pay taxes to the Chinese (Smirnov, Sokolov, and Zyryanov 1990, 10).

It is not clear what these rock carvings tell us about the historic status of snow leopard populations, but they clearly complicate the image of the snow leopard as a creature of wilderness. It seems that the ancient humans of central and south Asia had socialized snow leopards into a specific cultural system of meaning. Given the low density and relatively isolated nature of human settlements in snow leopard habitat, we do not see any range-wide cultural attitudes toward snow leopards. Even within Pakistan, a particular myth about snow leopards may be popular in one village, while in the next, no one has heard it. These kinds of issues of uneven diffusion of cultural traits in a region are specific to mountain areas.

The snow leopard belongs to the Panthera genus of *Pantherinae*, subfamily of Felidae, and family of the *Carnivora* order (Blomqvist 1980). Recent paleontology studies have shown that central Asia, rather than Africa, is the origin of the five big cats of the Panthera subfamily, which includes lions, jaguars, tigers, leopards, and snow leopards.[6] These five cats diverged a million years ago from the rest of the cat family tree, Felinae, which also includes cougars, lynxes, and domestic cats.

The vast high-mountain habitat of the snow leopard naturally raises some questions about subspeciation that may have occurred due to natural barriers. The possibility was first raised in the 1970s that because of a huge gap between its southern population in India, China, Nepal, and Pakistan and its northern population in Russia and Mongolia, the snow leopard might be a prime candidate for subspeciation (Kitchner, Meritt, and Rosenthal 1975). This proposition was not accepted, however, mainly because some scientists believed that snow leopards can travel five hundred miles, thus reducing the chances of isolation (Koshkarev 1990; Nowell et al. 1996). The issue was again raised when a snow leopard range-wide genetic study proposed that three subspecies of snow leopards exist globally (Janečka et al. 2017). This proposal has not yet been accepted by the IUCN, the international scientific body that conducts this classification.

During the 1990s, debate about the classification status of the snow leopard arose following the suggestion that because of the animal's behavior and its distinct morphology—skull shape, tooth shape, and limb proportions—it belonged in a genus separate from *Panthera* (Fox 1989).[7] Evolutionary biologists are studying phylogenetic relationships within the genus/subfamily *Panthera* to understand the pattern of big cat evolution and how it might have been deflected by major environmental changes. Genetic studies show that tigers and lions are not as closely related as had previously been thought; lions are more closely related to jaguars and leopards, while tigers are closer to snow leopards, possibly being the sister taxon (see Bininda-Emonds, Decker-Flum, Gittleman 2001; Yu and Zhang 2005).

In 2005 Chinese scholars Li Yu and Ya-ping Zhang published a study based on the molecular analysis of mitochondrial DNA of the snow leopard to show that snow leopards and common leopards ought to be considered sister species because of their relatively close evolutionary history. This claim was refuted by biologists who agreed with the earlier studies asserting that snow leopards and tigers (*Panther tigiris*) are sister species based on their estimate that both snow leopards and tigers diverged genetically around 3.2 million years ago (Davis, Li, and Murphy 2010, 74).

The snow leopard is considered the smallest in the big cat family. A fully grown adult weighs about 45–55 kilograms (100–120 pounds) and measures 120–200 centimeters (5–6.5 feet) from nose to tip of the tail; its tail is about 50 percent of its body length. Edward Percy Stebbings (1912), a British Army major and big game hunter, described the snow leopard's physical appearance:

> A beautiful skin has the snow leopard, the most handsome of the many beautiful ones possessed by the various cats. He is smaller than the panther, with a long tail in proportion to his length—the tail, too, is thicker and bushier. The black rosettes on the skin are of larger size and more open than those of the leopard. The general colouring of the animal is pale whitish grey, with at times yellowish tinge, above and pure white below. The whole animal is spotted with black, but the rosettes only appear on the back, sides and tail. The fur is long and very soft and downy to the touch." (165)

In most accounts of snow leopard sightings, especially by the British big game hunters of the nineteenth century, the tail commands the most attention. Biologists believe that in addition to giving warmth, the tail works as a balancing force as the snow leopard maneuvers in rocky and broken terrain. Like other striped and spotted cats, each individual snow leopard exhibits distinct patterns of spots that act as its unique barcode. Biologists use these signature spots to identify individual snow leopards in pictures taken from camera traps that show multiple angles of a cat's body. The snow leopard is viewed by local people as a master stalker. In one month, a snow leopard kills one or two large animals, such as wild or domesticated sheep or goats, as well as several small animals, such as pikas, marmot, and birds, which are mostly consumed in the summer. It is estimated that to survive a snow leopard needs to consume, on average, about twenty to twenty-five goats or sheep per year.

Snow leopards in captivity have been known to live as long as twenty-two years, but they die younger in the wild, at thirteen or fourteen years. A snow leopard can breed between the ages of two and twelve in captivity, with peak fecundity observed between the ages of six and seven.[8] Given the elusive nature of the animal and the difficulty of accessing its habitat, initial studies and knowledge about snow leopard morphology, anatomy and feeding, mating and marking behavior come from observations in captivity (Freeman 1982, 128; 1983, 17; Khalaf 1988, 61).[9] Helen Freeman, a biologist at Seattle's Woodland Park Zoo who went on to found the International Snow Leopard Trust, claimed that snow leopards mate for life and that males groom more than females. This claim was found not be true and was most likely a result of Freeman's emotional and empathetic attachment to the animals. Indeed very few studies have been conducted based on observation of snow leopard's behavior in the wild.[10]

Snow leopards are generally found at elevations of between 600 and 4,000 meters (2,000 and 14,000 feet) in the northern part of their range and between 1,800 and 5,800 meters (5,000 to 18,000 feet) in the southern part (Fox 1989). Snow leopards are well adapted to the high altitudes of their mountain habitats. Their relatively large nasal cavity, powerful chest muscles, and short and strong front legs allow them to move around their steep mountain abode with agility. The use of radio collars to study snow leopard habitat preference in western Nepal has shown that the cat favors non-forested steep and heavily broken terrain, with some scattered vegetation cover mainly comprising shrubs and bushes interspersed with patches of good foraging areas for wild and domestic goats (Jackson and Ahlborn 1989).[11] The snow leopard's home range is relatively small in best habitats with abundant natural prey, at between fifteen and thirty-nine square kilometers. In the extreme north of its range in the gentle rolling plains of the tundra of Mongolia and Russian Siberia the home range is larger, up to five hundred square kilometers. Similar habitat is found on the Tibetan plateau where the snow leopard lives in open country but at much higher elevations. Snow leopards are also found in the open coniferous forests of northern Russia (Schaller, Junrang, Mingjiang 1988). It is not clear if there are significant morphological changes in these relatively less steep and high-altitude terrains.

Information and knowledge about snow leopards has been difficult to come by and is at best incremental and patchy. When snow leopards became the subject of international protection in the 1970s, conservationists had very little information besides basic facts such as the animal's nocturnal and solitary habits. Its remote and harsh habitat made it difficult to study the snow leopard in its natural environment. These constraints are relevant even today, although research has benefited from the availability of remote camera technology, increase in genetic studies based on non-invasive methods, and a rising number of snow leopard ecologists. But the problem remains, or at least as per the standard conservation narrative. From almost every region where snow leopards are found, we read a familiar description such as this one from Siberia: "The so far scanty knowledge about the snow leopard within the limits of this region is due not only to its rarity, but also to the extremely difficult access to its habitats" (Smirnov, Sokolov, and Zyryanov 1990, 9).

George Schaller (1988), the famous American naturalist and one of the first biologists to photograph a snow leopard in the wild, said that most accounts of snow leopard sightings are anecdotal and contain very little useful information about the animal's ecology or behavior (16).

The first radio telemetry study of the snow leopard was conducted by the famous biologist and snow leopard conservationist Rodney Jackson in the early 1980s, when such studies had already become commonplace in large mammal research in the United States and elsewhere.[12] While this method of studying wild predators remotely worked well in the case of those predators whose habitat was relatively flat and easy to access, it was not easily adaptable to the case of the snow leopard and its mountain habitat.

The first difficulty is capturing a snow leopard in order to attach a collar, and the second is studying it in an area where, due to topography, radio signals are difficult to record. Advanced technology and remote methods are now available that make it easier to study the cat's movements, using satellite links to send signals from a radio-collared cat directly to a researcher's laptop.

Technology, however, has its own limitations, and some older-generation wildlife biologists lament the fact that reliance on remote technology has reduced the use of naturalistic techniques that require a researcher to be in the field for extended periods.[13] Moreover, not all technological advancements have led to new research directions; some have just improved the existing method of study, such as with radio telemetry. Advancements in molecular techniques, however, have led snow leopard research into new directions, making accessible information that was previously very difficult to obtain. Now, by using noninvasive methods, conservationists can ascertain the identity of the species and also its diet (Janečka et al. 2008). Both of these pieces of information have immense potential to reduce some of the ambiguity that belies snow leopard research and also to help shed new light on the standard conservation narrative.

WILD SNOW LEOPARDS IN WESTERN EUROPE

Western Europeans first learned about the snow leopard through Johann Christian Daniel von Schreber, a gentleman naturalist. Schreber was a contemporary of Carl Linnaeus, the eighteenth-century Swedish botanist and founder of the Linnaeus classification system, and the two frequently corresponded during the 1760s and 1770s. A Saxon aristocrat and professor of natural history, Schreber must have come across snow leopard pelts in Europe, as live animals did not reach Europe for another century. Schreber named the specimen *Panthera uncia*, under the Linnaeus classification system. The first live snow leopard was exhibited in Europe in 1872 by the Russian general Kaufmann at the Moscow Zoological Garden. It is most likely that Kaufmann got the cat from the Altay or Pamir Mountains of central Asia, the westernmost extent of the snow leopard habitat within the Russian empire. It was during the late nineteenth century that the Russian empire had conquered all of the central Asian Khanets and was knocking on the doors of British India. Almost two decades later, the British got their first live snow leopard from Bhutan, on the other side, the eastern edge, of the Himalayas. Richard Lydekker (1896), the naturalist of the Victorian era, reports that "the first living example brought to England was a young animal from Bhutan, purchased by the Zoological Society in 1891" (94). The cub did not survive, and three years later, the society ordered another specimen, an older animal. Lydekker reported that only one other snow leopard was reported in captivity, in the zoological gardens at Amsterdam in 1893.

The Helsinki Zoo in Finland periodically published the *International Pedigree Book of Snow Leopards*, which listed all the known captive leopards and their pedigrees. Volume seven of this series included a list of snow leopards kept in captivity between 1905 and 1996. This is not a comprehensive list because it is missing information from some regions, particularly China. But it shows that a total of 1,977 snow leopards had been kept in captivity in these ninety years, and of these 309 had been wild caught (Blomqvist 1998, 4). A quick analysis of the list shows that during the first half of this period there had been a steady flow of wild snow leopards into the domestic confines of European zoological gardens and menageries. Between 1905 and 1960, some 125 individuals had been kept in various zoos in Europe, of which 90 percent had been caught in the wild. The rest were born in captivity, beginning with a cub born in 1910 at the Leipzig Zoo in Germany. The origins of the wild-caught snow leopards between 1905 and 1930 is almost completely unknown, but from the 1930s to the 1960s, it seems from the scant information available that the Soviet Union was a steady supplier of wild-caught snow leopards to the western European zoos.

There also seemed to be a steady supply of snow leopard pelts for western European markets during the first half of the twentieth century. The two main sources of pelts: big game hunters and commercial trapping and curing of skins for European markets by some of the range states.[14] As in the case of wild-caught snow leopards, the main supplier of commercial snow leopard pelts during the first half of the twentieth century was the Soviet Union. It is almost impossible to know the number of pelts that were traded on a global scale, as there is hardly any record outside the former USSR. There are a few regional estimates, but they do not give much idea about the extent of this trade and its effect on snow leopard populations. In Russia a study by Soviet biologists showed that 120 snow leopard pelts were reported to have been tanned in 1920 alone (Heptner and Sludskii 1992, 318). While giving figures for Mongolia, biologist David Mallon (1984) states, "Mongolia for their fur, but as Bannikov remarked, it has little commercial significance, owing to its rarity. He quoted figures for the number of snow leopard skins obtained in Mongolia in the first part of the century: 80 in 1908; 40 in 1927; about 20 annually from 1929–1932; 10 in 1933; 40 in 1934, then 15–25 annually up to 1944. There are no figures for recent years but the totals are certainly low and the figure of 40–50 killed annually given by Kibbert (1968) must be considered an overestimate" (4). In China the government purchased snow leopard pelts from local herders and paid them bounty. An eastern Tibet official purchased 88 snow leopard pelts from herders in 1968 (Schaller 1988, 186). It seems that these pelts had multiple sources: state vermin eradication programs, herders taking bounty payments, and hunters wanting pelts for personal collection. The second supply source of pelts was the local *shikaris* (local hunting guides) in British India who trapped snow leopards and cured the pelts for sportsmen or for the tourists who came to Srinagar in Kashmir. It seems that this was not a systematic trade, and that its volume was low. Again, without quantitative data, it is difficult to assess either the numbers of pelts traded or the impact of the trade on the snow leopard population.

The supply of wild-caught snow leopards seemed to have declined in the second half of the twentieth century. Between 1960 and 1973, 270 more individuals were added to the snow leopard population in captivity, of which 118 or about 45 percent came from the wild. It is quite clear that during this period most of the snow leopards originated from the USSR. Between 1973 and 1980, about 300 more snow leopards were added to the captive population of which 45, or about 15 percent, came from the wild. During this period, China, especially the Xinjiang region, emerged as another source of wild-caught snow leopards bound for Europe. After 1980 the supply of wild-caught snow leopards dwindled almost completely. Between 1980 and 1996, another 1,300 snow leopards were added to the captive population, but of these, only 20, or about 1.5 percent, came from the wild.

What could be the reason for this decline in the arrival of wild-caught snow leopards to European zoos over the past hundred years? The most important factor was the introduction of environmental regulations across the world. Moreover, captive populations grew as more and more zoos initiated breeding programs, which decreased the need to rely on the constant injection of wild snow leopards.[15] Also, individual countries, particularly the USSR, started to call for a halt to the live and pelt trade of snow leopards. A study from the former USSR concluded that "For a long time, due to misunderstanding, the ounce [snow leopard] was considered a dangerous and harmful predator and hunting was permitted year-round by any method. Rewards were even offered for dead animals. In reality, as stated before, the harm done to livestock and game is insignificant, and the cat poses no danger whatsoever to man. The ounce is, in fact, a valuable treasure in our mountains and of great scientific interest as a highly specialized cat. In the world market live ounces are always in demand and their sale a profitable item in zoological exports." They continue, "Evidently the indiscriminate destruction of this animal should be banned everywhere. Catching ounces should be prohibited year-round in the Tarbagatai, Saur, Altai, and Sayans. In Tadzhikistan, Uzbekistan, Kirgizia, and Kazakhstan shooting ounces should be banned and catching them for the purpose of export only permitted from October through February. In 1950 in Kirgizia, the ounce was struck from the list of predators to be exterminated. Hunting was banned altogether and only the catch of live animals permitted. In this same republic capturing cubs and destroying dens with cubs prohibited" (Heptner and Sludskii 1992, 318–19). The USSR continued to be a source for wild-caught snow leopards for the zoos across the world. The snow leopard population suffered a decline after the disintegration of the USSR (Cunha 1997). It seems that poaching has been controlled significantly since 2010, as evidenced by the lack of supply of snow leopard pelts in the markets of central Asia.

EMPIRES AND PREDATORS

The British Empire had a special aversion to predators and made active efforts to eliminate them from areas where they ruled and settled. The historian Divyabhanusinh (2002), writing about the demise of Asiatic cheetah population in the subcontinent, states, "The British, like any other people, lived for the moment according to the tenets of their times. They did not see that their hunting and other pursuits inadvertently pushed the cheetah towards its final destiny on the subcontinent" (105). The elimination of predators served both the material and the ideological goals of the British. Elimination of vermin, symbolically, stood for British political discourse on the elimination of those political rivals who challenged their rule (Ranagrajan 2004, 210). Killing large predators had always been a sign of kingship and rule, so when the British arrived in India, they took up tiger hunting as much for clearing the landscape of vermin as for its symbolic value (A. Pandian 2001).

But the British also sought eradication of wild predators for a more immediate and practical reason. Attacks by such predators as tigers and leopards struck fear in villagers' hearts, causing them to refuse to work on their farms and perform state duties. By 1875 the problem of loss of revenues due to wildlife became so acute that the British started publishing statistics about it (Greenough 2001, 147). Colonial revenues depended on the expansion of agriculture into uncultivated areas, and the presence of wild predators made that difficult, leading to intense conflict between nature and society (Hussain 2012). By 1880 the British had established a system for bounty payments for the body parts of large predators—especially tigers and leopards—which were deemed vermin. The sport of tiger hunting served an administrative goal of eliminating wild predators. Moreover, any small or large predator was seen as an enemy of sportsmen, as it destroyed game and meat (Rangarajan 2004, 213). Hence tigers were persecuted for sport and because they were vermin. According to government bounty payout reports between 1879 and 1888, 16,573 tigers were killed in India (Hughes 2013, 60). Some 65,000 tigers were killed during the five decades between 1875 and 1925 (Rangarajan 2004, 285).[16]

The expansion of agriculture into tigers' and other predators' habitats initially benefited the carnivores. Tigers prefer disturbed habitats because their prey depends on vegetation created by disturbance. Similar trends were reported from other tiger habitats under colonial rule. For example, during Dutch colonial expansion in Indonesia, the frontier between uncultivated land and agricultural land was blurred, and tiger-human conflict was intense. It is plausible that when the (agri)cultural frontier was increasing, tigers benefited from the newly created conditions (Boomgaard 2001). Later, however, as human populations increased, the empire of culture devastated the empire of nature. A somewhat similar conclusion can be drawn from India about the effects of colonial agricultural expansion on cheetahs. In India cheetahs adapted to conditions very different from their natural habitat, so that in Chota Nagpur "the animal adapted itself to dense jungle which it did not originally belong by obtaining the easiest prey—village livestock—apart from *cheetal* and other wild animals such as hares" (Divyabhanusinh 2002,

103). For the cheetah, stalking livestock is easier than chasing wild antelope because of the former's lack of speed. But the flip side of this adaptation to modified habitats meant cheetahs were persecuted for killing domestic animals. Between 1880 and the 1920s, cheetah sightings became rare and signs of their presence also became less frequent (Divyabhanusinh 2002, 91–93).

Cheetahs were never hunted for trophies because they were also considered less destructive of livestock when compared with other predators, such as tigers, leopards, and wolves. They were shot mostly when a hunter came across them while stalking other game. Likewise, the snow leopard was not hunted as a trophy, although the government did pay rewards to hunters who shot them. The reason that snow leopards and cheetahs were never hunted as trophies was the same: both occurred in low densities and were elusive and physically difficult to hunt and shoot at, so sportsmen saw hunting them as not worth the time and effort.

There is, however, a major difference between the snow leopard and the cheetah that has perhaps given the former a better chance at survival and adaptation: a difference in the nature of their respective habitats. The snow leopard habitat is almost impossible to convert into something else, whereas cheetah habitat can be transformed relatively easily and completely. The broken, craggy, barren snow leopard habitat is generally composed of ice and rock and, at a stupendous height of three thousand meters (ten thousand feet) and above, is a hostile environment for humans.

For this reason the snow leopard range and habitat in Pakistan and worldwide has not decreased despite an explosion in population growth and technological advancement in south and central Asia.

Up until the early part of the twentieth century, tigers and lions were also found in Pakistan, mainly in the plains of the Indus River delta in the south, but they are gone now (Nowell et al. 1996, 37). They were eliminated not through hunting alone but primarily because their habitat was converted into agricultural fields and towns, cities, and roads.

In comparison to the snow leopard, the tiger is restricted to 7 percent of its historical range today, and its habitat has declined to less than 10 percent of its size in the nineteenth century (Sanderson et al. 2010). The threat of habitat degradation emanates from global climate changes induced by consumption and production by advanced industrial societies, not from the subsistence practices of local farmers. The standard conservation narrative would have us believe that snow leopards were abundant in the past, before their habitat was opened up to farms and villages, but have become locally extinct. If anything my own experience shows in the Baltistan region that the modernization process is resulting in a decline in pastoralism and, hence, less pressure is being put on protecting snow leopard habitat from humans. Here, pastoralism is the only activity that can sustain humans and even that has its limits in terms of time and space.[17] For example, pastures can be used during the summer when they are free of ice and snow. For this reason we cannot apply to the snow leopard the standard conservation narrative of perpetual decline of snow leopard habitat due to encroachment of human societies.

A second reason for challenging the standard conservation narrative is that snow leopard populations are naturally rare and elusive, so an abundant past is highly unlikely. A recent evolutionary study has shown that a major bottleneck in the snow leopard population occurred about six thousand years ago when a temporary period of warming occurred during the Holocene (Janečka et al. 2017). This event was not induced by human activity; rather, it was a natural event and since then the snow leopard population has remained low. Although we do not have reliable data from the past to decisively challenge the standard conservation narrative of an abundant past and depleted present, we have a source on the basis of which we can problematize the narrative to be looked at critically. This source is the accounts of big game hunters of the British Raj between 1850 and 1950 from the trans-Himalayan region of what is today Gilgit-Baltistan in northern Pakistan.

This literature shows that snow leopards have historically been elusive and hard to sight. But the authors of this literature did not link this fact with snow leopards' declining population, rather to its (elusive) nature. This elusive habit of the snow leopard was, in the 1970s crisis narrative, transformed into an indication of its declined or declining population. The rising awareness of environmental issues such as forest and wildlife loss brought about this qualitative shift in the ontological status of the snow leopard in the minds of conservationists and the general public. The "elusiveness" and "natural" quality of the snow leopard became augmented in officially classifying the snow leopard as a threatened species.

SNOW LEOPARD IN HUNTING ACCOUNTS OF BRITISH SPORTSMEN

In what is now the Gilgit-Baltistan region of Pakistan, we only first begin to see written records about snow leopards during the second half of the nineteenth century, when the sportsmen of the British Raj started penetrating the trans-Himalayan regions of Baltistan, Astor, and Gilgit—all then under the suzerainty of the Kashmir State. The British sportsmen sought the magnificent trophies of ibex and markhor, the most prized of all wild goats. The horns of ibex and markhor can grow as long as five feet, which is why they're considered the lodestar among big game hunters then *and* now. These nineteenth-century sportsmen of the British Empire thought that with the ritualization of hunting in England, the hunting experience had been tamed (MacKenzie 1988); they lamented the fact that true wild nature had been lost. The northern frontier of India, in addition to other places on the subcontinent and on other colonies, presented the opportunity for hunting in the wild, as it used to be.

Within the global geographical range of the snow leopard, the region that is known as Gilgit-Baltistan—or the expanse between the valley of Kashmir and the Karakoram watershed—was visited by big game hunters more than any other part of the animal's geographical range. Although official posting to the region in the nineteenth century was considered to be a harsh assignment by the officers of the British Raj, there were some clear tradeoffs, especially for those interested in shooting big game. As Major Charles Granville Bruce (1910) of the Fifth Gurkha Rifles wrote: "There are compensations for everything in this world, and trying as a long residence in Gilgit can be, it has great attractions for the sportsman, for there is no better sporting country in the Himalaya and Hindu Koosh; ibex, markhor, and oorial, and shapoo [sic] snow leopard and red bear are all obtainable" (138–39). Major Roger Lloyd Kennion (1910), another sportsman, said, "Baltistan famous for apricots, but here you found 'the wildest game animals in the world'" (42).

We have patchy accounts of sportsmen's encounters with snow leopards in this region.[18] Some of these references are literally a sentence or two long, while the longest cover two pages. These accounts appeared between 1850 and 1940, in a collection of hunting monographs, tallying around fifty to seventy books of uneven quality, and in journals, newspapers, and delivered lectures.[19] British sportsmen flocked to the best hunting valleys, renowned for harboring good populations of ibex and markhor in Baltistan, Astor, and parts of Gilgit, early on in the hunting season.[20] Most British sportsmen hunted within the valley of Kashmir, especially in the Pir Panjal Range, shooting mainly markhor, ibex, Kashmir stag, and black and brown bears. Here they sometimes also encountered snow leopards, which are found in the upper reaches of the Pir Panjal Range.

The British hunters admired the snow leopard for its aesthetic beauty but also despised it because it hunted ibex and markhor, which the big game hunters were after. Both of these opposing tendencies resulted in a desire to "bag" the cats and turn them into trophies. The sportsmen who came here varied in their level of skill, motivation, and intensity of seriousness about game. Some came mainly to trek in the mountains and carried a rifle with them by the way.[21] But serious sportsmen came specifically for trophies. The difficult terrain and the demanding conditions of the snow leopard's habitat made it among the hardest trophies to obtain. To a sportsman, such a trophy would represent an encounter with the wildest of the wild. Around this trophy he could weave remarkable tales of risk, endurance, and luck. For example, Bairnsfather (1914, 20) stated,

> Of these the most desirable of all for a trophy hunter is the snow leopard or Ounce—desirable not only, from the sportsman's point of view, for the difficulty of obtaining specimen, but also aesthetically for the beauty of his skin. But it is seldom indeed that one comes across him. I, personally, have been round dozens of times on sporting trips to the Himalayas, but never had the luck to see one. Yet, I suppose that, on almost all of these trips I have seen their tracks, and indeed one is often constrained to brand the whole tribe with important anathema for scaring the ibex out of our pet nullah which we had taken so much pains to secure.

Bairnsfather indicates that there were abundant signs of the snow leopard's presence thus emphasizing its elusive nature rather than its precarious status.

HABITAT AND DISTRIBUTION

British sportsmen frequently passed along general information about where snow leopards could be found in the wild and where their pelts could be purchased and at what price. In 1895 Walter Lawrence, the settlement officer of Kashmir, wrote the following: "The ounce is rare in the territory to which these remarks are confined. In Brariangan, and high up the Sind, are the only places I actually know of its occurrence, but a skin was brought to me in Lidarwat; this specimen was said to have been shot near Tar-Sar" (109). John Collet (1884), who wrote the first tourist guidebook to Kashmir, stated that the "skins of the white leopard are sometimes sold in Srinagar at from Rs. 20 to Rs. 30 each" (81). We know next to nothing about the trappers who provided these skins, as very little information exists on them and their profession. In most cases these skins were passed from the primary trapper in snow leopard range country to British sportsmen through the mediation of shikaris, professional hunting guides that sportsmen were required to hire. Some sportsmen-turned-naturalists also kept live snow leopards, which they might have obtained from the shikaris.

The hunters write their accounts in quasi-scientific or gentleman-scientist parlance. For instance, describing the extent of the snow leopard habitat, Gerald Burrard (1925) writes, "It is found from the Hindu Kush on the west to the extreme eastern end of the Great Himalayan Range, and extends right into, and probably throughout Tibet; but its southern boundary is generally the Great Himalayan Range, and it is not nearly so common on the southern slopes of the main axis as on the northern side. It extends in limited numbers a few miles along the Dhauladhar and Pir Panjal Ranges from their junctions with the Great Himalayan Range" (222). Col. Edward Stebbing (1912) described its habitat and range: "The snow leopard or ounce (*Felis uncia*) is an inhabitant of the high mountains, living up above 9000 feet (about), although it may possibly come lower down in winter. It is said to be more abundant on the Thibetan side of the snowy range, and it is met with on the upper Indus and upper waters of the Sutlej, and is said to be fairly common in Gilgit" (62–63).

Almost all of these accounts show that the sportsmen understood the distributional density of the snow leopards, knowledge gained from their personal experience and from hearing stories on hunting excursions.

GAME KILLER

British sportsmen invariably saw the snow leopard as a game killer, and they did not hide their negative feelings about it. There was thus a clear conflict between snow leopards and the sportsmen. In this time before ecosystems, trophic cascade, and apex predators were understood, one of the major threats to the snow leopard between 1850 and 1950 was sportsmen of the British Raj, because they saw it as a competitor for ibex and markhor. To the sportsmen, wild nature was simply a source of thrill.

Colonel Stebbing (1912) wrote, "The snow leopard is generally to be found in ibex and markhor ground.... In Baltistan there are many snow leopards, and they levy a heavy tax on the herds of small ibex" (181). A. E. Ward (1887) of the Bengal Staff Corps, an avid hunter who authored *The Sportsman's Guide to Kashmir and Ladak*, stated: "The destruction caused by these beasts of prey must be very great. Ibex, Burhel [a wild sheep] and Markhor are the chief victims" (85–86).

Both accounts describe ibex and markhor as "chief victims" of snow leopards, and their killing as "heavy tax." Snow leopards not only reduced the potential trophies that the sportsmen were after but they also sometimes spoiled the chase. In various accounts hunters express their frustration when their quarry is chased away by a snow leopard whom they often fail to see. As Captain Hugh Whistler (1924) wrote, "The presence of snow leopards in any particular nullah [a valley] is also apt to drive ibex out" (68). Major Kennion (1910) mentions how his stalk was spoiled by a snow leopard just as he was about to take a shot. After his quarry fled he went to the location of the ibex where "tracks of two snow-leopards had been seen, and they were supposed to be the cause of the fiasco" (116).

On the other hand, some hunters seemed to genuinely enjoy at least the spectacle of a snow leopard stalking its prey. Lt. Lionel B. Rundall (1915) was trumped by a snow leopard who attacked the ibex herd that he had been following. He writes,

> A sinister form had come slinking among the rocks above the little herd—a hungry snow-leopard creeping stealthily upwind, with the intention of stalking one of the sleek ibex which stood cropping the grass on the terrace. His beautiful skin was a clouded white-grey in color, mottled with big black spots. The powerful muscles rippled as he stole nearer to his quarry, and a fire smouldered deep in his smoke blue eyes. Nearer and nearer he came until he was crouching within a few paces of the fattest doe, which was preparing to lie down un-suspiciously under the shadow of the very rock upon which the enemy lay. Gathering himself together, the big cat suddenly shot down upon her like a stone from a sling, and . . . bit savagely through her neck. (35)

A sportsman who had missed a shot at the snow leopard remarked: "I have been fortunate enough to see a good number of these animals since, and have, I fear, expended a good deal of bad language upon them when time and again they have spoiled a stalk by disturbing game which I was after. I have on more than one occasion been lucky enough to see snow-leopards actually in pursuit of their quarry, which is as pretty a sight as a man could wish to see —provided his quarry and the leopards' are not one and the same animal" (Houghton 1913, 255).

For the sportsmen, encounters with snow leopards in the wild were about more than coming face to face with one's foe. It was also about a chance to catch sight of one of the finest specimens of nature, in nature. A stalking snow leopard was both admired and resented, and often in the same breath. For these authors, the wildness of the snow leopard was depicted in its full majesty when they were stalking and chasing their quarry—a type of description that is absent in the conservation literature today.

COVETED TROPHY

Despite appreciating their physical beauty, sportsmen did not hesitate to shoot snow leopards for their trophy collections. It seems that getting a good shot at a snow leopard was an extremely rare and lucky event because an encounter between a hunter and a snow leopard was always unplanned. For example, Major Kennion (1910) wrote, "An opportunity of bagging a snow-leopard was lost when I came face to face with one of these handsome beasts on a recently killed ram. My rifle was in its cover, and by the time I had got it out he was gone like a shadow up a boulder-covered hill, on top of which, like a great cat, he lay down to watch me, nor did all the craft of my stalker get me a shot at that embodiment of feline wariness" (169).

Burrard (1925), however, wrote, "Occasionally snow leopards are seen by day, and when this occurs they are frequently in pairs. If the sportsman is quick to appreciate the situation, and the rifle is at hand, he will have a chance of bagging a right and left" (223).

Sportsmen expressed great regret about missing shots at snow leopards. Henry Darrah, who butchered more than three dozen game animals in one season, regretted that he could not bag a snow leopard in Baltistan. Upon missing the shot, Darrah (1898) wrote: "On examining the ground there was no blood, and it was pretty clear that I had missed. I was naturally awfully disgusted, for a chance at a snow leopard is very rare" (188). Another sportsman wrote, "Next day the men went to fetch the dead burrell and found an 'ounce,' or, as it is more commonly called, a snow-leopard, at work on them. If the stupids had only had sense enough to leave one of the carcass as a bait, the beast would certainly have returned to it, and in all probability I should have got a shot at a rather rare animal I was most anxious to kill" (Macintyre 1889, 423).

Some, however, were lucky enough to have two shots in a year. Lt. Col. J. R. C. Gannon (1932), who traveled to Chitral in 1923, reported that the political agent of Chitral had a wonderful collection of trophies, including the pelts of two snow leopards that he had shot that same year. Unconcerned and unconstrained about the welfare of the game and moral laws, they shot snow leopards irrespective of age and sex. Col. Fred Markham (1854) wrote, "During several years, the summer and autumnal months of which Wilson spent chiefly in the higher regions, where [the snow leopard] is found, he only met with it three or four times, and succeeded in killing but one, and that a half-grown cub" (166).

Although it was difficult to organize a hunt specifically for snow leopards, some enthusiastic sportsmen suggested using live bait to bag one. These hunting accounts are as much narratives about their adventures as instructions for future hunters. For example, conflicting reports have been written about whether or not it is a good idea to sit and wait by a dead goat to bag a snow leopard, a method successfully tried in British India against other large predators, such as tigers and leopards. Gerald Burrard (1925) wrote, "If a fresh kill is ever found it would certainly be worth while sitting up, but this is not an amusement which will appeal to any but extreme enthusiasts on account of intense cold" (223). But Frederick George Aflalo (1904) wrote, "It is useless to spend time in trying to get to a shot at one, but you are sure to come across them sooner or later when after ibex" (182).

Despite some rare successes, the general experience of the sportsmen in bagging snow leopards could be summed up in the following commentary by Colonel Stebbing (1912): "The snow leopard, however, for all its reported abundance or commonness in certain localities, is not an easy animal either to see or to come across. At least I give this as my own personal experience, and shall have many to corroborate it. Whenever I have been in a locality where there was the remotest chance of my coming across one of these much-coveted animals I have worked hard and long for the beast. And yet my bag of snow leopards has been *nil*" (163–64; italics in original).

Snow leopard shooting was permitted as part of a multispecies shooting license issued to the sportsmen by the Kashmir Game Preservation Department at the cost of sixty rupees (Koenigsmarck 1910, 95). The British colonial officers frequently bought snow leopard pelts, perhaps later claiming to have shot the animals themselves. In *The Sportsman's Book for India* Aflalo (1904) mentions that in the late nineteenth century and first decade of the twentieth, the sale of skins of wild beasts such as bear and leopards was not regulated (184). About the shooting licenses issued by the preservation department, he states, "The holder of this license will not require any special permit to shoot wolves, lynxes, foxes or martens, and, if desired, the reward in force at the time can be recovered for the destruction of such vermin" (190). Snow leopards were considered vermin by the British, and a sportsman with a valid hunting license could pick up a bounty of ten rupees for shooting one. Aflalo mentions that in the 1900s, the Kashmir Game Preservation Department issued three kinds of licenses:

1. March 15 to November 15. A sportsman paid Rs. 60.00 as license fee and allowed to shoot about 42 animals of about 10 different species, mostly wild ungulates, and unlimited snow leopards.
2. Rs. 20 license, one can shoot unlimited amount of snow leopards, black bears and pigs.
3. Winter license November 15 to March 15. A sportsman paid Rs. 30.00 and allowed to shoot about 24 animals of 10 different species and unlimited snow leopards. (190)

It is clear from the above regulations that the snow leopard was not considered worth protecting; rather, its eradication was encouraged. George Schaller (1988) reported that A. W. Ward, a nineteenth-century game warden from the Kashmir Game Preservation Department, had shot five of the eight snow leopards he had seen—killing the predators who killed game animals. The tussle in the 1920s between sportsmen and conservationists shows that sportsmen often relied on their adherence to hunting codes as a way of placating the growing number of opponents of hunting as well as those demanding preservation (Mangan 1986). According to the sportsmen, hunting codes differentiated hunting from butchery (see also MacKenzie 1988). Unlike butchery, which the natives did, hunting entailed great physical danger and required stamina and courage on the part of the hunter. By that standard, no other predator or big cat invited that challenge more than the snow leopard. But the elusive nature of the snow leopard made its chase into a non-sport: snow leopards were shot by chance, as the by-product of hunting for other animals.

LIVESTOCK KILLER

Between the 1850s and 1950s, sportsmen seem to suggest that snow leopards killed domestic livestock regularly, while at other times they stated that snow leopards do not share habitat with humans and their livestock. Bairnsfather (1914) wrote of the cat's nocturnal habits: "He is, of course, one of those who walk and hunt by night or in the gloaming, and living at too high an altitude to be able to take toll of the tame flocks of the villagers, he generally confines his attention to the wild herds, be they goat or sheep" (21).

This statement can clearly support the current general position in conservation literature that there was no or little conflict between farmers and snow leopards in the past. But accounts from much earlier periods, when the region was almost unvisited by sportsmen and hence natural prey would have been even more abundant, show a different picture. For example, Fred Markham (1854), one of the first British sportsmen to have visited the region, wrote in the early 1850s,

> As it roams about apparently as much by day as by night, it is surprising and unaccountable how it evades observation; the more so as its principle resorts are above the limits of forests, where [there] is little or no cover, one would imagine, sufficient to conceal it from sight. Even the shepherds who pass the whole of the summer months, year after year, in the region it inhabits, but seldom see one; except when their flocks are attacked by night, which the white leopard occasionally does to some purpose. Everywhere their traces are to be found, often as if the animal has passed only a short time previously, but it is, as it were, invisible. (166)

The naturalist Richard Lydekker (1896) also reported the destructive behavior of snow leopards on livestock. He writes, "Domestic Sheep, Goats, and even Ponies, fall victim to the Snow-Leopard" (94). He also mentioned the particularly excessive killing methods of the snow leopard, stating that in 1874 a British officer of the Royal Artillery had seen what could be called the first evidence of surplus killing of ibex by snow leopards. Lydekker writes, "A sportsman in Pangi district, on the Chinab, came across the bodies of five or six male ibex lying within a few yards of each other; all of which had doubtless been killed by Snow Leopards. From the number of ibex destroyed in this instance, it is highly probable that the Ounce hunts in couples" (94).

Walter Lawrence (1895), the first settlement officer of the Kashmir State, thought that the snow leopard relied mainly on wild prey but occasionally attacked domestic herds: "The Kashmiris call it the Safed Chetah. Sah is a name given by some. . . . It now and again kills sheep, but is not nearly so destructive as the leopard. A couple of ounces frequent the hills above Narastan and evidently hunt the few ibexes that are left in Bra-iangan" (109).

Based on these anecdotal accounts, it could be argued that while conflict between the snow leopard and the farmer was not widespread, it was present. And where it did occur, it was quite severe. This conclusion about snow leopard–farmer conflict is not so different from the situation more than a century later. But today, according to the standard conservation narrative, snow leopards attack livestock only because farmers have depleted their natural prey, such as ibex and markhor.

ELUSIVE PREDATOR

Perhaps one of the most recurring themes in the accounts of sportsmen about their encounters (seen and unseen) with snow leopards is the idea of its elusiveness. For example, Burrard (1925) states, "When marching and shooting in the Zanskar Range I have day after day come on fresh tracks of these creatures, but I have never seen one, and I am sure that it is only on account of their nocturnal habits that they are so seldom encountered, not because they are in any way rare" (222). This important distinction is relevant to the modern conservationists' assumptions about the snow leopard's threatened status.

In 1850s Colonel Markham (1854) wrote, "Despite its actual elusiveness snow leopards signs were present everywhere in higher grounds where ibex and markhor roam. I have seen their fresh tracks day after day" (165–66). He further wrote, "We were lucky enough this day to see a white leopard, which galloped across the open. He may be considered as fortunate indeed, who during months of shooting on the snowy ranges, gets even a sight of the 'burrell-hag,' or the white leopard" (165). Writing in the same vein, Colonel Stebbing (1912) states, "In Astore they are plentiful, but very seldom seen" (181). Another British sportsman, General Alexander Kinloch (1892) wrote, "The Snow-Leopard is scattered all over the highest hills, but it is seldom that the English sportsman has the luck to meet with one; I have never had that good fortune during all my wanderings" (258).

Clearly, a sighting of a snow leopard then, as today, was very rare, but does that mean that it was also *actually* rare, even back then when hunting pressures and other human-induced factors had not affected its habitat? This would be a gross oversimplification. Although direct sightings of snow leopards were rare, evidence from hunters show that signs of its presence, such as tracks, were common; hence many sportsmen expressed their frustration at not "bagging" one. This might lead us to an opposite conclusion, that snow leopards were common in the nineteenth century but have become rare only recently. This, too, might be an oversimplification. The fact that the sportsmen were in prime ibex or markhor territories makes the high density of snow leopard signs expected. Without actually knowing the relative status of snow leopards in less suitable habitats—habitats that did not harbor its prey—in the two eras, it is difficult to assess true changes in its population. But as snow leopard ecologists from Russia (Smirnov, Sokolov, Zyryanov 1990, 10) surmise, "Because of the very severe environmental conditions . . .

the snow leopard is unlikely to have been numerous in our region in the remote past." We can apply this observation to the status of the species across its entire range.

What is interesting to note in the above passages is that sportsmen did not attribute the rarity of snow leopard sighting to its declining or low population level but rather to its ecological adaptation and behavior, such as nocturnal habits and elusive nature. In today's standard conservation narrative, the rarity of snow leopard sightings is often interpreted as evidence of its endangered status. The main factor contributing to this translation of its elusive nature as threatened is the popularity of the standard conservation narrative and the rise of ecological science as a discipline that concerns itself with nature conservation.

What can be said about the population of snow leopards based on these accounts? Not much, really. But we can look at other more subjective matters in historical context. For example, the fact that as far back as 1854 when Markham reported snow leopards attacking domestic livestock means that the conflict arose when humans settled in the region with their domestic animals. Although there is not accurate data on snow leopards' prey species from the late nineteenth century, it can be assumed that snow leopards did not have a dearth of "natural" or wild prey at that time. If the natural prey was available, then what motivated local people to trap and kill snow leopards, and why did British administrators mention their destructive behavior?

After the 1920s, hunting accounts from the Baltistan region almost dried up, however that does not mean that hunting of big game had stopped. After the British set up a permanent administrative system, the frontier became more restricted and access to it was mostly limited to the British officials serving in the Gilgit Agency, and it was they who continued to hunt and record their achievements in the Big Game Register of the Gilgit Agency. This register kept record of all the game species—ibex, markhor, Marco Polo sheep, urial, blue sheep—but not necessarily snow leopards. The representation of snow leopards as a species that caused irritation to game hunters, and thus as a good target, remained unchanged during the first half of the twentieth century as officers and sportsmen of the Raj continued to shoot the animals whenever they encountered them. Raleigh Trevelyan (1987), whose father was a military officer of the Gilgit Agency in the 1920s, shot a snow leopard in the vicinity of Gilgit town and donated the skin to the Natural History Museum in London.

At the end of the nineteenth century the social conditions did not exist in which a wild predator could be appreciated and conserved by a wider general population as is the case today. How did the predator become important and worth saving for human societies? One could write volumes describing the process. Historian Jon Coleman (2004), in his brilliant study of the history of the eradication of the gray wolf in North America, links the rise in sympathetic attitudes toward predators to the increasing industrialization and urbanization of the continent.[22] The wolf became the symbol of disappearing wilderness. With the rise of an ecological consciousness, the bounty hunter was replaced by conservationists (12). A somewhat similar transformation of the image of the snow leopard occurred in the second half of the twentieth century when it became a symbol of wilderness that remains.

CONCLUSION

The snow leopard was first listed as endangered by the Endangered Species Program of the US Fish and Wildlife Services in March 1972; the following year it was declared a protected species worldwide with the ban on trade in snow leopards under the Convention on International Trade in Endangered Species (CITES) in 1973. And it was declared a protected species in Pakistan under the Northern Areas Wildlife Preservation Act of 1975. The protected status of the snow leopard accompanied a peculiar change in the description and general characterization of the animal from the accounts of nineteenth-century sportsmen. For example, Tom Roberts (1997) wrote in *The Mammals of Pakistan*: "Of all the large cats the Snow Leopard is perhaps the *most beautiful*. Besides being thick and *deeply luxuriant*, its fur is *most handsomely* marked" (222; emphasis added). In the 1970s, George Schaller visited the northern mountain region of Pakistan. In his book about this trip, Schaller (1988) describes his encounter with the "mythical" and elusive cat in Chitral Gol National Park: "Casually I meandered up the slope, alternately sitting and drawing closer in a seemingly purposeless manner until at 250 feet I halted. Crouched on a boulder, she stared at me with frosty eyes" (22).[23] In 1978 the American writer Peter Matthiessen wrote his famous book *The Snow Leopard* about his travels in the Nepalese Himalayas. Matthiessen uses the snow leopard as a metaphor in his soul-searching journey through a transformative wilderness. He does not represent the snow leopard as game or as a killer of livestock but emphasizes its elusiveness and rarity, now resignified as an indicator of declining population.

Under the influence of Matthiessen's and Schaller's writings, the image of the snow leopard that remerges in the standard conservation narrative in the 1970s is that of an iconic wilderness predator under threat. Across the world we see similar transformations in the image and representation of other large predators. Predators that were earlier discussed and embedded in a discourse of improvement, imperialism, and domination are now lodged into a new discourse of ecology, biodiversity, and an imperiled planet. This discourse reached Pakistan and India in the second half of the twentieth century. Predators that had been seen as useless and even threatening in earlier discourse of improvement and civilization have become the indicator species, the keystone, and the top predator species in a later discourse of global ecology.

CHAPTER TWO

Producing Wilderness Predators

I F, in general, wildlife benefited from the emergence of benign and sympathetic views toward it in the late nineteenth century, wild predators—especially large terrestrial predators—did not share this benefit until the second half of the twentieth century. From the seventeenth through the first half of the twentieth century, throughout Europe, America, and in the colonies, state administrators kept lists of bounty animals and their death records.

Eradication of predators was considered part of the civilizing process by the early Euro-American states, and no predator suffered more than the wolf. European society had an ambivalent relationship with the wolf, which was both feared and respected (Plukowski 2010). Wolves were common throughout Europe during the sixteenth century (Breitenmoser 1998), but by the 1850s, as population and agriculture expanded, they were completely eradicated from the southern and western Alps, Switzerland, the British Isles, Germany, Denmark, Belgium, the Netherlands, Luxembourg, and most of Scandinavia (Boitani 1992).[1] Wolves survived in small isolated populations in eastern and northern Europe (Breitenmoser 1998, 220). In America, the persecution of wolves continued well into the 1960s, and the conflict continues to this day. The early settlers to America saw the eradication of wolves and Native Americans as part of a clearing of the "wilderness" and settling of the frontier.

In Africa, the killing of leopards, lions, wild dogs, jackals, and hyenas increased dramatically during the colonial period and continued into the second half of the twentieth century (Sittirt 1998; Tropp 2002). In India, tigers and leopards were killed for bounty throughout the colonial period and into the first two decades after independence. At the end of the nineteenth century, British big game hunters and local farmers in Baltistan regarded the snow leopard as vermin that damaged game and livestock. At this time, snow leopard shooting and eradication was a matter of state policy for the British. In other words, predators had no place in human society.

Today, state administrators and international conservation organizations keep lists of species under threat of extinction. National and international institutions have been established specifically for the purpose of protecting large predators. Global programs, such as Project Tiger, which launched in India in the 1970s, became emblematic of human efforts to save wild predators and wild nature everywhere. The appearance of predators on these lists shows that their image in modern human society has undergone a radical transformation, almost an inversion: from threatening to being threatened. In the nineteenth century, society fought to eradicate wild predators; today society struggles within itself to protect them and keep them alive. Wild predators that were earlier seen as a threat to the order of society have now come to symbolize the threat society poses to the natural order. What are the reasons for this transformation?

This movement was only possible because of a fundamental shift that occurred in western society's conception of nature itself. In the eighteenth and nineteenth centuries, views of nature in Europe and America evolved from a utilitarian perspective in which nature is seen as something to be used for the material benefit of humans to a transcendental perspective in which nature has intrinsic and spiritual values. With the emergence of ecological sciences in the second half of the twentieth century, a third conceptualization of nature evolved: nature as an ecosystem in which wild predators played an important role in its function and maintenance. And most important, humans were conspicuously absent from this new conceptualization.

From a historical point of view, ecological and conservation discourses reintroduced wild predators into public discourse in a new way. In the utilitarian view, predators were simply in the way of progress and maximization of utility. In the transcendental view, predators had aesthetic value but no more than any other wild species. In the ecosystem view, which had become dominant by the late twentieth century, predators stood at the top of a natural ecosystem, the maintenance of which depended on their presence. Their roles and functions as caretakers of the ecosystem were reinscribed into the general popular consciousness. The literature produced about the snow leopards under ecological science and its cognate disciplines such as conservation biology "purified" the animal by representing it simply as a species connected to an ecosystem, thus deemphasizing its links with human society.

PREDATORS IN EARLY ENVIRONMENTAL MOVEMENTS

There are purportedly two different origins of the modern conservation movement, namely, the American experience of the New World and the European experience of the colonial world (Cronon 1995; Grove 1990).[2] The first was driven primarily by a concern to protect beautiful scenery, as manifested by the national parks movement of the nineteenth century—an aesthetic reason. The second was more concerned with the conservation of natural resources, mainly rivers, soil, and forests, by colonial authorities for revenue generation—a utilitarian reason (Oelschlaeger 1991; Grove 1990). Although one would be tempted to see these two strands of environmentalism based on two different—aesthetic and utilitarian—motives; doing so would be too simplistic. In the United States during the nineteenth century various laws for the protection of natural resources were introduced on utilitarian grounds.[3] Likewise, colonial views of conservation were also often inspired by aesthetic and cultural appeals, such as nostalgia for the homeland or as an escape from civilization.[4] Moreover, wild predators may be protected or persecuted for reasons other than their utilitarian value. For example, Lord Curzon refused to hunt lions in Junagarh because he thought it was a shame that such a magnificent animal was on the verge of extinction by colonial government policies (Divyabhanusinh 2002, 105).

What is important here is that neither of these strands of the environmental movement attempted to conserve wild predators but rather advocated for their active persecution, albeit on different grounds. In the colonial view, wild predators imposed economic burden on society, while in the American view, they did not belong in the purified "wilderness" of the nineteenth century, which comprised few game species. Wild predators were actively destroyed in national parks across the United States and Africa to increase the number of popular game species (Spence 1999, 116; Neumann 2002, 236) and also, perhaps, maintain the species that were safe for viewing by tourists.

The same attitude toward wild predators prevailed in colonial conservation practices across Asia and Africa up until the first half of the twentieth century. While game species were actively conserved, wild predators were actively eradicated. In India the first legal protection was provided to elephants in the 1874 Elephant Protection Act, which protected the elephant as an economic species. Perhaps the only exception to a universal dislike for predators were the indigenous traditions of totemism and the traditions of various princes in India who kept predators as symbols of the richness of biodiversity in their domains and as resources to build political capital by offering them for shooting to influential people in the colonial bureaucracy (Hughes 2013).[5]

ECOLOGICAL SCIENCE AND MAKING OF A WILDERNESS PREDATOR

A fundamental shift in attitudes toward wild predators came with the new field of ecological science (Worster 1994; Oelschlaeger 1991).[6] The rise of ecological sciences in the 1930s and its flowering into a fully developed discipline by the 1970s gave wild predators a new lease on life. The primary area of study in ecology, or ecological science, was how communities of different wild species are structured and how they mutually regulate each other (Fretwell 1987, 291). Ecological scientists examined nature as an ecosystem, as a collection of interrelated organisms in their physical habitat.[7] The idea of an ecosystem was first introduced through the concept of trophic levels by the English zoologist Charles Elton (Fretwell 1987, 292). Trophic levels comprise any group of organisms that share the same function in a food chain. For example, in a snow leopard–dominated ecosystem, all animals that are prey of a snow leopard share a trophic level. Writing in 1927 in his now famous book *Animal Ecology*, Elton speculated on the question of the links between food, trophic levels, and the broader ecological community. Elton described the ecosystem as a food-web and argued that life was stacked in a pyramid in which the biggest predators stood at the top (Elton 1927, 50).

The term *ecosystem* was coined by the English botanist Arthur Tensley in 1935, and it became a fully recognized concept through American ecologist and environmentalist Aldo Leopold's ([1949] 1990) idea of "thinking like a mountain," which combined scientific rigor with an ethical stance toward nature. In his famous book, *A Sand County Almanac*, Leopold puts forth the concept of a trophic cascade, wherein he realizes that killing a predator like a wolf carries serious implications for the rest of the ecosystem. Leopold emphasized interconnectedness as central to the idea of ecosystems in his oft repeated dictum: "A thing is right when it tends to preserve the integrity, stability, and beauty of the biotic community. It is wrong when it tends otherwise" (62). Here he is clearly talking about communities of species and their interaction with each other.

Ecologists have postulated the basic structure of a trophic cascade as one in which communities of plants and species are interlinked with each other in a food web. Plants turn the sun's energy into food, which sustains communities of herbivores, which in turn sustain the population of carnivores. There are different levels of organisms, with each level dependent on the preceding for its source of energy. Thus, the model is seen as bottom up, with the bottommost level of plants and animals serving as the foundation of the ecosystem and everything above determined by that level. In this model, top predators are considered the free riders of the ecosystem, as they feed no one.

This view was challenged in 1960 by ecologists who put forward a model that inverted the previous one, reasoning that the terrestrial world was green—meaning that it is largely covered in plants—because herbivores are kept from eating it all (Hairston, Smith, and Slobodkin 1960). And what kept those herbivores from turning the green world to dust, these authors suggested, were predators. This came to be known as Green World Hypothesis (Fretwell 1987; Beschta and Ripple 2009). Basically they said that it is not the communities at the bottom of the food chain that control the next higher level but rather the consumers at the higher trophic levels that limit the abundance of lower trophic levels. That is, the higher levels determine the lower levels, not the other way around.

This new way of thinking opened new avenues of ecological theory focusing on community-wide impacts of higher order predators on organisms at lower trophic levels (Steneck and Sala 2005, 15). Studies began to examine the role of predators rather than food servers. For example, in 1961 the Smithsonian Museum in Washington, DC, started the Serengeti Research Project to focus on the ecology and behavior of large predators in East Africa. In Isle Royale National Park in Michigan, researchers looked at the interactions between moose and wolves (McLaren and Peterson 1994). In 1966 Robert Paine of the University of Washington published a study in the *American Naturalist* on the effect of the absence of a marine predator on community ecology on the Olympic Peninsula in Washington. These works produced the idea of keystone species, which are species that greatly affect communities but constitute only a low proportion of the community biomass, mainly predators. Ecological science provided new methods of conservation through flagship theories such as the predator-prey theory (Holling 1959) and the theory of island biogeography (MacArthur and Wilson 1967).

The predator-prey theory maintains that large predators regulate the diversity and function of ecosystems through trophic cascade. The presence of large predators, such as gray wolves or cougars, in an ecosystem may affect both the behavior and population size of ungulate prey, such as elk and deer. This in turn reduces or limits ungulate herbivory, thus impacting the composition, structure, and functioning of native plant communities (Beschta and Ripple 2009). Along with wild predators, ecological sciences gave new importance to wild prey, which were previously important as game animals, as part of a food web. The theory became a prime vehicle through which wild predators could be discursively produced as scientific objects.

If predator-prey theory provided new theoretical leads and research directions to the merging field of ecological sciences, the theory of island biogeography provided it with policy direction upon which it could base the practice of conservation. The latter theory became the prime justification for the creation of a series of protected areas and their classification system during the 1960s. Taken together these two theories provided the foundation upon which the argument for the protection of wild predators could be made and the whole paradigm of modern conservation could be rested.

In addition to these studies, a general concern about the fate of wildlife in Africa emerged. Julian Huxley, the British evolutionary biologist and brother of Aldous Huxley, the author of *Brave New World*, went to Africa in the 1960s to study wildlife and came back alarmed by the conditions. Later on he founded the World Wildlife Fund. During the 1960s, studies of Serengeti lions by George Schaller and mountain gorillas by Dian Fossey further sparked the interest of scientists and the general public in wild predator conservation.

ECOLOGICAL SCIENCE AND THE PRODUCTION OF WILDERNESS PREDATORS

Ecology steadily evolved throughout the first half of the twentieth century to become an established academic discipline during the second. Scholars of environmental humanities Yrjö Haila and Peter Taylor (2001) explain, "Before the late 1960s and the environmental awakening, ecology hardly existed within academia as a coherent discipline at all but rather lived a shady life in the guise of disparate research traditions" (95). The first college-level course in ecology was taught at University College London in 1965. International collaborative research led to the establishment of research institutes in Uganda, Tanzania, Kenya, and India, focusing mainly on large predators during the 1960s and '70s. A further transformation occurred in ecological thinking with the rise of conservation biology and the idea of biodiversity in the 1990s, which provided new ways of thinking about and managing nature.[8]

The production of knowledge in the field of ecology provided scientific justification for the conservation of all wild species important to the functioning of an ecosystem. Ecological discourse reorganized the earlier science of natural history, zoology, and botany into conservation biology, which became more mission oriented: a science with a normative position and a goal. In the twentieth century we see for the first time a professional class that is fully committed to conservation and protection of nature as an ecosystem.

Today, as a result of the newly recognized importance of predators in ecological systems, "top-order predators are amongst the most studied wild organisms on the planet, and we know the natural history of many species in great detail, therefore, we have a deep understanding of their behavior and evolutionary ecology" (Hayward and Somers 2009, 2). Wild predators are the most frequently reintroduced category of animals in the wild (3), with the first predator reintroduced in the wild the Siberian lynx in Russia in 1941 (Schadt et al. 2002).[9] Moreover, there has been great amount of research on some iconic predators such as the wolf. Food habits or diet is the most studied aspect of wolf ecology (Pluskowski 2010).

But this increased research on wild predators and their influence on ecosystem dynamics was and continues to be conducted in national parks and protected areas. The reason for this choice is simple; these reserves provide a closed ecological system with minimal intrusion from humans, thus mimicking the laboratory conditions necessary for a scientific experiment. The more scientists are able to control the variables in the field, the more they are able to isolate the effect of predation on the wider structure and composition of communities. In other words, these studies have all been conducted in environments in which humans and their livestock were absent. The effect of the convention of studying predators in non-human environments, without predation of livestock, was that scientists did not build human impact into their studies, or when they did, it was only as disturbance. In addition to not paying enough attention to how predator ecology may be influenced by human practices, the ecological studies of large predators in the 1960s and '70s increasingly depended on remote methods such as tracking a radio-collared animal. Studying animals remotely has further exacerbated the affective divide between nature and culture and between the wild and the domesticated. The rise in remotely studying wildlife came from the ethos that "nature" should be observed but not subjected to intervention or experimentation. The idea was to study animals without being there, or without being an intruder (Benson 2010, 7).

Radio collaring became possible only in 1963 with the development of the science of immobilization during the 1950s. A New Zealand scientist, Colin Murdoch, invented a syringe and dart gun that could be used to administer vaccines to animals remotely. By the late 1950s, wildlife biologists in the United States were experimenting with darts for immobilizing animals to tag and enumerate them (Benson 2010, 65). One of the first attempts at immobilization of wild animals using a dart gun was carried out at the damming of the Zambezi River at Kariba by the Rhodesian government. It was called Operation Noah, named not only after its metaphorical similarity as a rescue mission but also for its literal similarity with the biblical event—a flood. The operation was launched by the Rhodesian government and led by the chief ranger of Rhodesia, Rupert Fothergill. This was the first translocation operation of its kind. From 1959 to 1964 over six thousand animals—elephants, antelopes, rhinos, lions, leopards, zebras, warthogs, small birds, and even snakes—were rescued and relocated. Fothergill pioneered the use of tranquilizer darts to subdue big game such as buffalo and rhino.

The invention of the dart and dart gun coincided with the invention of small radio transmitters that could be mounted on animals. Combined, these two technological developments allowed for remote study of wild animals. Twin brothers John and Frank Craighead studied the grizzly bears of Yellowstone National Park in the 1960s using radio collars for the first time (Craighead and Craighead 1971). In the following years, John Seidensticker put a radio collar on a mountain lion and studied its social behavior. Seidensticker (1976) later went on to radio collar tigers in Nepal.[10] This technique helped reinforce the ideal wilderness predator image, because now predators could be studied in their "natural" conditions, that is, or away from the gaze of an ever-present human eye. Physical separation between humans and predators became the new standard of research in predator ecology.

The anthropologist Julie Guthman (1997) has argued that the production of environmental knowledge and facts is "intimately connected to the production of interventions, and thus intrinsically bound up with power relations" (45). Thus, environmental knowledge not only enlarges our understanding of how nature works but also provides us with blueprints for how to save it. The early research on the importance of predators shows that the potential for human-wildlife conflict is built into the very process of production of knowledge about wildlife because the research process implicitly leaves out issues related to human presence in an ecosystem. This meant that when this research was translated into conservation action, it was ill suited to anticipate and take into account encounters between people and predators. And when conflict did occur, conservation programs blamed the locals for it. Eventually, this practice was transformed into established policy within conservation institutions and continues to be practiced today. The implication of this process of "wilderness predator" production is that predator conservation today continues to be advocated on the basis of a protected-areas approach because, ideally, they are devoid of human presence.[11]

PRODUCING THE SNOW LEOPARD AS WILDERNESS PREDATOR

Research on snow leopards has also been carried out mostly in national parks across its home range. The first study of snow leopards was conducted in Chitral Gol National Park in northern Pakistan by George Schaller in the early 1970s, who at the time worked for the Wildlife Conservation Society. Until this time there had been no scientific study of wild snow leopards, and the budding conservation community had very little knowledge about their distribution and home range, food habits, mating seasons, litter size, or habitat selection. Schaller wanted to know all of this and more. He was particularly interested in knowing the home range of the snow leopard to calculate the extent of their travel and the patterns of their territoriality. For this reason, Schaller wanted to put a radio collar on a snow leopard to study its movement. He chose Chitral Gol National Park to conduct his study because he thought that it harbored a healthy population of snow leopards, but he failed to trap a snow leopard for collaring so he gave up. He did, however, have his first encounter with a snow leopard in the wild. His description of his encounter with the snow leopard is poetic. It elevates the status of the snow leopard as an iconic wilderness predator. He writes, "Then I saw the snow leopard, a hundred and fifty feet away, peering at me from the spur, her body so well molded into the contours of the boulders that she seemed a part of them. Her smoky-gray coat sprinkled with black rosettes perfectly complemented the rocks and snowy wastes, and her pale eyes conveyed the image of immense solitude" (1988, 8–9). The last sentence rhetorically connects the snow leopard to the wilderness.

After Chitral, Schaller traveled up to Khunjerab and Shimshal Valleys in Upper Hunza, and then to Braldu Valley in Baltistan. He quickly surveyed these areas, looking for snow leopard signs, such as scat, spoor, scent mark, or claw rakes. Unable to find much wildlife, Schaller concluded that the snow leopard in Pakistan was in peril. In his book, with the metaphorical title *Stones of Silence*, Schaller wrote despairingly about the future of wildlife in the region. He quoted a passage from his previous book about his thoughts on the current state of wildlife in the Himalaya: "But the great age of mammals in the Himalaya need not be over unless we permit it to be. For epochs to come the peaks will still pierce the lonely vistas, but when the last snow leopard has stalked among the crags and the last markhor has stood on a promontory, his ruff waving in the breeze, a spark of life will have gone, turning the mountains into stones of silence" (1988, 2–3).

In these words Schaller was clearly laying a new vision on these mountains, a vision in which the snow leopard emerges as an imperiled species of this great wilderness. He estimated that no more than 250 snow leopards survived in the wild in Pakistan, and that to ensure their survival, the government should establish a set of protected areas. In hindsight it seems that this number was very conservative and pessimistic, but given how little time Schaller spent in the field, it is no surprise that he came up with this figure. The Karakoram, Himalayas, and Hindu Kush, the three mountain ranges that meet in northern Pakistan, constitute a vast landscape in which it is very difficult directly to observe wildlife. The sheer elevation of snow leopard habitat that is found between ten thousand and eighteen thousand feet coupled with the snow leopard's elusive nature make it impossible to judge its density in a mere two-week-long trip.

Schaller also studied the snow leopard in China, Nepal, and later in Mongolia, mainly focusing on its distribution, abundance, and diet. His research and writings introduced the snow leopard to the Western conservation community as an endangered species, threatened by humans, and to the general public as a ghost or mythical cat. Although Schaller found in his study of the Chitral Gol snow leopards in Pakistan that domestic livestock remains were found in almost half of the snow leopard scats, this fact did not weaken his adherence to the image of the snow leopard as "wilderness predator."

The first study of a radio-collared snow leopard was conducted by the biologist Rodney Jackson between 1981 and 1985 in the Langu River Gorge in northwestern Nepal, which provided an ideal snow leopard habitat. During this period, Jackson managed to put radio collars on five snow leopards and to observe their movements and behaviors. This was the first time a researcher had succeeded in collaring a snow leopard. As a memento of this remarkable feat, Jackson was also bitten by a snow leopard that was only partially sedated. The study made the cover of the *National Geographic* magazine in 1986.

Jackson was looking for the same basic answers about snow leopard ecology and behavior that motivated Schaller. He wanted to know if snow leopards are solitary animals, and if so, how they communicate with each other, the size of their home range, whether they defend territories, what they hunt and how frequently, and how much they travel (Hillard 1989, 26). Jackson spent four seasons in Nepal's Langu Gorge, systematically recording radio-collared animals' home ranges, mating cycles, hunting patterns, and habitat preferences and use. He found that the cat's home range in the Langu Gorge was between seventeen and thirty-nine square kilometers. The cat was active mostly during the day and used mostly broken terrain. Jackson's study provided much-needed information to the scientific community and spurred further work in determining home ranges and distribution of snow leopards.

Based on this study Jackson's partner, Darla Hillard, wrote a wonderful account titled *Vanishing Tracks*. Jackson was ahead of his time in seeing the trend that conservation biology should take. Although trained as an ecologist at University College in London in the 1970s, Jackson was fully aware that successful conservation efforts lie not only in creating protected areas but also in working with local people. His philosophy and approach to snow leopard conservation was almost diametrically opposed to Schaller's. For example, Schaller believed, based on little to no discussion with local people, that they killed snow leopards simply because the animals presented a suitable target. Jackson preferred to get a more informed and contextual explanation for why local people killed snow leopards.

Hillard (1989) recalls that Jackson said, "I wonder what would happen if we had to live here for the rest of our lives. . . . Working side by side with the Dolphas, herding yaks and farming, would we be any better at using the land wisely? How long would pass before we, too, stopped caring much about what happens to the snow leopards?" (304). While not exactly exonerating the local people for their behavior, Jackson was trying to put things in the context of the relationship between the conditions of livelihood and one's attitude toward nature. Jackson rightly acknowledged that in communities where personal and community survival is the most pressing issue, care of wildlife on intrinsic or cultural ground can take a back seat.

Another sustained study of snow leopards was carried out by the biologist Tom McCarthy, who started working with George Schaller in Mongolia in the 1990s. Between 1993 and 1999, McCarthy (1999) studied snow leopard movement and home range and concluded that it was much larger than Jackson had reported: 61 to 142 square kilometers for males and 58 to 1,590 square kilometers for females. McCarthy attributed this variation to the density of natural prey and the habitat conditions. He stated that in areas with low prey density, snow leopards command a large territory where they hunt and breed. In the area Jackson explored in Nepal, because of abundant natural prey, snow leopards defended a smaller territory than what McCarthy found in his study of a habitat that nomadic herders had traveled through and used extensively. Based on his survey, McCarthy concluded that there were perhaps eight hundred to seventeen hundred snow leopards in Mongolia.

In the 1990s Indian and Norwegian ecologists used radio telemetry studies in the Ladakh region of India to study snow leopard home range and feeding ecology. Raghu Chandwat tracked radio-collared snow leopards in Hemis National Park and based on his findings recommended that the size of the park be increased to accommodate snow leopard movement patterns.

What is notable about the early research is that almost all of it was conducted in protected areas and almost all of the researchers recommended establishment of more protected areas for snow leopards. We see this trend continue even to this day. Although there is certainly more recognition of the "human" problem, protected areas in one form or another continue to be the main approach to snow leopard conservation.

During the 1990s the International Snow Leopard Trust developed a standardized methodology for surveying and reporting snow leopard populations that included gathering information from local people. The method was called SLIMS—Snow Leopard Information Management System— which was an indexical method. SLIMS included information on snow leopard presence signs (tracks, spray and spoor marks, scrapes, claw rake, and scent marking), habitat quality, prey species quality and abundance, and information gathered from villagers.

SLIMS was widely used in the 1990s but in the early 2000s, it came under criticism from other snow leopard ecologists for its lack of applicability across the range. For example, among presence signs, it is very difficult to pick up tracks on a rocky trail or in areas where it rains a lot. Moreover, spray marks and spoor marks might appear more frequently in one habitat type than another without much difference in the relative abundance of the cat. Once SLIMS was discarded in the early 2000s, given its limitations, the opportunity for conservation scientists to interact with local people was also diminished.[12] The indigenous knowledge of the local people that had been taken seriously and incorporated into the scientific data and theories through SLIMS was no longer used, furthering the divide between local people and snow leopard scientists. Newer survey technology, based on remote cameras and the collection of snow leopard scat for genetic testing, meant that field-based scientists no longer had to talk to local people.

In the first decade of the twenty-first century, the use of genetic techniques and camera traps to determine snow leopard density became widespread. They became the benchmark against which the quality and reliability of data about snow leopard population was measured. Camera trap studies focused on the core problem of snow leopard conservation, namely, devising a method to estimate snow leopard population as accurately as possible.[13] In addition, noninvasive methods of DNA collection were developed by molecular biologists working in labs in Europe and America, which meant that the identity of a species could be determined by its scat. Since then, developments in sequencing techniques now make it possible to identify the prey remains in the scat accurately, eliminating any human subjective errors in visual identification of prey remains. These methods, while reducing the interaction between scientists and local people, have at the same time produced information that has confirmed some of the local knowledge. For example, we now know that snow leopards are not as threatened as we thought they were, and that a substantial portion of their diet in conflict-prone areas comes from domestic livestock.

SCIENTIFIC UNCERTAINTY AND CONSERVATION POLICY

Despite an explosion of research, many gaps remain in our knowledge about large predators, especially their behavior in human-dominated systems. The science of large predator conservation is hardly definitive because the switch from a competition-based model of community ecology to a predator-regulated model in itself remains contested (Ray 2005). The theory of trophic cascade has been validated for only seven of the thirty-one mammalian carnivores (Ripple et al. 2014, 151). Moreover, debate continues about the "path" predators take in changing an ecosystem, whether it is by controlling the population density of the prey by physical predation or the behavioral changes in the prey due to the presence of the predator (Ripple et al. 2014). Few studies have looked at the role of the snow leopard as the keystone predator, although almost all snow leopard conservation discourse is based on the assumption that the snow leopard *is* the keystone predator. The closest any study comes to looking at snow leopard effects on the ecosystem is at one level of the trophic cascade or, in other words, the predator-prey relationship. In this study ecologists have looked at how the recovery of snow leopards in Mount Everest National Park impacted the population of tahr, its natural prey (Ferretti et al. 2014). No systematic way exists to study how that might then affect the vegetation or bring about other changes in the next trophic level. This study was possible only because of the experiment-like conditions that were created with the absence and presence of the snow leopard. Other ecological studies look at interspecific competition and food and habitat preference for predators and foraging and browsing preference of wild and domestic ungulates. But none of them nail down the keystone predator role of the snow leopard. It is also not clear if snow leopards regulate behavior of the herbivores through predation or avoidance and what effects this has on vegetation diversity.

Whether or not the snow leopard is a keystone species, what is important to note here is that it is prima facie given that status primarily because it justifies its protection on ecological and scientific grounds. In some ways scientific research preempts its own results.[14]

While many experts recognize that there are questions about the predator-regulated model, they still make management and policy decisions as if it has been proven that predators regulate ecosystems through the top-down trophic cascade.[15] Conservation institutions and professionals may also advocate for conservation of predators not only for their assumed unique role in an ecosystem but also for a more pragmatic reason: it enables them to justify enlarging territories under conservation management (Ray 2005, 40–41). If predators are strategically identified as endangered, the public is more likely to pay attention than if less charismatic species are at risk. The establishment of a system of protected areas of wildlife preserves to protect tigers in India serves as a prime example of using wild predators to rationalize setting aside land for conservation.[16] The wilderness predator becomes a self-fulfilling prophecy. According to Luke Hunter (2011)—a biologist with Panthera, a leading international NGO working exclusively for the protection of the Panthera group of carnivores, which includes the snow leopard—"The key to saving most carnivores relies on the existence of large expanses of wilderness relatively free from human influences" (13). Hunter, however, cautions that even keeping habitat intact is meaningless as these habitats do not have enough prey species to sustain predator populations. Therefore, creating protected areas for large predators requires not only alienating land from other uses but also imposing a ban on killing wildlife species that people hunt for subsistence. Another way in which land is set aside for conservation of snow leopards is on the basis of its home range requirement. For example, a habitat study of the snow leopard states that "40% of the 170 protected areas in the global range of the snow leopard (*Panthera uncia*) are smaller than the home range of a single adult male and only 4–13% are large enough for a 90% probability of containing 15 or more adult females" (Johannsen et al. 2016, 1). These types of studies become the means for rallying support to set aside more protected areas.

TERRITORIALIZING CONSERVATION

Never before in the history of humanity have we had the kind of relationship with the natural world as we have now. Today, management plans and strategies for wild species exist. The various classification, enumeration, and monitoring efforts by scientists over the past century have resulted in a strict regime of surveillance and control. These classification systems constructed an order in the natural world. The emergence of ecological science and consciousness about the finitude of natural resources and the unending human desire to accumulate them produced another kind of classifications system: lists, plans, strategies, commission reports, and conventions and declarations for the protection of threatened wildlife and other living things. All of these social products of conservation practice classify nature according to degrees of threat. If one product attempts to curb international trade in endangered species, then the other safeguards their migration across state boundaries. The materiality of these products, as hard and bounded objects, creates an illusion of protection to species that exist in the wild.

In conservation practice, a wild species is something about which there exist certain scientific facts. The most important facts are about how species fit into ecology, such as its relative abundance and distribution. Other information such as behavior and habitat conditions are also important. When conservation biology journals disseminate knowledge of these wild landscapes and the species within, they reify these objects and grant them materiality. Whether or not a territory is worthy of conservation hinges on data such as animal densities, sightings, presence and absence, threat level, habitat suitability, and carrying capacity. Generally, there exists an inverse relationship between the threats to species and the appeal and legitimacy of these products: Threatened and fragile species confer stability to these products.

An example of how these products "manage" and "domesticate" wild landscapes and wildlife therein is the latest fad in snow leopard protection: a landscape-level approach to conservation. This approach is advocated by the Global Snow Leopard and Ecosystem Protection Program (GSLEP), which has set a target of establishing twenty snow leopard landscapes across the snow leopard range by the year 2020. Under this approach, conservation practice focuses on an entire landscape, consisting of both human and nonhuman species, but the main emphasis is to keep them apart while also talking about their overlap. In fact, this overlap becomes the problem of disturbance that needs to be solved. The emphasis on human population and its effects on wildlife should be seen not as the indicator of a more inclusionary conservation policy but as the opposite. The objective is to connect different protected areas by means of ecological corridors to conservation of a large landscape (ecosystem). Management and planning of these landscapes are conducted through resignification of the landscapes under a new system of knowledge and meaning. These landscapes have come into being in and through the act of planning. Making landscape-level management plans brings these theoretical landscapes into the administrative realm. It is the science that does the job: ecological science lays down the basic rules for these landscapes.

Just as landscape paintings are grounded in imagination, so are the landscape-level plans. But how does this work of imagination turn into concrete reality? Conservation discourse and practice domesticate a landscape in three steps. The first step is the initial apprehension and appropriation of a landscape as worthy of conservation. This usually happens when an area becomes famous for harboring an endangered and charismatic species, such as the mountain gorilla or snow leopard. Conservation institutions conduct initial surveys and prepare reports and research papers bringing the landscape within the discursive frame of conservation.

In the second step conservation institutions measure a potential landscape unit, define it in detail, identify its boundaries, and fix them physically. This is the stage of actual apprehension and appropriation of the landscape, mainly through regulatory means. Laws are passed to appropriate public land in the name of conservation. International treaties, conventions, and accords also play a role in this process, as they become reference points for justification of conservation action.

The third step occurs when conservation institutions give a territory a specific ecological numerical value and classification. So, for example, the GSLEP recommends creating twenty snow leopard landscapes across its range by the 2020, with each harboring at least a hundred breeding pairs of snow leopards (Snow Leopard Working Secretariat 2013, 15). The idea and the subtheme of connectivity between protected areas to create conservation landscapes have given rise to concepts such as "source" and "sink" populations, "corridors," "core zone," and "buffer zones." The end result is creating a landscape of conservation that stands for wild and untamed nature under threat from human populations.

It is these numbers, such as 100 breeding pairs and twenty landscapes, each of at least a certain size, that gives these landscapes a semblance of real existence. But what is the basis of these numbers? What is their basis for being grounded in environmental reality? For example, why should each snow leopard landscape harbor 100 pairs? Why not 74 or 127? Currently, Pakistan is proposing to prepare three such landscape-level plans that cover almost its entire snow leopard habitat. According to the GSLEP criteria, then, these three landscapes will harbor six hundred snow leopards. Recently, the scientists affiliated with GSLEP announced that only twenty-three snow leopards were left in Pakistan!

If science is about precision, its data reflect approximation, which is often taken as generalization. The fact is that these metrics may be based on an existing body of literature, but the problem with that argument is that our existing knowledge of predators is based on culturally modified landscapes, including protected areas. And these landscape-level conservation models and plans usually do not take this human influence into account. The final product of this exercise is a "domesticated" land where wildlife roams free of danger, and rural mountain farmers lose their land and its meaning.

The presence of signs of wildlife and other ecological parameters become potent in the context of a global biodiversity crisis. Snow leopards are territorial animals. They leave various kinds of calling cards throughout the territory they inhabit. They defend their territory against others, and the size of the territory they control varies with other factors, such as availability of prey and terrain suitability. Biologists use snow leopard territory-marking behavior as an index of its population density. Conservation institutions use density of snow leopard presence signs—tracks, scat, spoors and spray marks—to index landscapes under different classifications schemes. These mobilities of snow leopards as observed by biologists translate into "core zone," "corridors of connectivity," and "buffer zones." The idea of connectivity is redesigning territory in new ways. Some might call this reterritorialization.

If a surveying biologist finds snow leopard tracks more frequently in one territory than in another, then the territory with more signs becomes important from a conservation point of view. Areas with high densities of territorial markings get categorized as suitable snow leopard habitat. It comes under a different set of regulations than it had traditionally been under. This new use of territory as a space given to wild animals and their movements has resulted in displacement of many people across the world, creating environmental refugees, people without territory. Snow leopard signs become exclusionary signs, even though the best places to find snow leopard tracks are alongside human and livestock trails. Trails opened by humans and their livestock become, indirectly, vehicles of their own dispossession if snow leopards start using the same trails. Just as yak movements to new pastures and along new routes open up the possibility of extending and claiming territory for local communities, so does the movement of wild snow leopards for conservationists. This process runs parallel to the process of production of "wilderness predator," and the two go hand in hand.

CONCLUSION

While the shift in attitude among Euro-Americans and national elites has provided the snow leopard a new identity and protection, local views of the animal remain unchanged. They may even have become more negative because the snow leopard has now become a symbol of outsiders' agendas. In historical terms then, what was a genuinely snow leopard–human conflict has become a human-human conflict as more than 90 percent of snow leopard habitat is outside the protected areas (Nowell et al. 1996). This conflict has intensified with the introduction of modern technologies and poisons—and of conservation projects. Local people now have sophisticated tools to eliminate predators, along with new fears and anxieties.

Almost all studies that focus on the human-wildlife conflict seek to portray local peoples' attitudes toward wildlife. Perhaps a more meaningful approach would be to assess local attitudes toward conservationists and conservation institutions. Such a change in the focus would highlight the dissonance between the significance of wildness for local societies and for outside conservationists. This disjuncture is particularly acute in the debate over how to resolve the conflict between herders and the snow leopard. There seems to be a basic epistemological disagreement over the nature of the snow leopard and its basic ecological requirements.

At the end of the nineteenth century both British big game hunters and the local farmers of Baltistan and surrounding regions saw the snow leopard as an unwanted predator that preyed on game and livestock. By the end of the twentieth century, however, the outsiders' view of the snow leopard changed. While the big game sportsmen had been confined to some exclusive clubs, during the last half century a new class of outsiders—conservationists—emerged and has taken the role of advocates of wildlife rights and needs. These outsiders see the snow leopard as an indicator, a keystone species, and apex predator whose conflict with farmers reflects a threat to the ecosystem. The heart of the matter leads us to the construction of human-wildlife conflict.

CHAPTER THREE

Human-Wildlife Conflict

Human-wildlife conflict is generally understood in conservation biology literature as damage done by wildlife to humans and their property.[1] Within the profession of wildlife management, this conflict is a quantifiable and reducible phenomenon to which specific techniques can be applied. In addition to assessing the extent of financial damage that predators inflict and delineating ecological factors associated with crop or animal loss, conservation institutions concerned by human-wildlife conflict also study local attitudes toward wildlife.[2] Social scientists have defined human-wildlife conflict in a different way. The anthropologist John Knight (2000) argues that in human-wildlife conflict the real conflict is not between wildlife and people but rather between people with differing views about the proper place of wildlife in society. From a social sciences perspective, especially that of anthropology, human-wildlife conflict is a contest between different segments of society over the meaning and impact of nature and their relationships with it. Political ecologists regard conflict in the field of conservation as a struggle over how to manage nature and how to distribute its costs and benefits. They argue that modern conservation practices impose excessive costs on rural dwellers while dispossessing them of ecological knowledge and a moral relationship with nature.[3]

From the point of view of social sciences and political ecology, the standard conservation narrative about snow leopards is of their perpetual decline, and that is essential for the spectacle of snow leopards being under threat by farmers. This narrative presents the root of the conflict as not necessarily the predation of livestock by snow leopards but the retaliatory killings by farmers. This one-sided focus obfuscates and fetishizes the causal and historical relationship between the actions of snow leopards and the reactions of farmers. The specter of the snow leopard under attack by farmers is what haunts and preys on people's emotions, and the representation of this specter as a spectacle allows people to consume it and lighten their mental distress. "A twenty-dollar donation will stop farmers from killing snow leopards," a donor might think. But why snow leopards are killing domestic goats and why farmers are killing snow leopards will rarely cross his mind.

LEVEL OF PREDATION: SNOW LEOPARD SCAT STUDIES

Predation of domestic livestock by snow leopards is a major source of the animal's conflict with humans and arguably one of the greatest threats to its population. A recent study on global poaching of snow leopards showed that about half of the pelts that are traded on the global market have their origins in conflicts between snow leopards and farmers (Nowell et al. 2016). An assessment of the dietary preference of snow leopards from published papers has shown that domestic livestock—including cattle, yaks, domestic dogs, horses, donkeys, sheep, and goats—constitute about 25 percent of the total prey consumed by snow leopards globally (Lyngdoh et al. 2014, 9).

There are two sources of information on the extent of damage caused by snow leopards to farmers' livestock: attributed predation to snow leopards by local farmers and the actual remains of domestic livestock in snow leopards' diets. The first kind of information comes from villagers' contributions to interviews and surveys conducted by conservationists. The second comes from the frequency of prey remains in snow leopard scat analyzed by conservation scientists.

During the 1980s and 1990s, most studies of snow leopard diets used visual evidence to identify prey remains in snow leopard scat. In Chitral Gol National Park in northern Pakistan, about 45 percent of the snow leopard scat contained livestock remains, and studies in China showed similar proportions (Schaller 1988). In Nepal 25 percent of the biomass consumed by snow leopards came from domestic livestock (Oli et al. 1993). Remains of domestic livestock are less frequent in scats taken from more remote regions. For example, in the Langu Gorge in Nepal, wild prey remains were found in 82 percent of the scats (Jackson and Ahlborn 1989); this presumably means that the remaining 18 percent was domestic livestock.

In Mongolia about 31 percent of the snow leopard diet came from domestic livestock (Lhagvasuren and Munkhtsog 2000). A decade later, another study from another part of Mongolia reported that 27 percent of the snow leopard diet was domestic livestock (Johansson et al. 2015, 251). In Ladakh in the Indian Himalayas, a high proportion, 40 to 58 percent, of livestock was found in the snow leopard diet (Bagchi and Mishra 2006), and 38 percent of the total livestock losses was attributed to snow leopards (Namgail, Fox, and Bhatnagar 2007, 490). In the second decade of the twenty-first century, the snow leopard had returned to Sagarmatha National Park for the first time in three decades (Ferretti et al. 2014), and two years later a study published from the same region showed that about 27 percent of the snow leopard diet came from domestic livestock (Chetri, Odden, and Wegge 2017). This begs the obvious question about what role domestic livestock may have played in both the crash and recovery of the snow leopard population in central Nepal.

Looking for livestock remains in the snow leopard diet relies on the skills of the field biologist. There is always a chance of misclassifying scat from wolves, lynxes, or foxes as that of snow leopards. Field biologists use electronic microscopes to identify animal remains in scat by using a "key" in which body parts, especially the hair of wild ungulates, are compared with those found in the scat. Again, the reliability of this method depends on the skills of the researcher.

With DNA analyses becoming more and more accessible, estimates of the dietary contribution of domestic livestock have become more accurate. Our project, Baltistan Wildlife Conservation and Development Organization, conducted one of the first studies using the DNA method to identify snow leopard scat. This 2011 study found that of the hundred samples of scat collected as snow leopard scat, only fifty-seven were actually from snow leopards (Anwar et al. 2011). When these scats were analyzed, we found that about 70 percent of the biomass consumed by the snow leopard came from domestic livestock. These results showed a very high dependence on human domestic economy—evidence of the high subsidy provided by local farmers to the snow leopard population.[4]

While conservation institutions acknowledge in scientific papers that snow leopards subsist on domestic livestock, this fact does not seem to be translated into any concrete policy or practice on the ground. So, for example, a study of predation rates in Ladakh, in northern India, reported that snow leopards could be relying less on wild prey due to the availability of domestic prey: "Domestic ungulates must also be considered as diminishing snow leopard dependence on wild ungulates in some areas" (Fox et al. 1991, 293). Another way to describe this situation is that the snow leopard's dependence on domestic livestock diminishes the local peoples' capacity to survive in harsh mountain environments. But the situation is hardly ever described in this way as it inverts the institutional discourse that privileges wildlife over rural farmers, and indirectly the status quo. This is also relevant to the representation of predation as a problem of disturbance in the nature-culture boundary.

IDENTIFICATION OF THREATS TO THE SNOW LEOPARD

In May of 2002, the International Snow Leopard Trust organized the first Snow Leopard Summit in Seattle's Woodland Park Zoo. It was the culmination of a long process of collaboration by experts in all the home range countries.[5] Some sixty experts from the twelve home range countries participated in the summit, which the International Snow Leopard Trust declared a success in carving out a concerted plan to protect the snow leopard population.[6] This plan, the first Snow Leopard Survival Strategy (SLSS), was a comprehensive document that described the state of knowledge of the snow leopard, the threats facing its population, and the actions needed to mitigate those threats. In the years since, the SLSS has been periodically revised and continues to act as a guiding document for snow leopard conservationists all over the world.[7]

The SLSS 2003 identified twenty-one threats facing the snow leopard population. These threats across their range, which vary in degree and intensity, can be divided into four broad categories: habitat degradation and prey reduction, direct killings, lack of appropriate policy and awareness, and other issues such as war and climate change.

In 2013 the Global Snow Leopard and Ecosystem Protection Program (GSLEP), a truly global and consolidated international initiative, was launched to protect the snow leopard and its habitat. Backed by the World Bank and a consortium of snow leopard conservation organizations, GSLEP brought all twelve home range countries to one table. The program produced its own plan, the Global Snow Leopard and Ecosystem Protection Plan (also GSLEP), listing thirty-two threats to the snow leopard population, which were later included in the 2014 version of the Snow Leopard Survival Strategy. The GSLEP plan became the primary document for global action on snow leopard protection and is continuously being updated. Each of the home range countries has now produced its own National Snow Leopard Ecosystem Protection Plan to carry out protection at a national level. The list of threats to snow leopards, as identified in the SLSS 2003 and GSLEP 2013, are a representative sample of this institutional literature. In these documents several threats to snow leopard populations are identified and almost all of them result from its conflict with local people.

TABLE 3.1. Threats to the snow leopard

SLSS 2003 (21 THREATS)	GSLEP 2013 AND SLSS 2014 (32 THREATS)
Category 1: Habitat and Prey Related	**Category 1: Habitat and Prey Related**
1.1 Habitat degradation and fragmentation	1.1 Habitat degradation
1.2 Reduction of natural prey due to illegal or unregulated hunting	1.2 Habitat fragmentation
1.3 Reduction of natural prey due to legal hunting	1.3 Prey reduction due to illegal hunting
1.4 Reduction of natural prey due to competition with livestock	1.4 Prey reduction due to competition with livestock
1.5 Reduction of natural prey due to disease	1.5 Prey reduction due to legal hunting
1.6 Fencing that disrupts natural animal movements and migration	1.6 Prey reduction due to disease
	1.7 Fencing that disrupts movements/natural migration
Category 2: Direct Killing of Snow Leopards	**Category 2: Direct Killing or Removal of Snow Leopards**
2.1 Killing of snow leopards in retribution for livestock depredation loss	2.1 Retribution for livestock depredation
2.2 Poaching snow leopards for trade in hides or bones	2.2 Poaching for trade in hides or bones
2.3 Zoo and museum collection of live animals	2.3 Zoo and museum collection of live animals
2.4 Traditional hunting of snow leopards	2.4 Traditional hunting of snow leopards
2.5 Secondary poisoning and trapping of snow leopards	2.5 Secondary poisoning and trapping of snow leopards
2.6 Diseases of snow leopards	2.6 Diseases of snow leopards
	2.7 Potential threat from legal hunting of snow leopards
Category 3: Policy and Awareness	**Category 3: Policy and Awareness**
3.1 Lack of appropriate policy	3.1 Lack of appropriate policy
3.2 Lack of effective enforcement	3.2 Lack of effective enforcement
3.3 Lack of trans-boundary cooperation	3.3 Lack of transboundary cooperation
3.4 Lack of institutional capacity	3.4 Lack of institutional capacity
3.5 Lack of awareness among local people	3.5 Lack of awareness among local people
3.6 Lack of awareness among policy makers	3.6 Lack of awareness among policy makers

Category 4: Other Issues
- 4.1 War and related military activities
- 4.2 Climate change
- 4.3 Human population growth and poverty (indirect threat)

Category 4: Other Issues
- 4.1 War and related military activities
- 4.2 Human population growth (rapid)
- 4.3 Poverty (indirect threat)
- 4.4 Feral dogs attacking snow leopards and prey
- 4.5 Poaching and wildlife trade by migrant workers
- 4.6 Poaching by military personnel

Category 5. Emerging Threats
- 5.1 Climate change
- 5.2 Growing livestock populations and intensifying human-wildlife conflict
- 5.3 Large-scale development projects
- 5.4 Direct and indirect impacts due to mineral exploration/mining
- 5.5 Impacts due to hydroelectric projects
- 5.6 Impacts due to roads or railroads
- 5.7 Disturbance related to cordyceps collection

DISAGREEMENTS

The standard conservation narrative that frames the snow leopard–farmer conflict in the above two documents, and literature of the snow leopard in general, can be divided into two parts: human-induced habitat degradation and reduction of the snow leopard's wild prey due to illegal hunting, and the lack of awareness among farmers about the true ecological importance of the snow leopard. Although they are seemingly reasonable explanations for the conflict, they are not necessarily the complete truths and look less convincing and more questionable when examined in light of historical and currently available evidence. These explanations by conservation institutions, as constitutive of snow leopard–farmer conflict, amounts to four fundamental disagreements between conservation institutions and local farmers: the extent of damage to the snow leopard habitat, the ontology of the snow leopard and structure of its ecosystem, the extent to which causes of predation are to be blamed on society (farmers) or nature (snow leopards) (Dove and Khan 1995), and the extent of damage done by snow leopards to farmers' livelihoods.

Eventually, these disagreements have implications for how the impact of predation is to be remedied: through technical and spatial fixes, such as protected areas, or through structural changes, such as compensation and an inclusive policy. These disagreements and their consequences show a basic division between how the conservation institutions and farmers conceptualize nature.

Disagreement over the Extent of Damage to the Snow Leopard Habitat

Under habitat degradation and fragmentation, the Snow Leopard Survival Strategy identifies increased use by livestock of open rangeland. This depletes the snow leopard's natural prey population and thus results in increased attacks on domestic livestock.[8] The SLSS also states that the threat is exacerbated by increased human population and the illegal hunting of the snow leopard's wild (natural) prey by farmers, thus further reducing the availability of prey and inducing snow leopards to attack domestic livestock. But how severe is this encroachment and what is the current trend?[9]

There is a general impression given in the SLSS and conservation literature that throughout the snow leopard's home range, human population and livestock numbers are increasing, but there are not enough studies that show that this is universal.[10] In fact, evidence from Pakistan suggests that humans and livestock populations may even be declining in some valleys where snow leopards are found. For example, a report from Pakistan concludes, "The general trend seems to be that villages with higher employment outside the village are decreasing their share of livestock (Naqvi and Fatima 2012, 69).[11] Evidence from Shimshal, where I conducted my doctoral fieldwork, also suggests a decline in pastoralism. Since the last decade the number of yaks held by Shimshalis collectively has declined. But specific evidence apart from not being generalizable is also ignored by conservation organizations because it does not fit the institutional narrative of encroaching humans. It disrupts their story of the specter of humans ravaging the snow leopard's habitat.

Disagreement over Ontology of the Snow Leopard and the Structure of Its Ecosystem

Farmer-induced wild-prey deficiency is not the only explanation for the snow leopard's predation on livestock. Ample evidence shows that predators also frequently attack livestock in areas that are rich in wild prey, such as the edges of national parks.[12] Evidence from Baltistan, Pakistan, shows that one of the major problem valleys is Hushe, where the annual depredation rates by snow leopards are very high (8 percent of the total herd size) despite the valley's having one of the biggest populations of ibex in Pakistan.[13] A high population of snow leopards means that there is a high probability of encounters between snow leopards and domestic goats, resulting in higher predation. Lately some scientists have questioned the assumption that snow leopards kill domestic livestock only when there is a low density in its natural prey. Some have even revised their earlier positions on this issue. For example, a 2013 study suggests that predation of domestic livestock by snow leopards may actually be higher in areas where its natural prey is in higher densities.

> This is in contrast to our own earlier work where we have indicated that livestock depredation by snow leopards may decline with increase in wild-prey abundance (Bagchi and Mishra 2006). In fact, this premise has guided an important aspect of conflict management, viz., facilitating wild-prey population recovery (Mishra et al. 2003). Our present study, however, suggests that an increase in wild prey—a highly desirable conservation outcome considering their own endangerment and their functional role— would, in fact, lead to an increase in livestock depredation by snow leopards, presumably by supporting a greater abundance of the cat. We therefore hypothesize that the relationship between

snow leopard depredation of livestock and wild prey abundance may be bimodal. (Suryawanshi et al. 2013, 558)

Other explanations for snow leopards' attacks on domestic livestock include snow leopard–specific factors, especially the age and health of an individual. Most predators or large cats that attack livestock can be categorized as either subadults or as old and diseased or injured animals. In Gir Forest in the Indian state of Gujrat, most livestock killed by lions happened outside the protected wildlife reserve and in most cases subadults of both sexes were implicated (Saberwal et al. 1994). No study on snow leopards shows the relationships between predation and age or sex and health of individual snow leopards. This inference is made based on observations on other predators in other regions, mainly lions in Africa.

Conservationists account for snow leopards' behavior when they attack domestic goats, despite the availability of abundant wild prey, by negating their own characterization of the snow leopard as a truly wild animal. On the one hand, a snow leopard is considered a wild animal with autonomous agency, but on the other hand, when this autonomous snow leopard behaves "badly" by killing domestic goats, its action is attributed not to its predatory nature but rather to the negligence of human society. In this view, it is generally farmers' lax herding techniques or their hunting of the snow leopard's natural prey that prompts snow leopards to attack their livestock (McCarthy and Chapron 2003; Khatiwada, Chalise, and Kyes 2007). According to snow leopard–farmer conflict literature, predation of domestic livestock by a snow leopard is an unnatural event because domestic livestock is not its natural prey. Thus, in some ways, conservationists simultaneously classify and deny the snow leopard as an autonomous being with independent agency—that is, a truly wild animal. Despite this contradiction, the image of the snow leopard as an iconic species of wilderness persists among conservation professionals and society as it continues to be produced scientifically.

It is a conventional belief in conservation institutions that the ignorance of local people about how an ecosystem functions lies at the heart of the snow leopard–farmer conflict. For example, the Snow Leopard Survival Strategy of 2003 states, "From a broader perspective, conservation is a poorly understood concept for many people who live in snow leopard habitat. The reasons for conserving a large predator which impacts their lives by taking livestock have not been adequately conveyed to most local people" (McCarthy and Chapron 2003, 32). It is implied in the above passage that farmers might stop killing snow leopards, irrespective of livestock damage, if their ignorance of the ecological role of snow leopards were overcome. But, "if conservation strategies distress human populations, especially those who are less powerful, politically marginalized, and poor, little that conservationists argue on behalf of biodiversity makes sense" (Agrawal and Redford 2009, 3).

There seems to be a fundamental disagreement here between farmers and snow leopard conservation institutions about the reality of the snow leopard and its place in the ecosystem. This disagreement is represented as a behavioral problem among farmers, namely, their lack of tolerance for predators. When conservation institutions promote tolerance among farmers, they ignore the cost incurred by these local farmers. The structural issue of unfair distribution of cost and benefit among conservationists and local people is transformed into an issue of lack of knowledge. This lack can be targeted using specific technical interventions, such as awareness-raising campaigns and programs. While these campaigns and programs are necessary in any good conservation program, they are not highly suitable for resolving the specific problem of human-wildlife conflict, especially when implemented in isolation from other tools, such as compensation or insurance.

Many communities that incur financial loss because of predators have little interest in the ecosystem functions of these species or, rather, the ways in which this function is thought about in ecological sciences. They are concerned about the economic costs of predators to themselves.[14] People may understand the abstract concept of trophic cascade and the interlinked nature of different species, but that knowledge does not necessarily alter their aversion to those species if they cause harm.

In fact, their view of local ecology is quite different when snow leopards have a small role to play. For example, in the conventional ecological narrative, snow leopards are important for an ecosystem because they regulate the population and behavior of other species. According to this logic, a healthy predator is essential for a healthy prey population. This view is different from what Shakoor from Sadpara village in Baltistan described to me. He said that ibex like peace of mind. They don't want to live under the threat of predation by snow leopards. He said happy ibex were also healthy ibex. On another occasion, Shakoor told me that my explanation of the purported role of snow leopards in maintaining a healthy stock of wild ibex and markhor was incorrect. He said that it is rather the quality of pasturage available in a valley that determines the health of the ibex population. He then gave examples of Ho Nallah in Shigar and Nar-Ghoro Nallah in Skardu. Both places are reputed to have the biggest heads of ibex in the region. For Shakoor the ecology of the region was bottom-driven, not predator-driven. So he may listen to the ecological rationale for conserving predators, but he may not agree with it.[15]

Thus the disagreement shows that while conservation institutions place the snow leopard at the top of the rural ecosystem, the farmers place the quality of their pasture at the top. This disagreement is an outcome of an implicit disagreement over what kind of place a snow leopard habitat or landscape is. From the perspective of conservation institutions, it is an uninhabited wilderness and a natural ecosystem, but from farmers' perspectives, the snow leopard habitat is part of their agrarian landscape. It is these two opposing views—domesticated and wilderness—of a single landscape that dictates where snow leopards are placed in the local ecology.

Disagreement over Causes of Predation

In conservation biology literature, another explanation for farmer-induced conflict is that farmers are not vigilant against predators when herding their goats on high pastures. In a study in the livestock-dominated landscape of Mongolia, the authors stated, "Predation on livestock largely appeared to result from chance encounters with free-ranging livestock, stragglers that got left behind in pastures overnight, or herded animals grazing in broken terrain that were out of view of the herder. Our data suggest that livestock predation could be reduced considerably by reducing the number of stragglers and avoiding grazing in very rugged terrain that provides cover for snow leopards. Such adjustments in herding practices, in combination with the use of predator-proof corrals at night, can substantially reduce livestock predation" (Johansson et al. 2015, 256–57).

Another study from Nepal concluded that a combination of "lax guarding practices, favorable cover and habitat conditions, and high snow leopard density are primarily responsible for the high depredation rates observed in ACAP [Annapurna Conservation Area Project]" (Jackson et al. 1996, 245). The ecologists Wang and Macdonald (2006) reported from Bhutan that "a disadvantage of strict conservation policies combined with a lax herding system within the park is the loss of livestock to wild carnivores" (563). They continue on to say, "Improved animal husbandry practices need to be encouraged to alleviate the socio-economic impact of livestock predation and ensure adequate protection for predators. These include greater vigilance during grazing, proper penning and tethering of livestock, switching to more secure and productive stall-fed cattle, and avoidance of grazing in predation hotspots" (567).

Wang and Macdonald construct predation of livestock by snow leopards as a problem induced exclusively by farmers' practices. Representations of local farmers as lazy and ignorant have a much deeper genealogy that goes back to the colonial era (Blaikie 1985; Dove 2011). Balti farmers, on the other hand, do not attribute snow leopard attacks on their domestic livestock to their own carelessness. Rather, they attribute it to the agency of the snow leopards, or even of their goats, who sometimes run away. In explaining predation of their livestock, Balti farmers refer to the agility, cunning, and elusive nature of snow leopards against which guarding livestock is almost impossible. By representing livestock predation by the snow leopard as a preventable problem, the onus of responsibility is shifted from the snow leopard to the farmers. But at a more subtle level, it is the institutional responsibility that is shifted away from conservation organizations to do something meaningful about the problem of predation.

An implicit assumption in conservation institutions is that herders should voluntarily adapt their subsistence practices to protect the snow leopard. Often described as negligent in conservation biology literature, the farmers are doubly damned: for being anti-environmentalists and for being lazy and inexpert at what they have done for centuries. Herding goats and sheep on open, high pastures is a difficult proposition. At the pasture, when the goats and sheep are let loose to graze on the open range, theoretically the herder should stay with them, keeping an ever-watchful eye. But this is not what happens in practice. Often, after reaching the grazing area where the animals go in different directions as they compete for good forage, the herder finds a spot to relax and rest, periodically checking the location of his herd. Goats and sheep mimic behavior of the snow leopard's natural prey, ibex, and thus appear as the snow leopard's "natural" prey. It is absolutely impossible to keep an eye on all animals as a matter of duty.[16] In my discussions with local people, I raised the issue of vigilance many times, and every time I got a look of astonishment and annoyance when I inquired why herders can't be more vigilant. Herders replied that no one knows when a snow leopard will strike, so how can one guard against such a predator? On one occasion a disgruntled herder asked me if one can guard against a suicide bomber.

A common practice across many villages in the region is to send one's livestock with the collective herd of the village under the charge of four or five men. When such arrangements are made, the owner of the livestock has to give a certain amount of ration (food) to the herders, according to his herd size, and the owner collects a portion of the dairy produce at the end of the summer. The unstated rule about losing livestock to snow leopard predation is that the herders are not responsible; the owner does not and cannot hold the herder responsible for any losses. The expectation is that the predation is out of the herder's control. Usually predation is attributed to just pure bad luck, an occupational hazard.

Goats grazing on a pasture. Photo by Thierry Grobet/Rolex.

Disagreement over Extent of Damage Done by Snow Leopards to Farmers' Livelihoods

Although they do acknowledge that domestic livestock supplement the snow leopard's diet, literature produced by conservation scientists, institutions, and state agencies often imply that farmers often exaggerate predation rates, misreport causes of livestock mortality, or misreport the identity of the predator.[17] Most conservation biologists contend that while predation by snow leopards does occur, it is not as frequent as farmers claim. Conservationists usually conduct studies and surveys to assess the severity of the damage and financial loss caused by predators to human property. Doing damage assessment surveys can be very tricky for a number of reasons. One challenge is the recall bias; a respondent tends to forget details of events that happened a relatively long time ago. Farmers don't keep track of the exact numbers of livestock each one of them has lost in the previous, say, five years.[18] In my more than two decades of research in the Baltistan, whenever I have asked villagers' opinions about snow leopards, they say that they kill their livestock. I, too, have heard exaggerated claims in the field, but I take these exaggerations as signs of discomfort and a source of worry among farmers for having a snow leopard in their surroundings, rather than their dishonesty.[19]

From the perspective of the farmers, there is a cost to having a snow leopard in the environment that goes beyond the actual loss of livestock. It is the psychological cost of harboring perceptions of threat in their minds when grazing livestock on high pastures and the experience of carrying the weight of the threat that lurks in their environment. Thus it is not only the physical labor that is demanded of the farmers by conservation institutions, but it is the affective labor of dealing with feelings of threat and danger. Mental stress, caused by the awareness of an ever-present threat, often translates into an exaggeration of the numbers of lost goats. Predation causes fear of losing livestock, and farmers overreact to that fear and exaggerate events, such as predation, that are spectacular in nature and rare. Perhaps they downplay common threats such as disease and other causes of livestock mortality. They think that rare risks are more common than they actually are, just as people in America tend to be more afraid of dying in an airplane crash than in a car crash.

There is an acute lack of information and few case studies on the hidden costs of human-wildlife conflict, as this topic is poorly researched (Barua, Bhagwat, and Jadhav 2013). A study of hidden psychological costs that are not traditionally accounted for in human-wildlife conflict research shows that "the shift in conservation to a systems view of the environment, coupled with spatial planning, have fostered modes of landscape management that are detached from individual experiences and concerns. Although necessary and of great value for systematic conservation planning, this type of management may ignore intimate scales of analysis that are needed to address people's anxieties and concerns" (Barua, Bhagwat, and Jadhav 2013, 313). The same study showed that unearthing these hidden costs of human-wildlife conflicts requires an interdisciplinary approach, which is rare in conservation institutions.

Furthermore, in the context of an inquiry—a conservation project doing damage-assessment surveys—it can be expected that some farmers will exaggerate the number of predations. What they expect from exaggeration is some relief.[20] In this scenario, the numbers game proves disadvantageous for the villagers because they are discredited, and their larger and deeper concerns are ignored. But the numbers game is empowering for conservation institutions for precisely the same reasons: they can reduce these concerns to technical issues, such as getting an exact mortality or loss count while they ignore larger structural concerns.[21] The insinuations of exaggeration by local people do not show up in conservation literature or official documents, however. Rather, such assertions are made in informal conversations at the dinner table or during smoke breaks during conferences and workshops, thus illuminating continuity between formal and informal processes. In the official literature such charges are mellowed using academically appropriate language. For example, while discussing the extent of snow leopard damage to the farmers' livelihoods in Mongolia, the ecologists Shehzad et al. (2012) state, "A better understanding of the diet of the snow leopard will allow us to more accurately assess the level of conflict between the cats and pastoralists who rightly or *wrongly* attribute their livestock depredation losses to snow leopards. Mitigating measures can then be designed that address a *real*, as opposed to a *perceived*, conflict" (4; emphasis added).

By adding the words *wrongly* and *perceived*, Shehzad et al. imply an element of doubt about the farmers' claim that the snow leopard threatens their livelihoods, despite the fact that their own research shows that 20 percent of the snow leopard diet comes from domestic livestock. Do we see the same kind of language used by conservationists when they describe scientific theories about predators' roles in an ecosystem? Would they say, for example, "snow leopards are rightly or wrongly considered important for their role as a keystone predator in the Himalayan ecosystem, and their population may or may not be declining?" I don't think so.[22]

SOLUTION: INVOKING TRADITIONAL BELIEFS AND RAISING AWARENESS

Conservation biologists and institutions generally agree that increasing the tolerance level of those who live close to predators, such as snow leopards, will reduce human-wildlife conflict. What causes debates among wildlife biologists and wildlife policy scientists are questions about which factors impact people's tolerance for wild predators. Are economic and livelihood considerations paramount, or do social and cultural factors largely shape tolerance for wildlife?

Evidence from China suggests that local attitudes toward predators directly correlate with real or perceived predation. For example, the local people of Gansu Province had very positive attitudes toward snow leopards; according to them they accounted for less than 8 percent of all predations. The lynx was the number one killer. Thus the economic impact of a predator correlates directly with how well it is tolerated (Alexander et al. 2015). In areas where snow leopards are considered major destroyers of livestock, they are viewed in negative terms, and their persecution is also heavy. In Mongolia snow leopards are thought to be among the major killers of livestock, which results in hostility toward the animals from local communities and retribution killings of snow leopards. In a survey conducted in the four regions of Mongolia, 14 percent of livestock holders have admitted to carrying out retaliatory killings of snow leopards (Shehzad et al. 2012, 2). In my own experience, local people's tolerance for snow leopards waxed and waned with incidences of predation. In 1994 a snow leopard attacked goats in broad daylight in Sadpara village, and strong negative sentiments lingered in the village for the next few years. As attacks became less frequent, the risk perception also waned. One can almost map these sentiments on the presence of snow leopards in a region. Where snow leopards are locally rare, one notices almost no bad feelings toward the species.

Despite acknowledging economic factors as shaping the tolerance of farmers toward snow leopards, conservation institutions and organizations prefer and recommend tweaking culture factors. Techniques that are frequently recommended for the resolution of human-wildlife conflict in conservation literature include invoking traditional beliefs, which presume that local people have forgotten these beliefs that protect snow leopard and the fact that conflict exists means that economic loss has trumped those beliefs. But rather than asking how we can revive forgotten beliefs about animal care and tolerance, we should ask why and when these beliefs were abandoned. Commenting on the degree to which the traditional Buddhist belief system shaped peoples' attitude toward predators in Ladakh, Fox and Chundawat reported in 1988 that the community tolerated low levels of predation, but after a snow leopard jumped into a corral and killed fifty goats, even the Buddhist ethic of non-violence gave way to retributory killing (139). Another study states, "Culture has certainly advanced the limit of tolerance to economic losses, but cannot do so indefinitely. Economics has begun to eclipse cultural symbolism in this age of markets and one must recognize this reality in conserving large mammals" (Madhusudan 2003, 474).[23] In Bhutan, Buddhist sanctions against killing predators were often violated when they killed livestock (Rajaratnam, Vernes, Sangay 2016).[24] It is not to argue that cultural beliefs cannot lead to tolerance of predators despite predation, but to say that even those beliefs are not always effective. And even if they are, how sustainable are they?

Identifying a lack of tolerance among farmers for snow leopards as arising from a lack of knowledge and awareness makes the task of conservationists easier. The implicit assumption of awareness-raising programs using cultural references is that these programs bring about long-term non-reversible transformations in the ways in which people view, think about, and act upon nature. Although there are very few ways to quantitatively measure the impact of awareness-raising programs on actual biodiversity conservation, project documents assume that their impact is self-evident. Without addressing the basic foundation upon which these beliefs are held, these transformations, if they do occur, cannot be long lasting or sustainable. The beliefs among local farmers about predators such as snow leopards arise in the context of specific subsistence practices that these farmers engage in. To undo these beliefs would require a change in the ways in which farmers' labor and snow leopards' natural history is interconnected.

Even if the actual effects of interventions, such as reviving traditional beliefs and awareness-raising, are dubious, they have a powerful effect on policy makers and donors who are mostly seduced by the simplification process through which the complexity of a conservation problem is reduced to a problem of "culture." In comparison to this, social scientists trained in anthropology, human geography, or sociology recognize from the outset that the problem is complex. Theories and methods from the emerging field of social ecology, which is both theoretically informed and mission oriented, are specifically aimed at understanding this complexity. The social and political ecology literature argues that culture is not a power to which causation can be attributed, rather, it is a context in which actions are interpreted.

SOLUTION: COMPENSATION PROGRAMS

Compensation programs that pay money directly to the farmers for their losses are perhaps the most contested solution to snow leopard–farmer conflicts. The oft quoted objections to these programs are that they are inefficient to run and require a constant supply of money from outside sources, as in the case of compensation used against snow leopard predation in China: "Compensation is often recommended as a conflict mitigation measure and, in China, it is the primary strategy currently in place. However, compensation schemes are often criticized as they are not financially sustainable and they suffer from a number of operational difficulties such as lack of clear guidelines, failure to ensure timely payments, and inability to measure success. Their effectiveness in reducing conflicts still requires validation" (Alexander et al. 2015, 8).

One straightforward reason is that many opponents of conservation are concerned about sustainability of these programs. For example, a report by the Food and Agriculture Organization (Lamarque et al. 2009) stated that compensation is "not sustainable as it depends heavily on the budget of the local governing bodies and/or non-governmental organization (NGO) support" (39). A similar conclusion is drawn by the Africa Wildlife Foundation (2005), which accepts that although compensation schemes meet the demand of local people to be financially compensated for the loss, they have their own problems. They are difficult to manage, requiring for example reliable and mobile personnel on the ground to verify claims. They can also be expensive. In the case of a pilot compensation scheme introduced by a voluntary conservation group, Friends of Nairobi National Park, to compensate Maasai livestock owners in the event of predation by the Park's lions, leopards or cheetah, the scheme proved too expensive to continue. A similar privately funded scheme operating in Amboseli National Park to compensate Maasai herders in the event that elephants kill livestock, for example at water holes during the dry season, has proved to be more affordable and sustainable because such occurrences are relatively rare. (8)

These comments are quite telling when their further implications are drawn. Here the issue of compensation is turned from political and economic—who should pay for conservation and why—to technical and apolitical—a budgetary constraint. In both instances above, the implicit institutional positions are that the compensation systems are unsustainable because they depend on financial support from NGOs and governments or other outside sources. The implication is that for compensation programs to be sustainable, they must not rely on outside sources.

But what sources of money should they rely on, then? Although not stated explicitly in the passages above, the expectation is that the cost of mitigating the conflict should be borne by local people, because, after all, they are the source of this conflict. This element of the narrative is also important for completing the specter. But from the perspective of the local Balti farmers (and presumably Maasai herders), compensation programs need to be sustained by outside support because conservation of snow leopards is the priority of outsiders. So rather than saying that the compensation program proved too expensive to continue, one could say that the Food and Agriculture Organization or the Friends of Nairobi National Park could not, or did not want to, bear the financial burden of conservation. Notice that the program in Nairobi National Park was called problematic because it was expensive. Does that mean that it was expensive because there was more predation hence more compensation was needed? Or was it expensive because it was inefficient? If the latter, then it's a technical issue and nothing to do with the ethical issue of unequal cost and benefit. But if the former, then it means something completely different. If it is not a technical issue, it is an issue of

HUMAN-WILDLIFE CONFLICT 75

acceptability and acknowledgment of responsibility of causing harm to other people who are not culpable in any crime. Compared to the Nairobi National Park case, the authors of the AWF working paper write approvingly of the program in Amboseli National Park to compensate for elephant damage. They argue that the Amboseli scheme was sustainable because predation was low. According to this logic, conservation NGOs will consent to compensate farmers not according to the actual damage incurred by predators but rather according to the funds available to them specifically for this purpose. If there is a mismatch between the two, then compensation schemes should be abandoned. But the funds allocated to compensation are not decided in isolation; they are decided with the costs of more traditional approaches to conservation in mind.

It seems that all programs that are popular with farmers are expensive from the perspective of the conservation NGOs. What if this situation was reversed? What if villagers said to conservation organizations, "We will need to cut down the population of snow leopards to the level at which we can afford to sustain the predation incidences?"[25] The villagers would most likely refuse to fully subsidize the snow leopard population, just as the conservation community is less than willing to compensate farmers *fully* for their losses.

All of these operational shortcomings can be addressed *if* conservationists allocate resources to these programs. Clearly, the risk of such programs becoming corrupt at the official level is not to be overlooked. But a program can be more transparent and accountable if local communities are involved financially and economically. Without allocation of resources and a realistic approach that accepts dependence on outside sources of money, compensation programs are designed to fail.

How does this negative evaluation of compensations programs, based on the criteria of financial and institutional sustainability, compare with other conservation interventions? It is quite clear that the conventional protected areas approach is equally, if not more, problematic when it comes to operational activities and funding needs. For example, when evaluating the existing institutional capacity of conventional approaches to conservation based on protected areas, the SLSS 2014 states,

> All of the snow leopard range countries report they have insufficient numbers of trained conservation practitioners at all levels, from frontline PA staff to game managers and wildlife law enforcement personnel, to research scientists. Moreover, and

even where conservation staff levels may be adequate, such as in some scientific institutions, low funding limits their effectiveness. In particular, range countries lack people trained to address the needs of communities and develop community programs. In large part, this is due to insufficient country budgets for snow leopard conservation and for conservation in general, given most range countries are developing nations and some are extremely poor. Donor funding is generally time-limited and insufficient to scale-up successful practices. Most of the range countries need greater financial and technical support from the international community for successful snow leopard conservation. (SLN 2014, 30)

Despite these shortcoming and weaknesses, the conservation community has not abandoned the protected areas approach. Nor have they declared, "The effectiveness of protected areas in conserving biodiversity and preventing conflict still needs validation," as they have about compensation schemes. And while the shortcomings of the protected area approach are considered resolvable with more funding—as stated above—they never say that compensations programs might work more effectively with additional support and funding. There has to be some other reason why conservationists generally dislike monetary transfers to farmers to compensate livestock lost to snow leopard predation.

Some Sociological Reasons for the Failure of Compensation Programs

Apart from financial issues and efficiency in delivery there may be structural reasons for the failure of compensation programs. In such situations, scholars view human-wildlife conflict as less about economic losses than about social and emotional factors. As Hill, Osborn, and Plumptre (2002) argue, "Evidence here suggests that when farmers complain about wildlife causing damage to crops the issue is not just about the degree of damage they experience—they are also making a statement about the fact that they consider that by no longer having the legal right to hunt they have (i) lost access to a valuable resource (wild meat) and (ii) have lost the right to adopt a method of controlling crop raiding species that they consider effective" (appendix I).[26] Social factors such as group norms, government policy addressing human-wildlife conflict, and the history of a community are more important than economic incentives in shaping people's tolerance for wild predators (Treves and Bruskotter 2014, 476). Many farmers and ranchers in Wyoming adhere to a culture of localism and do not respond to compensation programs that mainly come from outside the state (Clark, Rutherford, and Casey 2005). They see outsiders, especially city dwellers and representatives of the federal government, as a threat to their way of culture and livelihoods.[27]

There are, then, a number of competing scenarios for the efficacy of compensation programs. One can use a general and crude rule to assess whether compensation will work in a community: when a community is suspicious and unsure about the long-term intentions of an outside conservation organization, it generally does not accept the offer of compensation programs. For example, our experience shows that communities in Baltistan, such as Arandu in Shigar Valley, which are near the national parks whose boundaries are contested, have not been very interested in compensation programs despite experiencing high predation rates. For these communities, the question of compensation for immediate losses was trumped by the larger and bigger threat of losing all land and livelihood to the national park. They suspect that compensation programs are just a ruse for the government or NGOs to get a foothold in the village and eventually take over the land for conservation.

The history of a region also strongly influences attitudes toward compensation programs. Local resistance is a side effect of larger, historical concerns. For example, people in the western United States see the efforts of outside people and agencies that protect predators as negating the work of their ancestors, who eradicated predators to make the country habitable (Clark, Rutherford, and Casey 2013). They would like as little intervention as possible from the federal government; although they would not object to receiving other federal subsidies. Granted, the historical context of the human-wildlife conflict in the western United States is different than in the western Himalayas and central Karakoram valleys in Pakistan and elsewhere for that matter. In the United States, historically, wild predators were eliminated to make way for European settlements, while Himalayan farmers and agro-pastoralists never eliminated wildlife.

In addition to historical differences in the settlement process, class differences affect responses to compensation programs. Studies among relatively poor farmers indicate their tolerance of wildlife increased as their losses were compensated, whereas the attitudes of larger farmers remained unchanged (Ogada et al. 2003; Holmern, Nyahongo, and Røskaft 2007; Rosen et al. 2012). Madhusudan (2003) noted that in rural southern India, villagers "seemed willing to make small investments to protect their livestock and crops from wildlife" (474). A similar program has been successfully implemented in India through a partnership between a local NGO and WWF-India to provide supplementary "on the spot" compensation to farmers when livestock is killed by tigers near Corbett National Park (qtd. in Ogra and Badola 2008). On a larger scale, a study of ninety-three protected areas in twenty-two tropical countries suggests that compensation to local communities is positively associated with increased park effectiveness (Bruner 2001).

Compensation: Another Perspective

Despite a general aversion to the idea of compensation, voices within the conservation community regard conservation not only as a technical issue but as a social and ethical issue. This literature does not focus on the design of compensation programs but on what it views as the responsibility of conservation institutions to provide such programs. Verdale and Campos (2004) argue that compensation should be seen as a subsidy that society pays for "keeping the wildlife alive" (3). Nyhus and Tilson (2004), reporting on tiger-human conflict in the Sumatra region of Indonesia, suggest, "If carried out effectively, compensation can shift the economic responsibility for carnivore conservation away from farmers toward the supporters of carnivore conservation" (72). Others who may not necessarily favor compensation as a tool regard fair distribution of costs and benefits as essential to conservation success.

Amy Dickman and her colleagues, while reviewing mechanisms to resolve human-wildlife conflict, strongly urged the conservation community to address the issue of the economic burden borne by farmers due to conservation-related interventions. They write, "Overall, human-carnivore coexistence imposes substantial, diverse costs on local people, and although carnivore populations can generate considerable revenue, many existing revenue streams in developing countries are diverted externally rather than being captured locally, posing significant obstacles to incentivizing effective 'on-the-ground' conservation. This poor cost-benefit ratio at a local level leads to people extirpating such species from human-dominated land, and this has been one of the most significant drivers of the widespread declines in carnivore populations described earlier" (Dickman, Macdonald, and Macdonald 2011, 13938).

They make a very loud and clear argument that it is unfair to expect local people to absorb the costs of predation and still protect threatening animals: "If external beneficiaries want the long-term conservation of globally iconic but locally problematic species, they will have to develop and fund strategies to outweigh the local costs incurred, which will require significant investment from stakeholders such as governments and conservation agencies" (13943).

What Happens if Livestock Subsidy Is Removed?

Some of the authors who study snow leopard diets speculated on the possible role of livestock in sustaining snow leopard populations while protecting that of their natural prey. Such studies are framed within the overall problem of humans as part of the landscape, but only as a disturbance. They ask how snow leopards and their prey population would be affected if livestock were removed from their habitat. For example, the ecologists Raghu Chundawat and G. S. Rawat (1994) recognized that livestock present an alternative to wild prey and thus takes some pressure off the former. They write,

> at an annual increment of 29 individuals the blue sheep population of 220 to 240 in Rumbak Valley can sustain the predation pressure of four snow leopards. Thus, during our study duration predation by snow leopard alone was not a substantial threat to the blue sheep population in Rumbak Valley. This equation would change drastically, however, if all the domestic animals were to be removed from the study area. The presence of competing predators can also produce a negative impact on the blue sheep population. In such a situation alternate prey will play a crucial role in the dynamics of predation by snow leopard. (131)

In 2009 the snow leopard returned to Sagarmatha National Park (SNP) after twenty-five years. This concerned ecologists who thought that because of this return the wild Himalayan tahr, the snow leopard's natural prey, may become nearly extinct in the park:

> Small populations of wild *Caprinae*, for example, the Himalayan tahr population in SNP, are sensitive to stochastic predation events and may be led to almost local extinction. If predation on livestock keeps growing, together with the decrease of Himalayan tahr, retaliatory killing of snow leopards by local people may be expected, and the snow leopard could again be at risk of local extinction. Restoration of biodiversity through the return of a large predator has to be monitored carefully, especially in areas affected by humans, where the lack of important

environmental components, for example key prey species, may make the return of a predator a challenging event. (Lovari et al. 2009, 559)

Another study of the snow leopard's diet, based on DNA analysis of prey in scats, showed that about 42 percent of the snow leopard's diet came from domestic livestock (Wegge, Shrestha, and Flagstad 2012). In this study, the authors concluded that given the high reliance of snow leopards on domestic livestock and the concurrent lack of natural prey, reducing snow leopard access to domestic livestock may harm snow leopards in the long term. They write, "Among innovative management schemes now being implemented throughout the species' range, compensation and insurance programs coupled with other incentive measures are encouraged, rather than measures to reduce the snow leopard's access to livestock. In areas like the Phu valley, where the natural prey base consists mainly of one ungulate species that is already heavily preyed upon, the latter approach, if implemented, will lead to increased predation on this prey, which over time may suppress it" (131).

Although they acknowledge the importance of domestic livestock in the snow leopard diet, the authors still see this situation as "non-natural." They write,

> Current conservation of snow leopards focuses more on compensation and incentive programmes than on preventing livestock from being killed. Maintaining wildlife populations by *supplementary, non-natural food* is controversial, and allowing livestock to be killed for the purpose of conserving an endangered species such as the snow leopard is certainly not a viable, *ultimate solution*. Thus, long-term conservation of this charismatic animal requires measures that can sustain local numbers without predation of livestock. This is a difficult challenge, particularly in areas like the Phu valley where the main wild prey consists of only one species and where this food source is already being exploited to near its sustainable limit. (139; emphasis added)

The arguments of Wegge, Shrestha, and Flagstad are important to this discussion for many reasons because here, again, the conceptual divide between the wild and the domesticated and between nature and culture is being brought to bear on the problem of human-wildlife conflict. Wegge and his coauthors describe livestock as "non-natural food" of the snow leopards and refer to the reliance on livestock as "not a viable ultimate solution." They state, "Thus, long-term conservation of this charismatic animal requires measures that can sustain local numbers without predation of livestock" (141).

Clearly, anti-predatory measures are needed along with compensation to reduce the conflict, but it is foolish to expect that predation may never occur again. The search for an "ultimate solution," where snow leopards no longer eat domestic livestock, can only lie in establishing protected areas, which means removal of local people and their livestock from snow leopard habitats. But even that would not be the *ultimate* solution, in fact, fully operational protected areas could lead to higher predation rates. Some studies raise questions about the link between increases in natural prey and snow leopard abundance and a subsequent fall in livestock depredation. For example, the ecologists Johanssen et al. (2015) argue that "if conservation efforts lead to increased snow leopard densities as suggested by Suryawanshi et al. (2013), that could lead to increased livestock predation and should therefore be accompanied with efforts to better protect livestock and improve vigilance through better herding practices" (257).[28] What is interesting in the commentary above is that Johanssen et al. do not mention direct compensation, despite addressing better protection and vigilance. Clearly, vigilance here is considered a cost-free activity that the villagers should undertake, whatever its impact on their daily work routine.

A study of relationships between livestock and snow leopard densities and the rate of predation from Nepal shows that though the livestock loss is correlated to high snow leopard sign density, it was also related to blue sheep density (Sharma et al. 2006). The authors of the study state, "For example, Ngoru block showed the lowest sign density (3.9sign/km^2) with the lowest livestock depredation (10.3%), but blue sheep density was medium (4.7/km^2) amongst three blocks. Though it is presumed that livestock depredation may be minimal if sufficient natural prey is available to local predators, it was speculated that there could be other factors such as season, habitat quality and livestock *guarding pattern* which leads snow leopards to kill livestock" (184; emphasis added).

This implicit demand by the conservation industry of asking people to spend more time and resources guarding their animals or changing grazing patterns is a hidden cost of conservation that is expected to be borne by the farmers.

The claim by Wegge et al. (2012) that conservation efforts focus more on compensation and incentives and less on preventing livestock from being killed may not be true outside of the Nepal example. Many projects that run compensation and insurance programs, like the Baltistan Wildlife Conservation and Development Organization, also carry out activities such as building predator-proof corrals.

Why Conservationists Oppose Compensation

Wegge's opposition to compensation points to the durability of the idea of the division between nature and culture. It is important to understand the hold of this idea on the imagination and worldview of conservationists. Because compensation programs somewhat normalize and legitimize a flow of resources across the boundaries between nature and culture—wild and domesticated—they challenge the fundamental assumption in the conservation community that these two realms must remain separate, and so are never entirely acceptable. At best, they may be accepted as an interim measure, as we move toward the natural state of affairs in which there is no crossing of boundaries.

In addition to the challenge to the fundamental belief in the separation of nature and culture, the resistance of conservationists to compensation programs could be due to the threat that such an intervention poses to the status quo in relationships between local communities and outside conservationists. Direct payments to farmers for their support for snow leopard conservation has the potential to subvert the current asymmetrical relations in which outside conservationists have a privileged position. By maintaining their role as providers of technical help and expert advice along with some financial resources, outside conservation organizations can portray themselves as indispensable partners. Conservation organizations make it seem that protection of the snow leopard is possible only because of their presence. Moreover, more money directed toward compensating farmers may mean less money for conservation institutions.

Direct payments have the potential to recalibrate this unequal relationship. In my experience running a village-based insurance program that compensated farmers for their losses of livestock to snow leopard predation, direct payments were the most effective and sustainable way of protecting snow leopard populations. But direct payment had the potential to represent conservationists and local people as equals, as rational, and as mutually dependent partners in conservation. That is, villagers "exchanged" their good behavior and tolerant attitudes toward snow leopards for continued direct financial support from the outside. This constituted a transaction, such as the ones that anthropologists observe in the exchange of gifts in virtually all societies (Mauss 1954). Just as parties in gift exchanges create a mutual obligation through reciprocity and trust, so can direct payments create the same dynamic, one in which both parties have equal status.

Finally, the aversion to compensation programs by conservation institutions relates to the fact that such programs are seen as not in the realm of standard conservation practices, but rather in that of standard development practice. Payments for the sake of conservation build on the legacy of 1980s community-based conservation and sustainable-use projects. This policy had been only partially accepted by some conservation institutions, who, despite officially acknowledging the role of communities in conservation, marginalized social scientists such as anthropologists and human geographers.

Conservation biologists, however, are not the only source of opposition to compensation programs; there are other academics who somewhat surprisingly oppose it. Many well-intentioned social scientists see compensation as a way of introducing neoliberal, market-based ethics into a society. I encountered this view when I gave a lecture on insurance schemes at an elite college in Lahore in the winter of 2013. My main point was that we should not displace the cost of the conservation of snow leopards onto local farmers; rather, we should pay them for the subsidy *they* provide to snow leopards. After my talk, a professor from the college said that this kind of arrangement—paying compensation to the local farmers—will induce a monetary culture in the society and will lead to a capitalist ethos. This characterization is wrong for two reasons: First, like a subsidy that outsiders give to the local people, it is not a price that is put on a species to turn it into a commodity. What is being priced is not a snow leopard but the loss it incurs—the goat—which is already a commodity to a considerable extent. Second, this characterization imagines another boundary familiar in the social sciences, the boundary between traditional and modern societies. Balti farmers, like professors, depend on money too and like to have it when they can.

Contrary to the claims made by some social scientists, many communities embrace market-based conservation policies without associating them with cultural loss, as long as they can control the outcome. These communities engage in market economies voluntarily and sometimes eagerly, because they want to improve their economic position. The Pakistan trophy-hunting program is a case in point; communities participated because of the strong economic incentive it provided. The nature of the program was such that many communities saw it in their favor. The government had stipulated that 80 percent of the money from the sale of the license would go to participating villages, which did actually happen. In the end, the program proved detrimental to the conservation of predators such as snow leopards because

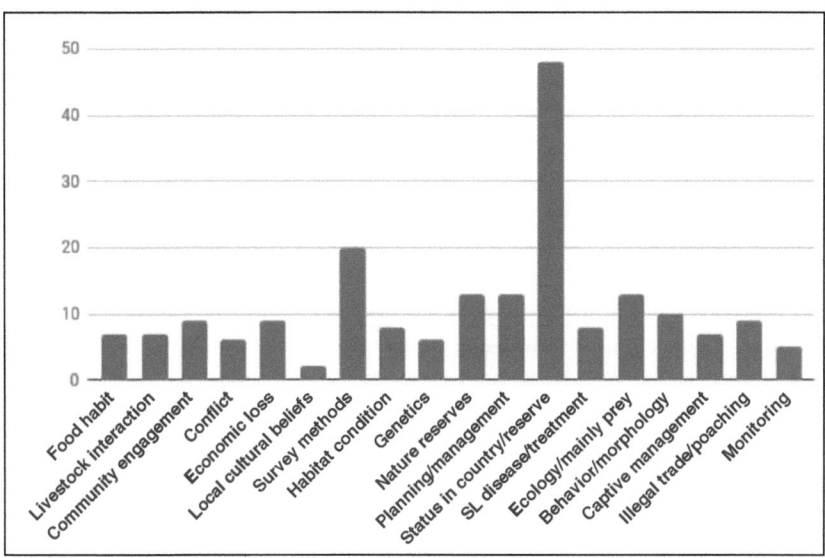

Research themes represented in literature on snow leopards, 1979–2019

the villagers started seeing the snow leopards as a threat to the prized ungulates that were now seen as having monetary value.

SPECTACULAR ACCUMULATION

In order to examine the topics on which conservation scholars have focused most, in 2017 I surveyed publications—journal articles, book chapters, field reports, institutional publications—on snow leopards over the last three decades. I drew on a database of about fourteen hundred publications on the bibliography list of the Snow Leopard Network. These publications are listed serial-wise from most current to the earliest. Approximately a thousand journal articles, in addition to four hundred grey publications, have been published since 1987. I surveyed 20 percent of these articles by doing systematic random sampling, picking every fifth article on this list. I read the abstract of all two hundred and categorized them according to specific themes. These specific and minor themes were as simple as "camera trapping technique" or "genetics" or "SLIMS." It is important to make this point about the "main" focus because many studies that manifestly do not include any aspect of human culture in their research will nonetheless say something about it in the concluding section.

This brief survey found a strong emphasis on snow leopard distribution and habitat, ecology, survey methodology, and planning and assessment of

TABLE 3.2. Financial resources allocated in Global Snow Leopard and Ecosystem Protection Program budget, 2013–2020

GSLEP THEMATIC AREAS	TOTAL DOLLAR AMOUNT (% TOTAL BUDGET)
Engaging local communities and reducing human-wildlife conflict 1. Reduction in livestock predation and mortality, decreased killing of snow leopard and prey	$16.0 million (9%)
Controlling poaching of snow leopards and prey 1. Threats halted; populations of snow leopard and prey base increased	$41.4 million (24%)
Managing habitat and prey 1. Extent of snow leopard habitats protection, management, and connectivity surveyed, documented, and increased 2. Habitat quality and connectivity and gene flow between populations maintained or restored	$50.3 million (30%)
Research and monitoring 1. Major knowledge gaps studied. Range, key reproduction sites, existing and potential connecting corridors for snow leopard populations identified and incorporated into landscape level-planning of management interventionsBetter coordination and decision making 2. Enables setting of baselines to track progress and effectiveness of conservation	$33.7 million (18%)
Transboundary management and enforcement, engaging industry, awareness and communication	$14.0 million (7%)
Strengthening policies and institutions and strengthening capacity of national and local institutions 1. Strengthened policy and institutional environment for deterrence of wildlife crime and enacting incentives for local communities to protect and conserve	$21.0 million (7%)

nature reserves. Relatively few studies are about snow leopard food habits and diet. The ecologists Lyngdoh et al. (2014) write, "As they are difficult to observe and follow, there is a dearth of published information on snow leopard diet, as well as other aspects of its ecology, in comparison to other charismatic large carnivores" (1). This preference for continued research on topics such as distribution and abundance is the bread and butter of conservation scientists. Intense emphasis on surveys and counting numbers and exploring habitat quality and prey availability creates a specter of the snow leopard as under threat of extinction, with local people identified as the main threat and conservation organizations identified as the saviors. The use of this specter in media communications to the general public, and potential donors, creates a spectacle that generates giving, or spectacular accumulation.

The preference for certain types of studies is also reflected in the allocation of budgets in snow leopard conservation projects. One example is the current proposed budget of the Global Snow Leopard and Ecosystem Protection Program. Despite listing retaliatory killings by farmers as a primary threat to snow leopards, only 9 percent of the resources in the program are allocated to management of human-wildlife conflict and community engagement. Lack of awareness is also mentioned as a primary threat in half of the snow leopard's home range, and only 1 percent is allocated to that. Not surprisingly a hefty proportion of money is allocated for activities that continue the current trend of spending money and resources on surveys, creating reserves, writing plans and reports, and doing monitoring and research. Among the on-the-ground activities, again, a high proportion of money is allocated to stopping poaching, controlling local peoples' access, and managing habitat and prey. The last two activities lead to the contemporary policy of creating more reserves and conservation areas by keeping out or controlling their access. These financial resources sustain conservation institutions as most of the activities help them keep doing what they know best, that is, surveys and assessments and advocating for and managing more reserves.

Despite the fact that snow leopard–farmer conflict is considered a major threat to the snow leopards, only 3 percent of the studies were dedicated to this topic. Coupled with how the budget was allocated in the GSLEP program, we see how the spectacle works in reality, which means a trumped-up threat in order to garner political and financial support. The actual money is not spent on understanding the problem (only 3 percent of the total studies) or solving the problem (only 9 percent allocated).

CONCLUSION

The politics of compensation cannot be separated from the social and scientific construction of the snow leopard as a wilderness predator. As long as there is a particular kind of snow leopard that is produced in conservation biology literature, conservation communities will continue to oppose compensation. That socially constructed snow leopard is one that does not attack livestock if left undisturbed. In other words, the snow leopard that emerges in anti-compensation debates is one that is truly wild, a wild ideal type—with no connection to the domestic realm. Constructing a "purified" snow leopard, one unable to kill domestic livestock or one that kills domestic livestock only when provoked, means that livestock predation will always be the fault of the farmers.

Not all conservation institutions overtly oppose compensation programs. Some accept them half-heartedly, as a second-best option. But more important, in the eyes of the conservationists, predation of livestock by snow leopards is not a normal, natural phenomenon but rather a nuisance created by the bad behavior of farmers. If they are being compensated for the losses of livestock, they are being done a favor. If, on the other hand, we imagine a snow leopard that is, as science says, an opportunistic and cunning predator that does not respect the boundary between the wild and the domesticated worlds, then the blame for the conflict can be displaced from bad behavior of the farmers to the agency of snow leopards. Such a situation, where snow leopard attacks on domestic livestock are considered normal, is unacceptable to conservation biologists. The continued reluctance of conservation institutions to recognize this issue and to compensate farmers has heightened the conflict between the two, making it hard to find common ground.[29] In the conservation imagination, an intervention that makes the human presence absent or at least invisible is considered natural, whereas human interventions that make these connections visible are considered unnatural.

CHAPTER FOUR

Domesticating Landscapes

BALTISTAN is part of the Gilgit-Baltistan region of northern Pakistan. The region is dominated by high mountains and cut by numerous rivers and streams (including the Indus and several of its tributaries) that form narrow valleys. Mostly lacking soil cover, the terrain is naturally unstable, and mudslides and rockfalls are commonplace. Baltistan has a dry, temperate climate with extremes of temperature (from −20°C to 40°C; −4°F to 104°F) that range from extreme cold at and above the snow line to high summer temperatures in the valley bottom. Rainfall is sparse, as the area lies outside the Himalayan monsoon belt. The endangered snow leopard is found throughout the higher elevations in Baltistan and preys on wild goats and on domestic livestock.

There are four main valleys in Baltistan in addition to Skardu. Kharmang is located along the Indus in the eastern part of the region, closest to the line of control between India and Pakistan. Khaplu is the valley of the Shayok River, which drains into the Indus at Keris. In the north of the region is the Shigar Valley through which the Shigar River flows and meets the Indus behind the sand dunes in the Skardu Valley. And the Rondu Valley is located west of the town of Skardu and connects Baltistan with Gilgit and the down country.

The Baltistan region is one of the poorest in Pakistan in terms of economic and social indictors, with per capita gross domestic product at only 60 percent of the national average (currently US$1,450). About 75 percent of the population engages in some form of transhumance farming. Due to climatic conditions and the poor quality of the soil, land under cultivation is scarce. Climatic conditions in the high mountains are greatly influenced by altitudinal differences. The main limiting factor for human settlement is water, and the area's sparse rainfall necessitates irrigation. Streams carry plentiful meltwater from the snowfields of the high mountains, and water from the streams is redirected through irrigation channels to the fields, sometimes over considerable distances of several kilometers and along steep slopes.

Production is low for all three major components of farming: crops, livestock-raising, and fuel wood collection and forestry, which include timber production. The region produces only half the grain it needs, while the government supplies subsidized grain to make up for the shortfall. Natural pastures provide the grazing grounds for livestock, while scattered stands of juniper, birch, and wild willow only partially fulfill the fuel wood needs of local people. Additional fodder and fuel wood are grown on arable land around villages. Villagers fulfill their dairy and meat requirements by raising goats, sheep, cows, yaks, and dzo (a yak and cow hybrid). The animals also act as sources of security in times of crisis.

On average, a single household has about a half acre of arable land, and farmers plant mostly wheat, maize, millet, barley, buckwheat, or rice. Local people plant crops in the best soil and grow fodder and trees on sloping and marginal land. Alfalfa is the main fodder crop, while the area under potato cultivation (particularly seed potato) is increasing. Virtually all the cultivated land is terraced to facilitate irrigation. Ploughing is done exclusively by men using pairs of bullocks; although, farmers also use small tractors in areas capable of supporting them and communally use wheat threshers. They normally sow crops in April and May, shortly before herding their livestock to high summer pastures, and they harvest crops just before the return of livestock to the village in September or October. They also cut grass during this period as winter fodder for stall feeding.

High-altitude pastures, or *broq*, are located near glaciers and snowfields. On high pastures, livestock are permitted to graze freely where they become semi-wild during this period. Goats predominate in the transhumant cycle, while carefully differentiated interbreeding between yaks and cows has created the dzo, which is adapted to narrowly defined altitude zones. Animals are able to graze in temperatures above 5°C (41°F), but lower temperatures necessitate stabling, sometimes within human shelters. An increase in fodder production has enabled villagers to stall feed their livestock, reducing the number of animals grazing on rangelands. Nutritious fodder crops, such as alfalfa, have had a positive effect on animal health (especially for milk animals), and stall feeding and increased access to veterinarians has reduced animal mortality rates.

Human settlements have brought major changes in the physical environment. Settlers have transformed once undeveloped and uncultivated land into oases with trees, meadows, and crop fields that are interspersed with stone houses. Cultivated land in Baltistan is privately owned, whereas

Balti herder and his cattle

pasture areas are generally communal, with grazing rights being accorded to all villagers. Property rights on most barren land are not clearly defined; in cases where undeveloped lands have been reclaimed (i.e., by constructing irrigation channels), local residents often claim ownership. Holding patterns for agricultural land are generally equitable, with very few landless farmers or large landowners.

THE PEOPLE OF BALTISTAN

Currently, four hundred thousand people live in Baltistan, spread among some two hundred villages. Skardu, the capital, is a bustling town with a population of sixty thousand in the winter and about a hundred thousand in the summer when tourists throng to the region. The people of the region historically practiced the animistic Bon religion. In the third century CE, Buddhism was introduced to the area and invasion by the Tibetan empire in the seventh century CE also brought a strong Buddhist influence to Baltistan; Tibetan script was adopted, and Buddhism partially replaced the older Bon religion. Islam reached the region through central Asia as well as through

Kashmir in the fifteenth century CE. At present, the majority of the population is Shia Muslim with a small Sunni minority. The local culture still bears signs of past belief systems, however. Mosques are built in the traditional Tibetan style of a chorten, but the influence of Kashmiri architectural styles and motifs is also present. The local language, folklore, and myths still hold legends of the past ages.

The main ethnic group in Baltistan is Balti and a small minority of Shin, whose villages are mostly located in the Himalayan belt, on the southern bank of the Indus. The Balti usually refer to the Shin as *broq-pa*, meaning "people of the pasture," or "hillbillies." The representation of the Shin as unsophisticated people is very much present in the Balti-Shin relationship and usually forms the basis of Balti jokes and banter. The Baltis consider the broq-pa uncouth and irascible. This representation of the Shins by the Baltis is contrasted with their own self-representation as people who observe etiquettes and civility. Baltis emphasize that due to Baltistan's direct geographical connection with the valley of Kashmir and the rest of India, civilization arrived here before it climbed to remote *nallahs* (narrow valleys), where the broq-pa lived. Moreover, according to the local oral history, the Balti rajas of the past centuries settled broq-pa in their territories as guards on the high mountain passes to prevent would-be invaders from entering the country. The broq-pa were expected to withstand the rough conditions better than the local Baltis, and the task suited their supposedly violent temperament. The Shin, on the other hand, regard the Balti to be effeminate and subservient people.

Nineteenth-century British explorers wrote about the Baltis as a docile race that had remained unchanged for centuries. They were generally considered more peaceful than the Shins but at the same time intransigent and stubborn characters. Today, most Pakistanis in Lahore, Karachi, and Islamabad meet Baltis for the first time in their kitchens, as cooks. Most foreigners meet them in the mountains as porters and high-altitude guides. They have different registers of identity, which accords with patterns of their encounters in pursuit of livelihoods.

In 1974 Prime Minister Zulfiqar Ali Bhutto abolished local princely states and incorporated Baltistan under the administration of the federal government. But the historical connection of Baltistan with the former state of Kashmir was, and still is, the major sticking point preventing Baltistan from achieving fully fledged membership in the Pakistani state. The Pakistani government's position on Gilgit-Baltistan has been that any final or unilateral settlement of the region will give a signal to India that Pakistan has abandoned its claim over the Indian-held areas of Kashmir.

Political and geographic isolation had largely been responsible for the historically slow development of socio-economic infrastructure and services in the region. And accessibility and connectivity have been a major determinant of socio-economic change in Baltistan. This improved access to the rest of the country has been made possible, ironically, by Baltistan's location on the Line of Control with India. The Pakistan Army needs to build roads to keep a strategic advantage over its archrival. Construction of these roads to carry military equipment has also meant a transformation in diet, clothing, farming practices, technology, and introduction of new modes of communications. The continued failure of the Pakistani state to respond positively to the political demands of the people of the Gilgit-Baltistan region has spawned an atmosphere of disenchantment and disdain. People show their frustration with the Pakistani state's failure to fully implement political reforms, leaving them without any constitutional status or position to defend their economic and political rights in the region.

HISTORICAL CONTEXT OF BALTI VIEW OF NATURE

Baltis do not view the landscape and the species therein as strictly divided between the wild and the domesticated; rather, in their view these categories often intertwine and mix. They see high pastures—where they graze animals during the summer months or hunt during the winter months—as semi-domesticated places, about which myths exist in local folklore that can be traced back to pre-Islamic beliefs. The Balti view of wildlife and wild places reflects a syncretic mix of pre-Islamic and Islamic beliefs. But lately pre-Islamic beliefs have given way to an Islamic view of animals and the human relationship to them.

The pre-Islamic beliefs are based on the Bon religion, which has now become extinct in the region. Bon, or Bonism, is a pan-Tibetan religion that expanded to Mongolia and Siberia and Manchuria; it existed before the Buddhist era (Francke 1901). According to the Bon belief system, the universe is ruled by two opposing forces, good and bad. The good force is a powerful deity, Hla, who protects society from evil, Hlu, but Hla also unleashes Hlu on people who disobey the basic principles of Bonism.

The objective of social life in Bonism is the correct relationship with these hidden forces. A shaman mediates the everyday relationship between the hidden reality and society. The natural world is animate and fluid in the sense that wild animals are not only sentient beings with consciousness and agency but are able to change shapes.

Bonism has no concept of an afterlife, but the world is animated with good and bad spirits that are manifested in things such as wild animals, mountains, glaciers, rivers, and streams. In this way the Bon belief about other beings is based on animism, in which non-human beings are given an interiority similar to that of human beings. In the Bon belief system, then, appearances are misleading, and reality constitutes both what is revealed and what is hidden. According to a local myth in the Hushe Valley, a hunter once saw an ibex with his naked eye in the distance, but when he looked at the ibex through his binoculars, he saw a beautiful woman. This myth perhaps reflects residual Bon beliefs about the illusory nature of appearances. The binoculars, in this instance, acted as a medium through which an alternative reality could be experienced visually and an already existing myth could be validated.

In Bonism, ritual life is organized around nature worship, propitiation of the evil Hlu, and celebration of the changing seasons. A major part of Bon beliefs surrounds the life of a cultural hero called Kesar. An epic revolves around the adventures and governance of Kesar, apparently a commoner but belonging to the royal family, who lays the foundation of the fairly just, secular, and prosperous kingdom in Tibet during the pre-Buddhist era. The story of Kesar is full of parables and allegories in which animals and people transmogrify to deceive each other. The epic is surprising as a "religious" script in the sense that Kesar, the main protagonist of the epic, is not a totally ethical being who is guided by morals. Rather, he succeeds through deceit and blackmail as much as through wisdom and generosity. According to a local historian, Kesar was a secular king who did not preach religion; he was more interested in expansion. He states that the Qatal gah, the location of the central mosque in Skardu town, is the site of an original Bon structure.[1]

Bonism, as a pan-Tibetan religion, has many regional variations that also overlap with Buddhist belief systems. In the Balti version of Bonism, a snow leopard, k'chun, is a creature of the highest and purest realm, signifying the Hla itself. But sometimes the snow leopard also acts on Hlu's behalf as a destroyer of livestock. Thus, in Bonism, the snow leopard commanded a respectable, but not wholly benevolent, place.[2] According to Bonism, ibex, or s'kin, is another being with a soul and communities like a human. The great spirit, Hla, occasionally manifests itself in the form of a special kind of ibex, Hla-s'kin. Hla-s'kin is distinguishable from other ibex by some special feature, such as having only one horn or a special marking on its body. In Bonism, Hla manifests itself to people so that they will be impressed by and worship him.

ISLAM AND CONTEMPORARY VIEWS OF NATURE

Today, when Baltis talk about their "cultural" views of wildlife and nature, they usually mean those beliefs from Bonism that remain. Although these views are current, Baltis talk about them as if they have passed out of local cultural tradition. They usually begin by saying, "In the old days, people used to think" such and such. They remember that in folklore an ibex with one horn is considered to possess supernatural powers.

Contemporary Balti beliefs about the natural world, its ontological order, and its relationship with human society are informed, predominantly, by Islamic beliefs and philosophy. But there are general similarities between Bonism and the Islamic view of nature that Baltis draw upon when they discuss nature. The Islamic belief system bestows consciousness and souls to animals, and in this way it is similar to the animistic belief system of Bonism. Just as the God of Bonism, Hla, manifested itself in an ibex, Allah too manifests itself, symbolically, in the beauty of nature.

In Islam, animals are recognized as sentient beings with souls (Wescoat 1995; Mikhail 2013). In the overall structure of creation, human beings are considered the highest being because of their superior intellect. Other animals and plants are arranged in a trophic order that also becomes the basis for a "natural" social order. In this order, smaller animals and plants exist only as food for higher creatures. Among higher creatures, herbivores exist as food for carnivores, whereas they all exist to serve mankind and Allah. In Islamic beliefs, animals are allies of humans as well as their foes; some of them have been promised heaven, while others have been condemned to hell.

In Islamic belief, while wild and domesticated animals are linked in a trophic cascade, they also exist in worlds parallel to those of human beings and other beings, all answerable to the same God. Animals are thought to form communities just like humans and to manage their affairs as such. Islam explains its injunctions against cruelty to animals in matters that assign them personhood. According to some Hadiths (sayings of the Prophet Mohammad), on the Day of Judgment animals will testify against those humans who have killed them pointlessly. In other instances, some religious scholars have argued that animals will have their own accountability and will be punished or rewarded accordingly.

The use of an Islamic ethic to frame discussions of interest in wildlife management issues is a modern phenomenon in Baltistan that is directly linked to conservation and development projects in the region in the 1980s and 1990s. Conservation organizations and state officials in Baltistan promote protection of nature on religious grounds. For example, they often state that natural beauty is a gift of God that needs to be protected.[3] Conservation of predators has introduced Baltis to the concept of the ecosystem, which when decoded through the prevailing Islamic beliefs translates into *Mahoul*.[4] Conservation organizations and state officials tell the Baltis that predators are good for Mahoul; they are pretty, and pretty things must be conserved because Allah has entrusted us to take care of them. Village conservation leaders often invoke conservation in the name of upholding a simple Islamic principle, such as not randomly killing wild animals because they are a part of the larger kingdom of Allah. These overlaps, contrived and accidental, make it easier for Baltis to articulate Bon and Islamic beliefs with conservation objectives and rhetoric.[5]

The use of an Islamic framework to advocate for the protection of nature strikes a chord with people in leadership roles of village governing bodies and who had been trained in Islamic seminaries abroad and within Pakistan. Religious leaders play an active role in the social and communal affairs of their villages in Shia Baltistan. In more conservative parts of the Gilgit-Baltistan region, where stricter forms of Deobandi and Wahabi Islam are practiced, religious leaders often give injunctions against working with NGOs on the grounds that they represent non-Islamic beliefs. They see these organizations as conspiring to undermine Islam by spreading secular culture and values. Such misgivings are relatively less prevalent in the predominantly Shia region of Baltistan. In Baltistan, historically, opposition from religious leaders to the work of NGOs has come from the outside.

Most of the current village leaders were groomed during the early days of the Aga Khan Rural Support Program (AKRSP). This local leadership group was trained in basic community management and administrative skills, such as calling and holding monthly meetings, bookkeeping, drafting resolutions, taking minutes of a meeting, and so on. The local leadership not only worked with AKRSP but also built institutional linkages with other NGOs working in the social development and environmental conservation sectors.

In Gilgit-Baltistan, religious leaders have been prominent in public life as brokers of political power and state resources for their communities. At the local level, those who have been trained in good oratory skills in seminaries have assumed leadership of local social and political institutions, and in Baltistan, religious views on nature and wildlife were popularized by this class of people. Even for those locals who have been trained in secular institutions, an image of religiosity and piety is more important than their academic achievements. Displays of piety and moral rectitude according to Islamic doctrine is the habitus of many men in leadership positions in

Baltistan. Leadership is thus not just about mental and intellectual capabilities to lead, but also judged on the basis of personal conduct and adherence to the Islamic faith. In a 2013 survey in which seventy individuals from five villages were interviewed, sixty-four (over 90 percent) stated that it is their religious duty to protect snow leopards.

In 2014 I met Qazi, a man of thirty-five. He had been to Karachi and Islamabad for his studies and work and had just returned to the village after completing a master's degree in social work from a well-reputed national university. He also studied for four years at a religious school in Islamabad run by a Shia scholar from Baltistan. Hailing from a poor village of Krabathang, Qazi was well-spoken and well-respected. He repeated to me many verses from Quran in which Allah told humans to be kind to animals and to not kill them or punish them unnecessarily. Most of the injunctions in the Quran about treating animals with care and compassion are directed to domesticated animals. *Darinda* (wild animals) are, however, treated in the same manner as in the other major Abrahamic religions of the world: with disdain.

THE BALTI VIEW OF THE WILD AND THE DOMESTICATED

The Balti view of the wild and the domesticated is informed by their everyday interactions with nature. Grazing domestic livestock on high pastures, collecting fuel wood, and going on hunting excursions bring Baltis face to face with nature and its elements. In the Balti view of the landscape and "ecosystem," both wild and domesticated species are represented. The high mountains and inaccessible valleys, though easily visible by the naked eye, are hard-to-reach places. Snow leopards and ibex live in these stupendous places, where they are encountered by a wandering herder or a keen hunter. Thus the local landscape is at once agrarian and wild, where subsistence activities dictate various relationships with nature. Because the Balti see their surroundings as a fluid continuum between nature and culture, they also see the categories of the wild and domesticated as less rigid and complete than conservationists.[6] But this does not mean that they do not recognize the categories of wild and domesticated and their respective attributes. For example, wild meat is considered tastier than the meat of a domestic goat.

In the winter of 2013, I was conducting snow leopard presence-absence surveys in Rondu Valley with members of the Krabathang Village Conservation Committee.[7] I climbed a steep cliff face and was completely out of breath. In the cold and frigid air of the Karakoram, my breath was forming icicles around my overgrown mustache. Around us were tall cliffs, whose faces were broken, forming craggy outcrops where a few juniper bushes and some artemisia clung. Along the path were scattered bushes of wild rose and willow that had been chopped and grazed upon by goats. I was following Mehdi, a middle-aged farmer from Krabathang, who was at least fifteen minutes ahead of me. We were out looking for his goat that he lost earlier that year. Mehdi's nephew, who had installed a remote camera, told me that he had seen the black-and-white female goat near a *spang* (grassy meadow) situated at the flank of a rocky outcrop at fourteen thousand feet. It was November and it had been two months since Mehdi had last seen his goat, which had become *rashore*, a Balti term for goats that have "gone wild." For the Baltis this was a nuisance and a problem of boundary crossing against which they must guard.

It was late afternoon when we reached spang, and there was no sign of the goat. Then at once, Mehdi shouted and pointed to the movement of animals farther up the mountain. By my pace, the location of those animals was another two hours of strenuous walking. I sat down and asked Mehdi to take out the binoculars to see what the animals were. They were ibex, and amid them was Mehdi's goat. The goat and the ibex were grazing together and tended to move along with the same agility and rhythm. We were unable to catch Mehdi's goat, and it was never seen again.

In 2010 I conducted a survey in the Hushe, Krabathang, Basha, and Basho Valleys to assess how local people differentiate between wild and domestic animals.[8] The survey showed that while defining the distinction between wild and domesticated, some of the informants stated that if they don't look after domestic animals, they will become wild. Thus domestication was not seen as fixed but rather as an ongoing process. In discussions with Balti herders about this topic, they often refer to traces of wild goats in their domestic goats by pointing out the shape of the horns and the color and pattern of their pelage.

In Hushe, my main informant Ghulam Ali, recounted to me how domesticated animals cross over into wildness and sometimes goats become part of the ibex herd and run away. Ali says,

> the meat of the goat is very tasty. It is so because it eats the same grasses as ibex. It is only the goats who [become wild] because they look like ibex, whereas the sheep does not. The goat has the same hair as the ibex. The sheep when runs away it does not survive the winter. When a goat runs away, people go to the mountain and try to separate the goats from the [ibex] herd. Last year there was someone in the village whose four

or five goats ran away, and only a couple returned, while the others become part of the wild herd.

Ali also said that similarly a dog becomes part of a wolf pack and goes wild and starts barking like the wolves. This tendency of domesticated goats to become wild is equally matched by the opposite tendency. In Baltistan, it is commonplace to hear stories about wild ibex becoming part of domestic livestock herds and finding their way into a corral. On many occasions I have seen a lone ibex in villages across Baltistan. Baltis usually keep an ibex with the expectation of breeding it with their domestic herd and claim that the offspring of such mating are very strong and fit. Local people say that they can feel the spirit of wildness in these offspring.

This perception of wild and domesticated has also found its way into everyday Balti language and communication. *Lo'shore*, a Balti term used for a sheep that goes wild, is sometimes used for a person who has gone mad. Just as the domestic animals that go wild seem possessed, a person who does not regard social norms is also seen as possessed, with the spirit of wildness.

THE *BROQ*: A SEMI-WILD PLACE

For the Baltis, a *broq*, or a "high pasture settlement," is a special place. Located, on average, between one and three days' walk from the permanently settled village, a broq is a temporary settlement, generally occupied between May and October. Strategically located near good pasturage, water, and fuelwood on a relatively flat piece of ground, the settlement can range from a few to many stone huts and several animal corrals. The main huts are divided into living quarters for cooking and sleeping, and a set of open and closed corrals for different ages and sexes of animals. Usually located just below the tree line, herders control the entire summer grazing operation from the broq. An average-sized broq of a village in Baltistan commands an area of about twenty square kilometers. Each broq is claimed by a village as part of its *shamlat*, or "common land," guaranteed under the current land settlement laws. The boundaries of the broq are strictly monitored and controlled, and conflict over broq boundaries and rights is one of the most common sources of disputes among villages in Baltistan.

A broq is a semi-domesticated place, sometimes referred to as jungle. But *jungle* here does not mean a thick forest of wooded trees; rather it is a place to get wood for winter heating and cooking.[9] It is a confined and domesticated place. Repeat visits to the broq invest it with memories, and it becomes the basis for the collective identity of Balti communities.

Ghulam Rasool at Skoyo broq

Baltis' encounters with wild nature are facilitated by their domestic animals grazing on the broq. It is the domestic animals that make the Balti herders traverse between the two worlds of semi-wild pastures and domesticated villages. When at the broq, Baltis follow the paths of their goats, sheep, dzo, and dzomo (female dzo) and in the process go to places where no other human would go because those places are so remote from human settlements. Balti herders told me that they sometimes spend days out in the area looking for their lost animals; such trips usually become the settings where mythical and folk stories take place.

Do Balti farmers hate wild nature or wildlife in general, as some people would have us believe? Perhaps not. Some anthropologists have argued that forest people often hate and fear wildlife (Bird-David 1990, 190; Boomgard 2001, 17). The Zafiminary of Madagascar, for example, have an indifferent and even hostile relationship with nature (Bloch 1995). For the Baltis, though, wild nature is part of Allah's creation, and it also has a right to exist. But there are elements of wild nature that are to be avoided, rather than feared and worshipped, because they cause material damage. If in the Bon belief system damage caused by snow leopards was considered by the Baltis to be a punishment, under the Islamic belief system it is considered an occupational hazard, against which people must take precautions.

THE BALTIS AND THE SNOW LEOPARD

Oral history and ethno-ecological studies show that snow leopard hunters enjoyed high status in the Balti society and were often exempt from the local tax of *begaar* (forced labor demanded by the state) (Roberts 1997). The local people used a variety of methods to trap and kill snow leopards, including using leg snares, poisoning carcasses of livestock, and shooting. There is no known tradition of using a pelt as a trophy or as an object worth collecting for its intrinsic value. But snow leopard pelts are used among certain communities in Nepal and Mongolia in ritual ceremonies where the pelt acts as a mode of transportation for shamans to travel to other worlds and change shapes.

Balti encounters with snow leopards are almost always by accident. They describe such an encounter as a significant event that leaves a mark on their memory. Some describe the snow leopard as a *robdar* animal, meaning an animal with "significant presence," one that commands respect and radiates a social power and influence over others. Others have depicted their encounters in opposite terms. For example, two farmers from Hushe, Afzal and Ghulam Ali, recounted a story to me in the winter of 2013 in which they purportedly played with a full-grown snow leopard all day. Afzal said, "We were young, may be ten or eleven years old. We were grazing goats in Aling Nallah when we encountered a snow leopard. We did not know at the time that it was a snow leopard; it played hide-and-seek with us. Then some old people approached us and saw that we had been playing with a snow leopard all day long as if it was a domesticated cat. When it saw the grown-up men approaching, it ran away."

Haji from Hushe explained that on one occasion, he was going to the forest to collect fuel wood with his eyes fixed on the path. "From the opposite direction a snow leopard was coming, with its eye fixed on the path too. When we came right in front of each other, then we both lifted our eyes from the path and saw each other and we both ran away in opposite directions. We both got scared," recalled Haji.

THE GHOST PREDATOR

The elusive nature of snow leopards makes them equally mysterious in the eyes of Baltis and of conservationists. They appear to have adapted equally to the wandering herders and wondering field biologists. For this reason it is so difficult to guard against them. I spent one week in the summer of 2007 on the Skoyo broq with a couple of herders from the village who were tending the village herd. They were guarding a total of about two hundred goats and about hundred sheep. In addition, there were about thirty cows and dzo. The Skoyo broq was at 12,000 feet (3,800 meters) at a relatively flat ground that was the size of a couple of football fields. The pasture settlement, which was a collection of log huts in really bad condition, was bounded by high mountains and deep ravines. The south end of the pasture settlement looked at the 18,000-foot-high Takht-e-Sulieman, or Throne of Solomon. The north end of the valley descended steeply to where the Indus flowed.

It was early August and the heat was intense. After a light breakfast of local bread and salt tea, I sat under the shade of a log hut and started interviewing Ghulam Rasool, a local herder who spend most of his summers here. Ghulam Rasool narrated numerous stories of snow leopard attacks on his herd. He said, "[The snow leopard] is like a suicide bomber; it takes the goat right in front of your eyes and you can't do anything about it." As our discussion progressed, Ghulam Rasool kept an eye out on the goats and sheep that were scattered on the surrounding mountains. Ghulam Rasool could still see most of the animals, but a few had gone down into a ravine. He got up and threw a stone at them to call them back in his sight.

The sun was now at is most intense, and both humans and beasts searched for shade. I was watching a Himalaya chough (a yellow-billed bird in the crow family) chasing a Lammergeier vulture while Ghulam Rasool was shaking a goatskin full of yak milk in a rhythmic motion to churn it into butter. A few stubborn and persistent flies were hovering around my face and trying to land on my nose and eyes. There was a gentle breeze, and a few small clouds floated in sky. I don't know when I fell asleep, but I was awakened by frantic shouting by Ghulam Rasool. There was a snow leopard attack taking place—right there—in front of me. I felt adrenaline rushing through my body. Here was my chance to see the snow leopard, finally. I ran toward the herd under attack, following Ghulam Rasool, who was now waving his stick and calling "ho, ho, ho" as loud as he could. The fanfare lasted just about two minutes, and then there was a silence. I did not see the snow leopard; it had come and gone truly as a ghost cat. There were no casualties so Ghulam Rasool was lucky this time. The incident made me realize how difficult it is to guard against such attacks. It would require immense manpower to truly keep the animals safe from attacks just by watching over them. The Baltis realize this fact, and when probed as to why they can't be more vigilant, they often laugh off the suggestions.

Many stories from local herders show that the herder who lost his livestock this year because he could not be bothered to keep a vigilant eye had successfully protected his herd against a snow leopard attack three years ago. In snow leopard conservation literature, what gets recorded are the number of successful attacks by snow leopards—which is an important datum to collect in itself because it helps compensation programs assess the extent of damage—but the number of unsuccessful attacks are never recorded or even discussed. Such case studies or data will clearly complicate the picture of herders as not just lazy or careless but perhaps as normal human beings. A focus on attacks successfully warded off by local people would have another implication: shifting the main focus of inquiry from farmers' laziness to behavior of the snow leopard and its stealthy and predatory nature, not fully known even to herders who spend their time in the pasture and in its habitat.

THE SNOW LEOPARD AND THE OTTER

Sitting under an apricot tree in the windy Skardu town in the summer of 2009, I was listening to Shakoor as he was telling me a strange story about snow leopards and otters. A man of small stature in his late fifties, Shakoor was a local fisheries guard who looked after the fishing activities at Sadpara Lake near Skardu; his job mainly consisted of issuing daily licenses to local anglers. He took a great pride in the fact that he slept all by himself during cold winter nights in his government-allotted "hut" (a small dingy room) at the lake when the outside temperature would read −30°C (−22°F).

That evening in Skardu, Shakoor was trying to borrow a remote camera trap from me. He said that he often heard snow leopard calls around his hut, and when he checked the snow for pugmarks, it would confirm that snow leopards had been circling his hut. Shakoor claimed that he often saw snow leopards "playing" on the far bank of the Sadpara Lake. He wanted a camera so he could prove his point. I was not interested in finding out about snow leopard presence around Sadpara Lake, as I had spent many moons on the lake, in all seasons, and I knew for sure that snow leopards did occasionally come down to the lake and its surroundings. But without any ibex population to sustain snow leopards, there were no permanent occupants of the valley.

After his unsuccessful attempt at getting a camera from me, Shakoor started narrating an old myth about snow leopards that I had first heard in 1993 and have since heard in villages all across Baltistan.[10] According to Shakoor, when a female snow leopard comes into heat on a full moon night, she goes to the edge of a lake or a river and calls a male otter. The otter emerges from the water and mates with the snow leopard. After copulation, the female returns to the mountains, and the otter goes back into the water. From that point I have heard two versions about the offspring of this interspecies breeding. According to the first version, at the end of her pregnancy, the snow leopard comes again to the edge of the water and gives birth. A newborn male cub goes into the water and becomes an otter, while a female cub leaves with her mother for the mountains. According to the second version, both the male and female cubs are born and stay in the wild, but the male is sterile.

The myth about the mating of the snow leopard and otter circulates as gossip in which a proverbial old hunter of the village, now deceased or shifted to another village, has seen the mating or has seen the snow leopard coming to the water on a full moon night. In general, Baltis talk about this as a myth from "old times," but it takes on a new meaning in the Islamic and conservation discourse on nature.

We can interpret this myth by putting it in the wider Balti cultural, historical, and ecological contexts. First, in its cultural context to clarify what kind of myth we are dealing with. Another regional myth holds that if a person recites the saga of Kesar to fellow villagers, Kesar, as a token of his appreciation, leaves an ibex at the door of the person who recited the story. This myth is about human-nature interaction and reflects the institution of reciprocity or gift exchange.[11] Such myths are studied by anthropologists who look at the symbolic meaning conveyed in them by a community. Myths about animals, such as totems, are processes of group identity and solidarity formation. In this myth, the animal society is considered a reflection of the human society.

The myth of the snow leopard's mating with an otter, however, is a different kind of myth, one about relationship within nature, or about nature. Rather than looking at this myth as a symbolic expression of society, we should look at it literally, as something about nature itself—that is, the "native's" view of nature. The otter–snow leopard story is about a quirk of nature and a special design of nature.

In the historical context, the story of an otter and snow leopard is most likely a localized relic of the Bon-era belief system. In this pre-Islamic religion, stories of Kesar and shape-shifting animals were commonplace. A British colonial officer, David Lorimer, who served in Hunza in the 1930s, says that the figure of King Kesar, as a cultural hero, spans many central Asian and Tibetan societies. The local version in Hunza is represented in the stories of "Gesar Khan" (Lorimer 1931, 105). In the Kesar saga, the natural and the social worlds are intertwined, and the boundaries of categories are not fixed.

The third context within which this myth could be understood is local ecological context. In ecological sciences, the snow leopard is a keystone predator. A keystone predator occurs in low density in nature and commands a large prey base and hence a large territory. In the ecological view, if the number of snow leopards increases in nature, their natural prey populations decline. Like scientists, Balti farmers see snow leopard numbers as limited by nature, but for a different reason—that they don't cause damage to farmers or livestock—one that shows that the Balti conception of the ecosystem includes wild as well as domestic ungulates. In the Balti worldview, the local ecosystem limits snow leopard abundance in an unusual but natural way: by making it mate with otters.

According to the myth, the snow leopard male is either missing or sterile, while female is not, hence the need for the female to be inseminated by a male of another species. The male offspring of cross-species mating are, as expected, sterile, thus completing the cycle. According to the Baltis, if male snow leopards were not sterile, they would breed like rabbits and create a huge problem for livestock and wild ungulates. The cultural, historical, and ecological context of the myth suggests that Baltis see their landscape as a mixture of domesticated and wild species that often cross boundaries. When I challenged Shakoor by contending that two different species cannot breed and produce offspring, he replied, "Don't we cross breed yaks and cows?" He said that just as the dzo, the male offspring of a yak and a domestic cow, is sterile so are the male offspring when snow leopards mate with otters. For the Balti, there is precedent in the practice of their domestic economy that makes the snow leopard–otter mating story believable.

CONCLUSION

Despite their interest in conservation on utilitarian grounds, villagers often complain about the new regime of governance that has been imposed upon them. For example, grazing restrictions and bans on collecting fuelwood and timber hurt the local livelihood base directly. Some even complained about conservation programs that were in high demand by communities. For example, Taqi, an elderly man from Basho Valley, said that the difference between wild and domesticated animals is that his forefathers used to hunt wild animal for meat, but now the conservation NGOs have come and asked villagers to protect and not hunt them, so they don't benefit from them. He quipped that what Allah made halal, NGOs and government made haram, pointing to the disjuncture between Islamic and state law.[12]

The widespread belief among Balti farmers is that under the guise of protecting animals, conservation institutions will take away their land. Haji from Hushe told me, "There is no competition between wildlife and goats. Also, if we decrease the number of livestock, pressure on ibex and markhor will increase." He looked at conservation practices more cynically, pointing to the political economy of nature conservation. In the 2014 survey, 50 percent of the people in the villages thought that conservation NGOs will either take over their pastures or their access to them.

According to the standard conservation narrative, farmers and their livestock in Baltistan have transformed the local wild landscape. But the farmers see the transformation taking place not in the biophysical environment but in the snow leopard itself. From the perspectives of the local people, it is not only that their tolerance toward snow leopards has decreased in recent years but that the tolerance of snow leopards toward humans has increased. From the perspective of the local people, with the provision of protection, snow leopards now do not care about humans and are not afraid of them. All of the above is true for snow leopards. Local people often state that snow leopards now kill their livestock in broad daylight. In Hushe village this perception about the change in snow leopard behavior is perhaps most acute, and with a certain degree of empirical basis. I visited Hushe between 2013 and 2015, and on each occasion I found fresh snow leopard tracks on the outskirts of the village. It seemed that the cats patrolled the boundary of the village hoping to come upon a stray goat. Studies from diverse geographical locations, dealing with many species and communities, show that local people often ascribe behavioral changes in animal species under conservation as an effect of conservation efforts.[13] Snow leopards are learning to be less tolerant of human presence. In some ways, the farmers see the relationship between their well-being and that of the snow leopard as inversely related.

One result of this threat of appropriation of local landscapes at the hand of extra-local institutions is the emergence of a new discourse among local farmers about wildlife. The commentary of local Balti farmers on the "attitude" of certain wild species, especially the snow leopard, toward them and their livestock shows their views about the state and its priorities. Local people see wildlife under conservation management as becoming more wild and uncaring toward them.

CHAPTER FIVE

Modernization and the Transactional Mode of Conservation

BALTISTAN Wildlife Conservation and Development Organization (BWCDO) runs a community-based livestock insurance program that compensates farmers who lose livestock to snow leopard predation. The organization seeks to resolve the snow leopard–farmer conflict by highlighting and rectifying the uneven distribution of costs and benefits involved in snow leopard conservation in the Karakoram and Himalayan mountains of northern Pakistan. Colleagues and I set up the organization in 1999 in the small, remote valley of Skoyo in the Baltistan region. Until 2007, it was known as Project Snow Leopard; we changed the name to reflect the fact that our work was about people as much as about wildlife.

The organization has three main activities: community-based livestock insurance program, construction of predator-proof corrals, and conservation education in schools. It aims to create optimal conditions for snow leopard conservation in northern Pakistan by providing an alternative to the current approach in conservation projects. Our approach is based on the conviction that successful conservation is not only about implementing technical solutions (national parks, in situ conservation and scientific management) but also about finding long-term "human" solutions.

This case shows that one possible response to the snow leopard–farmer conflict is to use a purely transactional approach in which villagers receive compensation for their losses. The transactional approach is particularly well suited to human-wildlife conflicts where a common vision of nature fails to emerge, as is the case in northern Pakistan. It is not possible, culturally or socially, to reconcile the opposite views of the snow leopard that are held by farmers and conservationists. The only way to change farmers' views of snow leopards as vermin is by eliminating the economic loss that drives this behavior. Retaliatory killing of the snow leopard can be stopped by enabling farmers to trade the negative cost of the snow leopard for economic security and peace of mind.

Baltistan and the entire northern region of Pakistan have a unique advantage that allows such a purely transactional relationship to work due to the long experience that the people of the region have of working with outside development and conservation organizations in the past. Many Baltis see development and conservation projects, especially community-based conservation, as a means of receiving financial and economic help from NGOs and government agencies. Such a transactional relationship is a logical outcome of the process of commodification of nature in the time of neoliberal economic policies. The kind of relationship that emerges when NGOs and farmers cooperate for conservation is based mostly on the instrumental rationality of both parties. There is little long-term commitment to each other on the basis of reciprocity or any other non-instrumental reasons. The main driver is the perception of cost and benefits that these relationships entail. Under neoliberal conservation policies when socio-natural entities such as ibex or pastures become commodities, the relationship also changes between farmers and ibex or pastures, resulting in these entities' acquiring a commodity-like character and entering a transactional relationship.

NEOLIBERAL NATURE AND COMMUNITY ETHICS

The biggest change in recent decades in Baltistan occurred with the arrival of the Aga Khan Rural Support Program (AKRSP) and the subsequent programs that have been built on its interventions. In 1986 multiple international, bilateral, and multilateral donors, including the Aga Khan Foundation, founded the AKRSP in Baltistan. Its aim was to "develop institutional and technical models for equitable development." It organized farmers into "broad-based, multi-purpose Village Organizations to overcome the handicap of subsistence holding." The Village Organization was to be "a coalition of those residents of a village whose common economic interest is best served by organizing as a group" (AKRSP 1993, 3).[1] During the first ten years, the program's main aim in Baltistan was formation of Village Organizations on a mass scale. By the end of 1995 the program had achieved something remarkable: it had established more than eight hundred Village Organizations in the Baltistan region and had started and completed nearly 95 percent of the eight hundred Productive Physical Infrastructure (PPI) projects, such as irrigation channels, water supply schemes, covering nearly 100 percent of the villages and 80 percent of the households (AKRSP 1996).

Under its various "packages," AKRSP supplied the "progressive farmers" of Baltistan with improved breeds of cattle, goats, and sheep at subsidized rates. It also provided seed, fertilizers, pest sprays—the whole green revolution package—to Village Organization members at subsidized rates. Under orchard improvement packages, AKRSP provided mostly local material for setting up small-scale commercial orchards.

The Village Organizations had a basic administrative structure with a president, manager, and general membership. Individual members were nominated by the general membership to be trained as specialists in forestry, livestock, agriculture, and accounting. The objective was for these specialists to teach their fellow members modern techniques of subsistence production.

The main responsibility of the Village Organization manager was to organize and chair the general membership meeting each month. And the main purpose of the meeting was to discuss village-wide development-related issues and to collect a monthly savings contribution from each member; an individual's membership was contingent upon their contribution to the savings fund, which went into a collective Village Organization savings pool. At first the Village Organizations used the savings pools as collateral to obtain low-interest loans from AKRSP, but later, due to pressure from donors, interest rates were raised.[2] The Village Organization manager was supposed to maintain two registers: one for recording the proceedings of monthly meetings and the other for recording individual members' savings. The program's Social Organizers were responsible for forming Village Organizations and visited them regularly to check their records of meetings and savings progress, "motivate" their members about new "packages," and bring back requests from Village Organizations to the technical sections such as forestry, livestock, and agriculture.

As mentioned above, one of the main interventions of AKRSP was its grants to create Productive Physical Infrastructures. In more than 70 percent of the cases, the funds were used to improve an irrigation channel or construct a new one. These channels are in many cases the lifeline of the village economy, allowing communities to cultivate communal land that would otherwise be barren due to lack of water. The land developed through this method was generally divided equally among Village Organization members. This means that in many cases villagers saw their landholdings suddenly double or triple in size.

I worked for AKRSP's Baltistan office between 1993 and 1996. During my time there the office was always full of villagers—Village Organization members, presidents, specialists—asking staff for advice, physical inputs, and training. It had the atmosphere of a Sunday agricultural market rather than a development office. People came not only to receive development assistance but also to make new proposals for infrastructure improvement or to complain to program engineers about the bad design or construction that they had overseen.

Trophy Hunting Program

Another program important to the socio-economic context of Baltistan was the Mountain Areas Conservancy Project, a trophy hunting program initiated in 1993. This two-phase US$15 million project was funded by Global Environment Facility and the United Nation Development Program. Although the project officially ended in 2007, the trophy hunting program initiated under it continues to this day. Under the program, the Pakistani government and the International Union for Conservation of Nature (the NGO partner) demonstrated a sustainable-use approach to conservation. It used the preexisting social infrastructure of Village Organizations to implement a community-based conservation project in which the local communities were asked to protect ibex and markhor in return for a share of revenue generated by the sale of hunting licenses.

International and Pakistani hunters were required to buy a license to shoot these animals. The local communities receive 80 percent of the license fee, and the provincial governments received 20 percent. In the 1990s the license fee for a markhor hunt was around US$25,000; in 2019 it was over US$100,000. The license fee for ibex is US$3,000 for international hunters, and 100,000 rupees (about US$1,000) for Pakistani nationals. No Pakistanis have purchased licenses for markhor given the high cost.

Each year around sixty hunting permits for ibex and four for markhor are issued in Gilgit-Baltistan. Out of the sixty hunting permits issued for ibex, about ten, or 15 percent, are reserved for Pakistani hunters.

In the initial years there were some hiccups in the program when some communities stopped getting their share of the revenue, but today the local communities reliably get paid within six months of the hunt. The money from trophy hunting is substantial and has served as a strong incentive for communities to protect the markhor and ibex in their areas.[3] Local communities throughout Baltistan and beyond who participate in this program have mostly respected the ban on individual hunting for subsistence, and the local wildlife department claims that the populations of ibex and markhor have increased significantly.[4]

Criticism of Trophy Hunting Program

A general criticism of market-based conservation programs such as trophy hunting is that commodification of nature transforms, in this case, an ibex from a socio-cultural object, governed by an ethic of reciprocity and sharing, to a commodity, governed by a market ethic. The concern is that it would result in the loss of an important cultural institution—sharing of hunted meat—and its accompanying social bonds. In one such critique of trophy hunting programs in Baltistan, Ken MacDonald (2004) warned that, "Ironically, this reconceptualization of ibex as a route to development retains the significance of ibex to community well-being. . . . But it is in the mediating role played by cash and the hope of development that a change in meaning, and a reaction, lies. Rather than its older significance in reinforcing social relations or bringing "natural" properties to institutions of authority in the village, ibex has become the route to individual gain. So, rather than strengthening community processes, capitalizing nature in Hushe has individualizing effects" (89).

MacDonald also argued that the commodification of the ibex was resulting in a transfer of control of the resources from village elders to a new set of younger actors who were interested in money and not the social relation that the exchange of ibex engenders. This critique of trophy hunting is justified to the extent that it is transferring control of ibex from one group of villagers to another. It is, however, perhaps not the case that this transfer is resulting in individualizing effects, (87) if by that MacDonald means reduction in collective action and decision making at the village level. The ethnographic evidence suggests that a monetary valuation of nature—or holding a purely instrumental view of nature—is as prevalent in rural societies as in urban ones. Moreover, these projects of commodification of nature also result in more communal labor and cohesion than one would expect.

In the summer of 2017, I took a group of university students from Lahore to Baltistan and Hunza, where I taught a six-week course. In Hunza my students surveyed local people about their perception of trophy hunting programs. The results were likely to be fairly representative of the attitudes of the people of Baltistan because Hunza and Baltistan have worked with the same set of NGOs and with government policies that have promoted a neoliberal approach to conservation and development. The students' field notes illustrate how people view the trophy hunting program:

> We were told by her uncle that in the 130 households in the village, everyone has a "share" of the hunt. Previously, the animal

would be brought to the village secretly, and was consumed by the family and acquaintances of the hunter, with no benefit to the rest of the village. He also told us that despite the losses the community faced, the benefits were much greater. If an animal is shot illegally, the entire village takes action and cases end up in court. Our informant then launched into a tale of how he accidentally shot from his gun while intoxicated, and despite being a resident of the village was fined 10,000 rupees. (Kulsoom Malik, July 28, 2017)

We started to discuss the trophy hunting program and were told that a "welfare committee" banned hunting in about 1991 [the dates in all interviews were not very precise], and then trophy hunting of ibex and markhor was introduced in about 1997 or 1998, in collaboration with this committee. Both men seemed to see greater benefit in the program. Foreigners have to pay the most for a license and usually come from America or Australia. The money made from these goes to a fund and then is used on a variety of projects. For example, a guesthouse was built—which our next informant told us cost 13 lakh rupees [about US$10,000]—it is used to fund healthcare, or to provide scholarships, or is loaned at low interest rates for people to start businesses such as grocery stores and small restaurants. (Kulsoom Malik, July 29, 2017)

We asked them about the benefits the village had received with trophy hunting. They told us that with the help of the money, Khyber had reaped a lot of benefits; they had constructed a community guest house (one we were sitting in), brought great improvement to their education, started a bank to cater for their people. The money was also used to help the needy. This had also resulted in an increase in the ibex population, "as now they can be easily seen, even in our fields. (Fatima Khan, July 28, 2017)

Regarding the benefits of trophy hunting, he told us how every member of the village had benefited with it. Every person in the community, man and woman, receives an equal share of the 75% of the trophy hunting money. He also told us about the irrigation canal project completed with the community paying 50 million rupees [about US$40,000] for it. The kids of the village are also sent for higher studies with the money. Later we were presented with a bag full of apricots to take with us. Next we visited an old man who used to be a hunter. When asked about the trophy hunting programme, he stated that he was happy. According to him, this was beneficial for the whole community, not only for the hunter and his family. Shah informed us that initially the hunters were not accepting this change but then a government official from Punjab convinced them to change their stance. Now, all the local "ex-hunters" accompany the hunter with the permit, to assist and monitor. (Fatima Khan, July 29, 2017)

The hunt takes place from the jeep, and 20 to 25 people from the village accompany the hunter, in case the animal needs to be retrieved after being shot. The hunter has three tries to shoot at the target animal. Moreover, the money from the license belongs to the village where the animal is shot and licenses have to be transferred to the village in case the animal is chased through territory. (Ali Aftab, July 29, 2017)

To a certain extent, a neoliberal ethic now governs most of the communities in Gilgit-Baltistan. As Laurie Medina shows in her work on commodification of protected areas in Belize, a new form of governance based on market calculation is appearing in local communities. Using Michel Foucault's thesis of governmentality, Medina (2015) shows how this market rationality is inculcated in local behavior. She writes, "As community members became incorporated into the global market for ecotourism . . . their conduct came to be governed through the market; more precisely, villagers came to apply 'the rationality of the market, the schemas of analysis it offers and the decision-making criteria it suggests' (Foucault 2008, 145) to govern their own conduct in relation to the sanctuary. Villagers thus abandoned hunting within the reserve to become collaborators in the ongoing production and sale of protected nature as commodity" (281).

Similarly, the experience of the Aga Khan Rural Support Program and the community-based conservation project under the Mountain Areas Conservancy Project have instilled an ethic of market rationality in the ways in which the Balti communities govern their relationship with nature *and* society. The program had actively sought to transform subsistence agriculture into commodity production, promote enterprise, provide access to financial credit and services, and privatize natural resources, which created the basic groundwork for this ethic that emerged. But it also emphasized group cohesion and the building of social capital, tendencies that go against individualizing effects in a society. It is for this reason, perhaps, we observe that in Baltistan and in Hunza commodification of nature seemingly has resulted in consensus and cohesion, or at least does not seem to have radically changed an existing collective ethos.[5]

It is important to understand how the new ethic based on market rationality emerges from a preexisting rationality based on reciprocity and cultural beliefs. So, for example, culturally, the Baltis have viewed the ibex as both meat and a means through which they mediate the relationship between society and nature at large. Ibex are seen as beings of a parallel world in which people must maintain an ethical relationship if they wish to ensure a continued supply of meat.

As mentioned by MacDonald (2004), Baltis also further social ties and bonds with each other by sharing ibex meat. But what happens if one tries to enlist both local cultural beliefs for the protection of ibex and local economic interest in ibex through trophy hunting? Essentially, the two rationalities, or ethics, that govern Balti farmers' relationship with ibex are mixed up. As soon as an ibex becomes a trophy rather than meat, the accompanying ethics governing its management and relationship to society also change in people's minds. The existing cultural ethic is no longer valid because the ibex is no longer meat or part of the wider cosmological order of the Balti universe. Here, a new ethic must appear to take over the management of the ibex as a trophy animal, and this ethic is governed by market rationality. It involves making decisions based on the instrumental value of things and not necessarily on their cultural and social value. As Foucault reminds us, the rationality of the market offers the schemas of analysis and criteria for decision-making (2008, 145). So when an ibex becomes a trophy, Macdonald asked a pertinent question about the clash of this new value with the preexisting value as a cultural and social object, governed under a different ethic, which is presumably based on more equal sharing of ibex meat, leading to community solidarity.

This means that market rationality governs the behavior of local people when it comes to dealing with nature that NGOs have asked them to protect, such as ibex and snow leopards. This is an important point. Nature is also dealt with in a non-transactional, or a reciprocal or ritualistic, way in Baltistan and across the region. As mentioned earlier, the local people practice vestiges of Bonism that combine with Islamic beliefs to form a moral ecology.

A dzo (cow and yak hybrid)

But when that nature is dealt with via an NGO edict or at an NGO's request, then it is dealt with in a transactional way. Thus what we see in Baltistan is a strange mix of Barthian transactional order, not so much overpowered by individual choices as by fairly collective choices. The new rationality that has emerged is based on instrumentalism, but it is also collective.

An important indicator of how trophy-hunting of ibex for conservation purposes has furthered a transactional approach among Baltis is the intensity of hatred toward predators, especially snow leopards. The unintended consequence of increasing the monetary value of ibex in the eyes of the villagers is the devaluation of snow leopards because they prey on ibex. In villages where the trophy-hunting program is working, villagers now claim that they have two reasons to kill snow leopards: to protect their livestock and to protect their ibex and markhor, which fetch a license fee for them. In Skoyo, villagers demanded that the government should either kill all the snow leopards or provide villagers compensation for any ibex or markhor killed by them. The Balti villagers often say, "The snow leopard is considered very important and unique by people in other countries." Here, outside countries mean, mainly, donor countries.

INSURANCE PROGRAMS AND SURVEYS

Between 1998 and 2000, I conducted extensive surveys in Baltistan and visited more than two dozen pasture settlements. At each pasture I asked the villagers about predation on their livestock and the identity of the predators, and at each pasture I received the same answer: predators were a menace, and the main culprits were snow leopards and wolves. Predation by these species was a constant and recurring problem and a part of pastoral life.

In 1999 I set up the first insurance program in the village of Skoyo in the Rondu Valley. This small village of twenty-six households is perched on a ledge that overhangs the Indus River. Because the terrain is dominated by jagged peaks and deep valleys, Skoyo and its surroundings are a prime habitat for snow leopard, ibex, and markhor. I was interested in Skoyo because I had heard about a famous, almost folkloric, tale of a male markhor jumping to its death into the icy water of the Indus while being chased by a snow leopard. The incident happened within Skoyo village, and it was witnessed by roadside spectators across the river. I would hear this story from the villagers for the next seventeen years! (The same incident happened again in January 2019.) But, more important, there had been reports from Skoyo and surrounding villages about livestock losses to snow leopards when I had worked for the Aga Khan Rural Support Program in the early 1990s. In 1999 a snow leopard had jumped into a livestock corral in Sari, a village just a few miles up the river from Skoyo. The farmer who found the snow leopard in the corral called the local authorities; they released the snow leopard, which had killed several animals, without compensating the farmers for his losses.

I had in mind an insurance program that would be fully funded by premiums paid by herders. In order to determine the premium rate per head of livestock, I calculated the annual predation rate in Skoyo and turned that into a monetary figure based on the estimated market value of killed animals in 1999. In Skoyo, the annual loss rate was about 2 percent of the total herd, and given that a goat cost a thousand rupees, I set a premium of twenty rupees (forty US cents) per head of goat. This amount would cover the average losses from predation in Skoyo without any outside funding. When I told the farmers from Skoyo about the amount they each would have to pay to join the program, they balked.[6]

The Skoyo villagers had worked with AKRSP for many years and had received fairly regular support and resources from it. Additionally, for the past six years, they had been getting significant financial returns from the government-sponsored trophy hunting program. People from Skoyo and other remote villages throughout Baltistan have long experienced dealing with development and conservation NGOs; the era of AKRSP was an era of development encounters for the Balti. They had learned the rhetoric of development and had adopted a language of marginality in order to attract resources.

The idea of self-help that the program promoted was closely linked to the idea of institutionalization of the development process. This meant establishing local entities that could carry forward the work of development beyond the program's support. AKRSP promoted the idea of partnerships and prepared local grassroots organizations for attracting funding from other sources—both from the state and the private sector. The Balti farmers were encouraged by program staff to view outside NGOs as sources of money and resources. The support network of NGOs in the NGO-village relationship is outside the traditional social structure of kinship and patron-client relationship that was once seen in villages across Baltistan. This is a new kind of relationship that it is purely transactional and governed by market rationality. Now, when national and international NGOs start working with local communities in Baltistan, the people ask about the "projects" that NGOs can bring to their villages. This social background in Skoyo explains their reluctance to ratify my suggestion and even their disgust at a proposal for a self-funded insurance scheme model. My "project" was asking *them* for money, rather than promising it to them.

It was not simply that the villagers had gotten used to receiving funds from outside sources, and, therefore, simply weren't willing to pay. Despite the efforts of AKRSP and other organizations, farmers remained extremely poor, particularly in terms of cash. An insurance model based on full premium contributions was not feasible in the region; therefore, we decided to negotiate the amount that villagers could pay. We thought it was important that they pay at least a nominal fee into the insurance fund because there was also a collective advantage in pooling the risk of predation.

We asked, "How much could you pay?" It was clear that compensation from an insurance program was not enough to soften their attitudes toward the snow leopard, especially if they were being asked to share the cost of the program. To convince the villagers that our project was interested in their wellbeing and not just that of the snow leopard, we told them the project would pay half of the premiums and fund social development projects in the village. In order to develop a sustainable source of funding for the insurance program over and above farmers' premium payments, the project decided to set up an ecotourism company called Full Moon Night Trekking, and the profits would subsidize the insurance premiums. We also hoped that enough funds would be raised through the trekking company to pay for other non-conservation-related projects, such as small-scale infrastructure projects. The project was right about the basic idea: farmers bear the cost of snow leopard conservation, and people who benefit from the snow leopard's survival may be willing to help pay for it.

The Design of the Insurance Program

All households in Skoyo village took out insurance on their goats. We decided to set the premium rate at 1 percent of a goat's current value. Indeed, given that the average annual loss in the previous five years had been 2 percent of the total value of herds and that this percentage was expected to remain constant in the coming years, the villagers' own premium payments could cover at least half of the costs of the average annual loss. The other half, we hoped would be covered by the ecotourism fund.

We decided to establish a two-tier financial design for the insurance program. Insurance premiums paid by the villagers went into Fund 1, kept in an account at a local bank. The money was held collectively, but individuals' payment records were kept separately in the village. The project had calculated that (in 1999) the average value per goat was 1,500 rupees (about US$30). (In 1999 the exchange rate was 54 rupees to US$1). At a rate of 1 percent, premiums had therefore been set at 15 rupees per goat. Fund 2, was set up to help cover the remaining costs of livestock losses; it was fed by proceeds from ecotourism activities run by the trekking company. Fund 2 was kept in a separate account at the local bank.

The Claim Process

The insurance program was meant to be largely self-sustaining and locally managed. A village insurance committee was set up, and villagers nominated the members of the committee. Claimants had to formally file applications, which verified the killings and made recommendations. If the committee recommended that a claimant be compensated, the following steps were taken: The claimant received an individual accumulated premium amount from Fund 1 as compensation. If the claimant's accumulated premium amount in Fund 1 did not cover the full value of the loss incurred, money was taken from Fund 2 to cover the remaining costs.

For example, a farmer has thirty goats. In the first year, he pays 450 rupees into Fund 1 (30 x 15 rupees). The same year, a snow leopard kills two of his goats, the value of which are 3,000 rupees (2 x 1,500 rupees). The village insurance committee verifies that the goats were killed by a snow leopard and approves the claim for compensation. To pay the amount agreed on, the committee uses the total premium amount the farmer has paid into Fund 1

(450 rupees). The remaining amount, 2,550 rupees, comes out of Fund 2. A member of the committee is the signatory on checks written from Fund 1. For Fund 2, a committee member and a Baltistan Wildlife Conservation and Development Organization staff member are cosignatories. Premiums are paid annually in March. Entitlement to money from Fund 2 is restricted to members of the community who have paid premiums into Fund 1. In the above case, because the farmer exhausted his contribution (premiums) paid into Fund 1 by receiving compensation, he must therefore make sure that he pays the premium on the remaining twenty-eight goats to insure them for the next year. In such a case, the premium rate for this second payment may be higher than 15 rupees as a result of his having filed a claim and received compensation in the first year.

One major advantage of this two-tier financial design is that unless the entire village colludes and decides to cheat, it is very difficult to abuse the program. Indeed, the villagers treat Fund 2 as their collective pool of money generated from "their" common resource—the snow leopard. Villagers have a strong incentive to let Fund 2 grow beyond a viable threshold that will allow surplus funds to be paid out in case of need and to fund projects in the village. This should constitute a collective disincentive to unnecessarily drain Fund 2 and ensure that only genuine cases will be filed by claimants and approved by the committee.

Full Moon Night Trekking generated modest income in the first two years and the Skoyo pilot program was more or less sustainable. And then 9/11 happened. Pakistan developed political instability that persists to this day. Tourism dried up, and the project failed. The possibility of such a collapse was something that I had anticipated in August 2000: "The principle of client-funded insurance rather than external compensation and the link with ecotourism activities are a means of ensuring that the project will be free of dependence on donors. However, there is a risk associated with the independent nature of the project: it is dependent on the fluctuating market for tourism. Real or perceived security risks arising from economic and political instability could reduce the flow of tourists to Pakistan, thus making the insurance scheme more vulnerable to financial crises" (Hussain 2000, 231).

Facing an almost complete halt in the flow of resources to subsidize the insurance program from snow leopard–based tourism, we switched our approach to raising money directly from private donors and conservation foundations. But rather than using the spectacle of snow leopard decline, we emphasized the plight of both the farmers and the snow leopard. We argued that donors should help us create a nature-for-social-services swap with the

TABLE 5.1. Snow leopard predation rate in Hushe and Rondu Valleys, 2007–2015

	Animals lost	
	HUSHE VALLEY	RONDU (KRABATHANG) VALLEY
2007	9	8
2008	45	1
2009	46	3
2010	25	0
2011	33	4
2012	17	2
2013	15	1
2014	26	6
2015	11	1

farmers: we would build water supply programs and finance school construction as long as villagers gave us their commitment to snow leopard conservation.

By 2016 the project had expanded: there were nineteen funds spread over twenty-six villages across three valleys in Baltistan. Between 2007 and 2015, Baltistan Wildlife Conservation and Development Organization disbursed around US$28,000 to village insurance programs and built more than forty predator-proof corrals worth more than US$70,000. Since 2006 we have compensated close to three hundred farmers for livestock losses.

By 2018 twelve out of eighteen insurance programs were functioning well and were considered active with members paying into the premium fund. The six dormant insurance funds had some major issues, mainly related to the villagers' frustration with the process of getting compensated. While these dormant funds are not currently operating, the premiums paid to date are still in the communal bank accounts. Another major problem was that many community members who did file claims could not get the Insurance Committee to do its work: verify the kill. The members of the committees have often complained to me that they lack the time the verification of a claim requires, which involves visiting the kill site and collecting evidence. Often such sites are far away from the village and can require a whole day of walking. Insurance Committee members, who serve on a volunteer basis, rightly argued that they should be compensated for their labor. Our organization, while fully cognizant of this subsidy that the Insurance Committee was providing, could not finance the verification process because of a lack of funding. Some of our major donors did not want their monies used for the insurance programs; rather they preferred to have it spent on predator-proof corrals and teaching local herders how to use other anti-predatory measures.

The evidence from compensation payouts suggests that Hushe Valley, which hosts both a high density of snow leopards and its prey species, also has the highest predation rates among all villages in the program. But we have also seen a reduction in predation cases reported to Insurance Committees, suggesting that predation on domestic livestock has slowed down somewhat over the past five years. We are not sure at this stage if we can attribute it to the construction of predator-proof corrals, and we do not know what impact, if any, this has had on the snow leopard population.

THE SEMIOTIC OF SURVEYS AND EFFECTIVENESS OF TRANSACTIONAL APPROACH

Information about snow leopard populations are estimated through three main methods: images and DNA identification based on scat collected in the field; sign density such as paw prints observed in the field; and interviews with local people recorded. Generally, conservation biologists prefer the first method, such as camera-trap photos or snow leopard DNA extracted from snow leopard scat. Population estimates based on the second method, such as paw prints, or spray and scrape marks left in the wild are considered less reliable, and estimates based on the third method, that is information gathered from local people, are considered the least reliable by most conservation scientists.

Between 1998 and 2001 we carried out snow leopard population surveys in Baltistan to ascertain its current populations. We repeated population-estimate surveys in 2007 and 2013 to look at the impact of the insurance scheme on snow leopard populations in the project areas. The 1998–2001 surveys were conducted using snow leopard sign density, while the two subsequent surveys were based on DNA identification. Our experience showed fruitful results from combining survey methodologies, using both snow leopard sign density and interviews with local people.

Estimating population density based on sign surveys alone is questionable. For example, commenting on the usefulness of this method, Jackson and Hunter (1996) state that the surveys based on "sign-density do not offer precise sign frequency/density conversion factors because of the many confounding factors involved, including differential marking rates with respect to individuals, time of year and habitat, and variation in sign longevity due

Looking for snow leopards in Hushe. Photo by the author.

to local environmental factors and disturbances. However, with consistent data recording and relatively large samples, it is possible to monitor population trends over time" (1996, 36).

In addition to following a standard set of protocols for conducting a sign-density-based population survey, we relied quite heavily on interviews with local people. We carefully selected members of a village who had either been hunters or herders. It was important to find people who regularly visited the upland areas around their village because, contrary to the conventional belief, one can easily find people in Balti villages who have never been to the village pasture. The interview process was open-ended; respondents talked about myths, told stories, and recounted hunting events. It seemed that the problem of predation was quite acute in certain valleys, especially in the Hushe and Rondu. Even in valleys where predation was not an acute problem, hunters and herders confirmed snow leopard presence. We came to recognize the knowledge of a seasoned hunter as invaluable in ascertaining estimates of environmental parameters. Most hunters were able to give more realistic figures than ordinary villagers. Hunters also gave reliable counts of ibex and markhor in their areas.

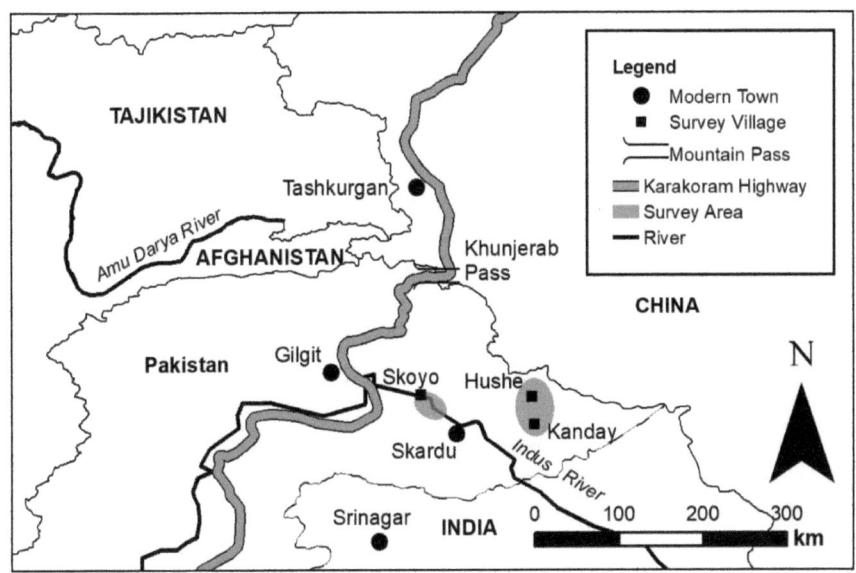

Snow leopard survey area, 1998–2014

While local reports helped us understand the absence or presence of snow leopards and the level of predation on domestic livestock in an area, I could not rely on the reports for snow leopard density or population estimates. Therefore, I augmented my sign surveys and interviews with local people by plugging in various ecological parameters to make some realistic assumptions. The most important ecological information required to estimate population density is the size and topography of the territory and the density of both wild and domesticated prey in it. The interviews in combination with sign density and ecological data allowed us to estimate population sizes. Based on these surveys, we made snow leopard population estimates for each valley, and from them, extrapolated numbers for the entire range in Pakistan. I published the results of this research estimating that there were between 300 and 420 snow leopards in Pakistan (Hussain 2003). Clearly, this estimate required a huge jumping of scale, but given my confidence that my micro data was correct, I was also confident of the macro level estimate.

Our results were substantially higher than those of George Schaller, who had estimated in 1975 that the total snow leopard population in Pakistan was not more than 200.[7] We began to wonder if the snow leopard population had flourished since Schaller's estimate, or if he had underestimated the population. But more important, we wondered if the snow leopard was really endangered in Pakistan, as it was officially classified.

We repeated the population surveys in the Hushe and Rondu Valleys in 2007 and 2013, this time using DNA collected from scat samples. In 2007 our team collected 102 samples of scat from six villages across three valleys in Baltistan. Half of each sample was brought to the United States for DNA identification of the species that produced the scat. The remaining samples were analyzed in a Pakistani laboratory to identify the species whose remains were found in the scat. We found that of the 102 samples, 57 belonged to snow leopards, and the rest were from wolves, foxes, and even a lynx.[8] Individual species identification showed that the 57 samples came from 19 different snow leopards. To our great surprise, the results of the analysis of the remains in the scat found that about 70 percent of the biomass in the snow leopards' diet came from domestic livestock, while the remaining 30 percent came from wild ungulates. We wondered, were the Balti farmers keeping the snow leopard at artificially high numbers by unwittingly feeding them their livestock? Was the snow leopard population responding to a decrease in wild ungulate population? A separate study published in 2017 in one of the valleys confirmed our findings, showing that about 66 percent of the biomass was domestic livestock (Bocci et al., 2017). I will try to address some of the questions that arose out of this research in the following sections.

Table 5.2 presents the baseline information on snow leopard populations that we have collected over the last eighteen years. (Note the differences in methodology and in the sizes of areas over which estimates of population are projected.) Our results show that despite recent misgivings about the relative density method based on sign surveys, its results corroborate genetics-based population assessments. In our 1998–2001 surveys, we estimated a population of between twenty-eight and forty snow leopards in our project area. In 2007 we conducted snow leopard population surveys using DNA extracted from scat samples. The DNA results confirmed estimates based on earlier methods and showed that at least nineteen snow leopards were present in the project area (Anwar et al. 2011).

The information in table 5.2 compares the population estimates across three different time periods, deploying two different survey methodologies in two locations in Baltistan, separated by a hundred miles of extremely rocky, mountainous terrain. The result shows the population trend and the possible methodological overlaps between the two survey techniques.

In the Hushe Valley the 2001 sign-density-based survey of an area of 1,500 square kilometers showed that there were between twenty and twenty-five snow leopards present. The 2007 and 2013 surveys of a 250-square-kilometer area around Hushe village, based on DNA analysis, showed eight snow leopards present in the valley in 2007 and seven in 2013. Looking at other

TABLE 5.2. Results of snow leopard population surveys in Hushe and Rondu Valleys, 1998–2014

					TOTAL SNOW LEOPARDS
			NO. OF SCATS		ESTIMATED/DETECTED
YEAR	METHODOLOGY	AREA	COLLECTED	TOTAL SCATS	

Hushe Valley

YEAR	METHODOLOGY	AREA	NO. OF SCATS COLLECTED	TOTAL SCATS	TOTAL SNOW LEOPARDS ESTIMATED/DETECTED
1998–2001	SLIMS	1,500 km²	NA	NA	20–25*
2007–2008	Genetics (DNA collected from scat)	250 km²	48	20	8
2013–2014	Genetics (DNA collected from scat)	250 km²	38	27	7

Rondu (Krabathang) Valley

YEAR	METHODOLOGY	AREA	NO. OF SCATS COLLECTED	TOTAL SCATS	TOTAL SNOW LEOPARDS ESTIMATED/DETECTED
1998–2001	SLIMS	500 km²	NA	NA	6–10
2007–2008	Genetics (DNA collected from scat)	350 km²	37	25	7
2013–2014	Genetics (DNA collected from scat)	350 km²	38	25	Results inconclusive

*This estimate is for both Hushe and Saltoro Valleys. See Hussain (2003, table p. 29).
NA: Scat-based genetic analyses were not done in 1998–2001.

ecological data, we can construct a picture of the carrying capacity of the valley. According to the recent surveys, there are close to eight hundred ibex in Hushe, while in Kanday Valley there are close to three hundred. These figures are available from the local district wildlife officer because the areas are under government-sponsored trophy-hunting programs, and the government officials survey the areas regularly to ascertain the population of trophy-sized animals. We have no information about the Soltoro Range and some of the other villages around Hushe, but the habitat in all of these locations is similar to Hushe, and it is likely to hold a good population of snow leopard and its natural prey.

Two factors appear to be important in determining snow leopard population density: habitat condition and availability of prey. It seems that more snow leopards can live in a relatively smaller space if that space is broken and craggy, thus providing physical niches rather than open and relatively flat terrain. Both Hushe and the surrounding Soltoro Range provide these conditions. We estimated that about sixteen hundred to two thousand ibex and about four times as many small livestock are present in the area. Counting 25 percent of the population of domestic livestock as potential prey, we can say that around four thousand ungulates are available, enough to sustain about twenty snow leopards.[9] If we assume that snow leopards supplement this food source with the availability of small-bodied prey, we get a full picture of the carrying capacity of the area.[10] Based on these figures, it is quite reasonable to say that perhaps an additional five more snow leopards can "fit" in this area, thus giving the area twenty-five snow leopards. This conclusion is not very different from the findings of the 2001 surveys based on sign density.[11]

The second set of data comes from the Rondu Valley, an area covering the villages of Krabathang, Skoyo, and Basingo on the southern bank of the Indus, and Bagicha and Saree north of the Indus. The 2001 sign-density-based survey of a five-hundred-square-kilometer area showed that there were between six and ten snow leopards present. In the 2007 survey, based on DNA identification from scat samples collected over an area of three hundred square kilometers, at least seven snow leopards were present. The figures for snow leopard natural prey density from the region are also reliable, because like Hushe, the entire southern bank of the Indus below Skardu Valley is under a trophy-hunting program. It is estimated that close to two hundred markhor and five hundred ibex are present, as well as about three thousand head of small livestock. Assuming 25 percent of livestock as additional prey is available to snow leopards, we get a figure of fifteen hundred head of ungulates, which puts the carrying capacity of the area at seven to eight snow leopards. If we include the availability of small-bodied prey, we can perhaps "add" another two to three snow leopards to this valley, bringing their numbers to ten. Here again, we see a very close match between the 2001 sign-density-based estimates and the 2007 and 2013 DNA-based estimates.

This also shows that between 2001 and 2014, the snow leopard population remained stable in the region. According to the 2001 survey, twenty to twenty-five snow leopards were estimated to be in Hushe Valley. This number was later confirmed in the 2007 and 2013–14 DNA-based estimates. In Skoyo, Krabathang, and Basingo, the figures are almost exactly the same. In the 2001 survey, we estimated that there were six to ten snow leopards in the area, confirmed again by the 2007 and 2013–14 DNA-based estimates that showed that there were at least eight snow leopards. Without having a control group to determine and isolate the effect of compensation programs, it is difficult to make a judgment on its success.

But other indirect indicators, such as eruption of conflict and protest, can be useful for determining the impact of compensation and insurance programs. For example, residents in the Hunza region have on several occasions trapped a snow leopard and then demanded compensation from the government. Such events are unheard of in our project valley despite predation. It may be due to the existence of compensation and insurance that people do not protest.

As mentioned in chapter 3, compensation programs will change people's attitude and make them more accepting of snow leopards. But I think it is futile to expect that people's attitudes will change for good. Rather, compensation and insurance make people indifferent to the snow leopard. But this change in attitude from lack of tolerance to indifference is not permanent; rather, it is temporary and ephemeral. Our compensation programs show that the sustainability of indifferent attitudes to snow leopards is tied to the sustainability of funding to mitigate farmers' losses to snow leopard predation.

CONCLUSION

The snow leopard population in our project area has been fairly stable over the last two decades. Can this stability be attributed to the successful implementation of the insurance program? It is difficult to say. One external evaluation of the project showed that people in the Hushe Valley were satisfied with the program and attributed the rising snow leopard population to the program's success. Does the transactional approach work? And if so, how do we assess its effectiveness? The approach is intended to bring about changes in local attitudes toward snow leopards, such that people stop killing the animals in retaliation. The only evidence that social sciences can offer to support the shift in actual behavior and actions of the Baltis is to look at the consequences of this shift. But it would be difficult to attribute the stability of snow leopard populations in project areas to a fundamental cultural shift in Balti society. Rather, what this indicates is that a delicate, momentary, and ephemeral balance between the interests of the local people and our conservation organization has been achieved in managing snow leopard–farmer conflict in Baltistan. A major criticism of transactional theory is that it pays insufficient attention to the structure of class and property relations in society, and it ignores the symbolic and cultural basis that might govern peoples' decisions in their social interactions. A transactional approach allows the reconciliation between the symbolic and the material domains of villagers' experiences of the snow leopard. The negative perceptions of the snow leopard among Balti villages are objectified, valued, and exchanged for material security and benefits.

The Baltis have learned how funds enter the community by working with outside NGOs over the last three decades, and they understand that snow leopard conservation is another source of funds. The whole region has become a desirable place for donors to invest their funds because the Baltis have become, like the people from Hunza, "deliverable communities"—communities that can deliver on development projects and secure continued funding. The interest of the Baltis in snow leopard conservation is not necessarily organic but is rather a derivative of modern conservation and its historic structure. It is the transactional approach that can forge a relationship between the Baltis and outside conservation institutions.

CHAPTER SIX

The Political Economy of the Snow Leopard

TWO cases involving snow leopards presented here show how they are implicated in international politics and how their conservation generates a struggle for resources and the need for alliances. Contrary to official discourse of cooperation and partnership, conservation efforts are pocked by divisions and rivalries in these cases. In the first, snow leopard conservation is entwined with the politics of global terrorism. In the summer of 2006, Leo, a Pakistani snow leopard, traveled to New York City as a goodwill ambassador and symbol of cooperation between Pakistan and the United States. The events that unfolded show that cooperation and partnership between the two countries remain as elusive as the snow leopard. In the second case, assessment of snow leopard status is tied to the politics of funding and resources. In 2013, when the Global Snow Leopard and Ecosystem Protection Program (GSLEP), spearheaded by the Kyrgyz republic with the backing of the World Bank, started, it was hoped that the initiative would unite snow leopard conservationists and institutions under a single umbrella. The events that unfolded show that the initiative created bitter relationships and deep fractures within the conservation community.

In both cases, cooperation was seriously undermined by struggles between different institutions and organizations over scientific facts, attribution of credit, and ultimately scarce financial resources for conservation. The consideration for conservation resources, institutional interests, and personal values often had implications for policy options and data interpretation.

In the first case, the Pakistani and US institutions involved ostensibly used the discourse of cooperation and friendship, while in reality disagreements over technical matters and misunderstanding over mutual financial obligations prevailed. The second shows that disagreement between various organizations over the official status of the snow leopard was due to specific articulations of scientific practice and political economy. As the anthropologist Michael Dove and his coauthor Mahmudul Huq Khan (1995) state in their study of the different perceptions of natural disaster in the Bangladeshi and international community, "The extent of disagreement suggests a reversal of normal empirical procedure: instead of data being used to settle arguments, the arguments became the means by which data (the reality of threat) were being settled" (446).

It became clear that in the end the status of the snow leopard rested not on data and facts but on how those data and facts were interpreted and applied.

CASE ONE: LEO AND TRANSNATIONAL RELATIONSHIPS

In the summer of 2005 a shepherd from the Naltar Valley in Gilgit informed the regional office of the World Wide Fund for Nature-Pakistan (WWF-Pakistan) that he was in possession of a male snow leopard cub. The exact events surrounding the capture of the cub are unclear. The "official" story is that the shepherd found the cub after it was abandoned by its mother. The more sinister story is that the shepherd killed the mother of the cub in order to capture it for sale. The team traveled to Naltar and brought the cub back to its office in Gilgit to examine it. It was found to be about seven weeks old at the time and in a healthy condition. The cub was named Leo by its attendant.

The WWF-Pakistan office notified the Gilgit-Baltistan Forest and Wildlife Department in Gilgit and the federal government in Islamabad. The Gilgit-Baltistan Forest and Wildlife Department then took custody of Leo and moved him to a security post near Khunjerab National Park farther north on the Karakoram Highway in northern Hunza. The department also deputized a wildlife guard to feed and look after Leo, who was kept in an empty room in its office at night. From time to time during the day Leo was tethered to a tree by the main Karakoram Highway. In August of 2006 when I saw Leo, he had been moved back to Gilgit and the office of the Directorate of Khunjerab National Park. Leo was then about fourteen months old, twenty-one inches (fifty-three centimeters) tall, and weighed about fifty-five pounds (twenty-five kilograms). The Gilgit-Baltistan Wildlife Department, the International Union for Conservation of Nature, and the World Wide Fund for Nature–Pakistan shared the maintenance expenses for Leo during this period.

In early 2006 the Wildlife Conservation Society (WCS), which runs the Bronx Zoo in New York City, requested the Ministry of Environment of the

Government of Pakistan through the US embassy in Islamabad to loan it Leo.[1] The society was interested in acquiring the snow leopard because it wanted to increase the genetic stock among its current snow leopard population of twelve animals by breeding it with new stock from the wild. In return for the leopard's potential insemination services, the society agreed to provide technical support to design a wildlife rehabilitation facility in Pakistan to enable the government to deal with the proper management of rescued wild animals. Under a Memorandum of Understanding signed between the Wildlife Conservation Society and the Pakistani government, the society agreed to support efforts to raise funds for the facility rather than providing funds directly from its own sources.[2] WCS also agreed to provide training for the Pakistani staff of the wildlife department who would manage the facility. The agreement, however, did not mention where training would take place or clarify who would pay for the trainees' travel and room and board if it were to be held out of Pakistan. The Memorandum of Understanding stated that Leo would remain the property of the government of Pakistan, under the Ministry of Environment, Office of the Inspector General of Forests. Leo flew to New York on August 9, 2006.

The event of Leo's transfer to the United States from Pakistan mobilized many debates and discourses that reflected the politics of the time and institutional interests of the various players. Debate over Leo's transfer to the United States became a source of introspection in Pakistani society about the nature of its relationship with the United States. In the United States, Leo's rescue from the wild lands of Pakistan became a heroic tale of American courage and care within the overall context of the war on terror in the post-9/11 political climate. At a time when the war on terror was not going well, the uplifting story of Leo offered an opportunity for the United States to frame its troubling relationship with Pakistan in a more positive light. The official narrative was international cooperation and collaboration, but it thinly concealed a discourse of distrust and claims and counterclaims of double-gaming and lack of long-term commitment to each other.

At the official diplomatic level, both the United States and Pakistan tried to gain as much political mileage as possible, while at the micro level, institutions within both countries tried to extract financial resources out of it. Leo became a source of struggles within Pakistan and between Pakistani state institutions and the Wildlife Conservation Society over the allocation of resources related to snow leopard management. This struggle revealed the deep structural relationship between Pakistan and the United States in which the former perceived that the latter has always called the shots. The nature of this alternative and non-official representation of the relationship between the two countries was expressed in informal discussions, stories, and jokes that pointed to the discourse of an asymmetrical power relationship and its awareness by the Pakistani officials.

To Send or Not to Send

From the beginning there were two opinions in Pakistan about whether or not the cub should be loaned to the Americans. The Gilgit-Baltistan government and International Union for Conservation of Nature–Pakistan supported the move, but the government of the neighboring province, Khyber-Pukhtunkhwa (KPK), which also has a sizeable snow leopard population, and WWF-Pakistan were against the transfer. The latter argued that the snow leopard should be handed over to the Pakistani government and urged Wildlife Conservation Society, WWF-US, the and Pakistani Ministry of Environment to build a facility in Gilgit-Baltistan. WWF-Pakistan wrote a letter to the inspector general of forests at the ministry to oppose the transfer and stated that it, along with the Gilgit-Baltistan government, had borne the cost of care and management of the cub. The KPK government argued that it had the appropriate facility and was planning to start a national captive breeding program for snow leopards. In reality the facility was extremely rudimentary, and the KPK government was hoping that with the transfer of a cub to its charge, the resources and training promised by WCS would come its way. IUCN-Pakistan and the Gilgit-Baltistan government lobbied with the Pakistani government to have the cub sent away.

WWF-Pakistan and the KPK government claimed that sending the snow leopard to the United States would give the outside world the impression that Pakistan was unable to manage even a single snow leopard, let alone its entire wildlife population. They were concerned that it would imply that the Pakistani government was not capable of controlling and looking after its people, that is, it was incapable of good governance. They stressed that Pakistan should try to project a positive image of itself as a responsible and mature nation, and that the transfer of the cub outside the country would undermine such an image. While the anti-transfer group saw failure to retain the snow leopard as symbolizing the failure of governance in Pakistan, the pro-transfer group saw the journey of the snow leopard as an opportunity to rehabilitate Pakistan's international image from that of a failed state.

The pro-transfer argument by IUCN-Pakistan and the Gilgit-Baltistan government struck a chord with the federal government. They contended that sending the snow leopard to the United States would overlay the image of Pakistan as place for breeding and exporting terrorists with one of a nation of compassionate people who breed and export a cuddly, charismatic, and endangered animal. Soon imaginations started to run wild among the members of the pro-transfer group, who professed that Pakistan could soon be identified with snow leopards just as China was with giant pandas. Pakistan's minister for the environment argued at a meeting held at the ministry that by creating a link between the snow leopard and Pakistan in the eyes of the international community, Pakistan could foster a new image as a country of environment-friendly and progressive people. According to this argument, nature conservation is not only about biodiversity and species but also about the cultivation and propagation of civility and its display among people.

It was also reported around this time that the minister for the environment was interested in developing a snow leopard conservation strategy for Pakistan.[3] The pro-transfer group also stated it was not practical to release the cub in the wild because it had been completely dependent on humans. Whereas zoos in Pakistan do not have the scientific expertise and resources to undertake rehabilitation programs, Leo would enjoy state-of-art facilities at the Bronx Zoo.

When it was officially decided that Leo would be transferred to the Bronx Zoo, the staff from the Gilgit-Baltistan Forest and Wildlife Department began to demand that since it was their snow leopard, one of them should go to the United States to hand the cub over to its new caretakers at the Bronx Zoo. Despite intense politicking and amid great expectations, the WCS turned down the offer. Zoo officials said that its staff would receive the leopard in Pakistan and take responsibility for it from there. In August 2006 WCS staff arrived in Gilgit to receive the cub at a local ceremony. The WCS kept the cub in an air-conditioned room in the best hotel in Gilgit (considerably posher than its previous home in the forestry department office). From here it was transported to Islamabad.

There, a national ceremony was held that was attended by the US ambassador and more than three hundred people, mostly invited by IUCN-Pakistan. It was a glitzy event, attended by the rich and powerful of Islamabad, including the diplomatic community, and extensively reported in the local TV news and print media. The story of Leo was simplified as vital action being taken to save a species under imminent threat of extinction; the event encapsulated this simple narrative and created a spectacle of conservation. The officials from WWF-Pakistan, Gilgit-Baltistan, and the KPK governments told me that they felt marginalized at the event. Even though the Gilgit-Baltistan government had supported the transfer, they were somewhat irritated by the fact that an international NGO, IUCN-Pakistan, seemed to take over responsibility for the process, sidelining not simply the KPK government but the Pakistani government in general. At this ceremony US ambassador Ryan Crocker made a speech that stressed the strong partnership between the United States and Pakistan. He said: "This truly is a win-win for all involved. The U.S. Government is pleased to have played a role supporting Pakistan's efforts to protect this endangered species, the Government of Pakistan will receive training and technical assistance, the Bronx Zoo will have the opportunity to study this rare animal, and the snow leopard gets to go on an expenses paid journey to the United States, where his only responsibilities will be eating, growing, and breeding snow leopard cubs. Maybe the snow leopard is the biggest winner of all."[4]

The ambassador also said the "Wildlife Conservation Society will also assist Pakistan establish a snow leopard care facility to tend to future snow leopard foundlings—in Pakistan."[5] He, however, did not clarify what "assist" meant. Many in Pakistan misunderstood it and thought the WCS would actually pay for the establishment of a rehabilitation center in Pakistan and the training of its staff abroad.

Crocker also joked that the cub was not traveling on an immigration visa—to make the point that it would eventually return to Pakistan.[6] By paying the expenses of the trip, the Americans communicated that the snow leopard was welcomed. This realization, as made explicit in Crocker's remarks, struck some Pakistanis as both unjust and ironic. International travel for many Pakistanis remained an unrealized dream, especially travel to the United States and to western European countries. For those privileged to travel, the representation of Pakistan in the world during the first decade of the twenty-first century as a hub for terrorist activities had made international travel for many Pakistanis not only difficult but also often humiliating. International visa regimes that scrutinized Pakistani nationals more than others in the wake of 9/11 had made smooth and unharassed travel a dream for many. A close friend of mine who works in a local NGO joked about the passport for Leo. "Which passport will he carry? It better not be a green one; you know what they will do to him." Given the times, US-government-sponsored travel for Leo made many government officials reflect on the nature of this travel. They wondered why the international community, especially the United States, cared more about the Pakistani snow leopards than about Pakistani people. Their engagement with this issue was also a commentary on western society at large and its perceived ethos of protecting wildlife over people.

In September 2006, after a month of quarantine, Leo was officially put on display. He was placed in the Himalayan Highland section of the Bronx Zoo during a ceremony attended by Sehba Musharraf, wife of Pakistani president Pervaiz Musharraf. This was a big show like the one in Islamabad. A letter from First Lady Laura Bush was read by a State Department official. In it, Bush described Leo as an ambassador of friendship between the two countries. The letter included platitudes about collective responsibility for saving the planet and putting Pakistan and the United States in a somewhat equal partnership regarding a seemingly politically neutral issue.[7] It has been reported that at the inauguration ceremony, like the goal of Pakistani-US friendship, Leo remained elusive, obdurately refusing to show himself to the public.

Reporting on Leo

Initially, in August 2006, the US embassy website in Islamabad stated, "The Wildlife Conservation Society (WCS), whose headquarters is at the Bronx Zoo, will supply training and technical assistance to the Pakistani animal care professionals who will be Leo's caretakers upon his eventual return from the United States." It remained unstated who would provide the funds. The issue of funding for the rehabilitation center was addressed by Sehba Musharraf in a speech she made at Leo's Bronx Zoo ceremony; she clarified that Pakistan would be responsible for this, with the support of the UN and in cooperation with the Bronx Zoo.[8] No date was given for Leo's return to Pakistan, but it was expected to be around five years. NBC news reported that "Patrick Thomas, curator of mammals at Bronx Zoo, said it would probably take three or four years before Leo and a female leopard would produce offspring. He said the zoo could send a female leopard back with Leo when he returns to Pakistan."[9]

International wildlife law required that Leo be officially categorized as a loan to allow him to be imported into the United States: "Lawfully taken and held endangered and threatened species may be shipped interstate as a bona fide gift or loan if there is no barter, credit, other form of compensation, or intent to profit or gain. A standard breeding loan, where no money or other consideration changes hands but some offspring are returned to the lender of a breeding animal, is not considered a commercial activity and, thus, is not prohibited by the Endangered Species Act and does not require a permit. Documentation of such an activity should accompany shipment."[10]

By 2007, it seemed that Leo was settling into his new home. A senior US official described Leo as "one of the most charismatic diplomats ever . . . Leo is thriving there and the WCS continues to work in Pakistan to develop the skills and the infrastructure needed to protect endangered species, like the snow leopard, in the wild."[11] In 2008 a US-based website reminded its readers that, "While the Bronx Zoo has bred more than 70 snow leopards in captivity, Leo will eventually return to Pakistan once an appropriate facility can be built."[12]

After a flurry of reports during Leo's first year at the Bronx Zoo, Leo remained out of the news for the next four years. During this period, I wrote periodic emails to the staff of WCS asking them when Leo would return to Pakistan and whether WCS had helped Pakistan in building a rehabilitation facility or trained Pakistani wildlife professionals for the eventual return of Leo. I did not get any replies.

Then, in 2011, an article appeared in Pakistan's daily *Dawn* in which it was claimed that Leo would likely not return to Pakistan. The newspaper reported,

> Officials in the Federal Ministry of Environment said that under the MoU the Society was responsible for construction of the conservation facility in Gilgit-Baltistan and training of the relevant staff in the US before bringing back Leo to its habitat.
>
> "Unfortunately, the WCS is yet to fulfill the terms and conditions mentioned in the MoU," an official said and added that Leo was the government's property and it could be brought back any time.
>
> Mary Dixon, representative of the WCS at Bronx Zoo, responded to an email, saying that "Leo has grown to be healthy and an amazing cat to care for. At this time, Leo has not yet bred, but he has matched up well with a female snow leopard here at the zoo and we hope that Leo and his mate will produce cubs in the near future. We have no further news except that Leo is doing great."

Regarding WCS's failure to fulfill its promise of building a rehabilitation facility and train the staff, the *Dawn* article continued,

> Information gathered by "Dawn" revealed that the WCS was responsible for raising funds for establishing the facility and providing training to conservators. However, the officials in the ministry demanded of the society to also pay airfare of the technicians to be sent abroad for training.
>
> A source familiar with the process told this correspondent that the real hindrance to bringing back Leo was at the Ministry of Environment, where efforts were underway to send some blue-eyed persons [sic] to collect the animal from the US.

"Ideally, a person from the Gilgit-Baltistan should go and bring the animal back home, but some elements also want to exploit this opportunity for a pleasure trip to the US," said the source.[13]

This claim of the *Dawn* reporter was incorrect. The actual terms and conditions as stipulated in the Memorandum of Understanding signed in 2006 between the Wildlife Conservation Society and the government of Pakistan (represented by the Ministry of Environment's office of the Inspector General of Forests) did not state that WCS was financially responsible for building a rehabilitation facility. The obligations of the WCS were covered under articles 2e, 2f, and 2g of the Memorandum of Understanding. These articles state:

2e: provide technical support to design and construct a wild founding care facility in Northern Areas, Pakistan with particular focus on care and management of founding snow leopards.
2f: support efforts to raise funds for the above facility and
2g: provide training to Pakistani specialists in the care and management of captive snow leopards.

Very little concrete information appeared in the agreement in terms of an actual commitment of funds from WCS. It is not clear who negotiated the terms of the agreement from the Pakistani side. To make the matter even more confusing, the Memorandum of Understanding was signed by the Pakistani secretary of Food, Agriculture and Forests of Northern Areas, "on behalf of the government."

Despite the Memorandum of Understanding and its clear stipulations that WCS was not financially obliged to help any Pakistan wildlife conservation agency, the wildlife and forest staff from both Gilgit-Baltistan and Khyber-Pukhtunkhwa expected WCS to finance the rehabilitation facility and pay for the training of Pakistani staff, preferably in the United States. A WCS official finally replied to my emails and clarified the society's position. He explained that WCS had agreed to help the Pakistani government by training its staff in the necessary skills to run a rehabilitation center and that it had created a series of training modules. WCS had offered to host a delegation from Pakistan, but despite sending invitations three times over the past few years, no delegation had ever been sent. The WCS official said the modules were still available and the society would be prepared to train the group whenever the Pakistani government sent them over. However, he also said that WCS never agreed to fund the construction of a rehab center but only to advise on its design and how to raise funds. He also raised some doubts about the likely conservation benefits of the center (Peter Zahler, email to author, August 12, 2014).

Clearly, there is a great difference between providing advice on how to obtain funding and actually providing funding. While the email sent to me from WCS did not say why Pakistani officials failed to show up three times, it is likely due to the fact that WCS expected to provide the training in the United States, but no funding was available to pay for the airfare and room and board of the participants, a matter raised in the 2011 *Dawn* article. What is interesting is that on the copy of the Memorandum of Understanding that I received from the office of WWF-Pakistan there are anonymous notations that raise these same questions. For example, under section 2g where it states that WCS will provide training for Pakistani specialists, a comment asks, "in Pakistan?"

What the WCS email did not mention was the agreement to return Leo. To date, the WCS remains tight-lipped about this issue. The Memorandum of Understanding states under 2b that "WCS will return the snow leopard to Pakistan at such a time that the Government requests the return or when it is mutually agreed that it is in the best interest for care and management of the cub."

But what was most interesting is that in the same email, the WCS official also posed similar questions that I had asked about the potential pitfalls of a rehab center, especially in terms of the kind of perverse incentives it might create to capture wild snow leopards. He raised issues about the uncertainty of success of such ventures and the high cost of running such facilities. Clearly, these considerations were not made explicit to the Pakistani government, or to the staff of the provincial wildlife department at the time WCS signed the Memorandum of Understanding in 2006. The question that comes to mind is whether WCS knew, when it was obtaining Leo in 2006 and signing a Memorandum of Understanding, that constructing a rehab center would be a bad idea for snow leopards? Did WCS's judgment about a rehab center for Pakistan change over the course of five years, so they were opposing it now? It seems that in 2006, amid the euphoria of getting a wild snow leopard, the WCS did not want to create any hurdles in the smooth transfer of Leo to the Bronx Zoo by raising concerns about the Gilgit-Baltistan government's demand for a rehab center. This also, perhaps, unwittingly built up the expectations of the Gilgit-Baltistan staff that the agreement could become a good source of revenues and a justification for personal trips in the future.

A rehab center, or an enclosure, for captured snow leopards was finally built in 2015 in Naltar, near Gilgit, with a grant from the US embassy in Islamabad. It was used to house a wild-caught snow leopard named Lolly. In just over a year, it became quite clear that the rehab center was built without much technical assistance or guidance. In January 2016, Lolly had to be rescued because it snowed so heavily and the enclosure was filled such that the cat was almost immobilized.

The saga of Leo shows that the parties signing the Memorandum of Understanding had quite different motives and interests. First, the Khyber-Pukhtunkhwa and Gilgit-Baltistan governments saw the snow leopard as an opportunity to secure resources mainly for training trips abroad. The struggle for resources reflects the lack of funding for wildlife departments in Pakistan. In this resource-deficient environment, Leo represented the goose that could lay golden eggs to benefit the wildlife department in the provinces. Some officials of these departments saw the loan of Leo as just the beginning. One staff member from the Gilgit-Baltistan Wildlife Department asked my opinion about the feasibility of the provincial wildlife department starting a small enterprise of supplying wild snow leopards to zoos across the world for breeding purposes in return for funds.

Leo was also implicated in the wider politics of representation in which care for nature became a symbol of cultural maturity. The way the federal government used the snow leopard articulated with views of rich Western countries about wildlife and nature. The federal government of Pakistan saw the snow leopard and its move to the United States from yet another perspective: an opportunity for major international PR and a restoration of Pakistan's public image—as the exporter of snow leopards, not terrorists.

From the perspective of the Pakistani government, its unflattering image in the West, especially in the United States, as a hotbed of Islamic fundamentalisms and international terrorism was simply a problem of misrepresentation. Pakistani officials imagined this problem could be solved by providing an alternative, positive image, using Leo as an ambassador of the Pakistani people's goodwill and friendship toward the American people.

But in practice that friendship remains as elusive as the cat that was used to forge it. The nature of the snow leopard is an apt analogy for the nature of cooperation between the two countries. And cooperation was not just elusive at the state-to-state level but also between smaller institutions. As discussed above, the miscommunication and lack of shared information between WCS and the various segments of the Pakistani bureaucracy was not the stuff that cooperation is made of.[14]

Another interesting event in Leo's story was the US publication of a children's book about Leo's "rescue." The 2010 book tells the story of Americans saving wildlife from a dangerous people in a dangerous place. A passage states, "When the Wildlife Conservation Society learned of Leo's plight, they knew they had to do something. There was a special place that could save Leo: the world-famous Bronx Zoo in New York. . . . After a rescue that involved treacherous, winding treks in the Himalayas, an extraordinary partnership between Pakistan and United States, and the help of dozens of dedicated people, Leo is making the Bronx Zoo his new home" (Hatkoff, Hatkoff, and Hatkoff 2010).

The account of Leo's dramatic "rescue" and his journey to safety is heavily adjusted to suit an American audience. The tale is a mix of scientific discovery and adventure that would not be out of place in a Disney movie. In the book, the shepherd who actually rescued Leo is not mentioned; rather it is the wildlife biologists of the WCS who drive on dangerous roads and trek along wild trails to rescue the rare snow leopard and carry him to the safety of the Bronx Zoo.

The Discourse of Powerlessness

The divide between how Pakistanis and Americans see the story of Leo relates to perceptions of structural power. Many Pakistanis with whom I spoke openly or subtly expressed their amusement at the fact that Leo was in demand because of his potential sexual services, the scientific raison d'etre, so to speak. This scientific discourse of "re-wilding" captive populations through constant interjection of new individuals was transformed into a sexual discourse and, eventually, into a power discourse. For many Pakistanis this aspect of the whole event was particularly exciting. They at once associated Leo with themselves: "our male leopard, their female leopard" (humara cheetah, unkee cheetiyan). This clear distinction between us and them was useful because it provided the frame for discussing issues that remained frustratingly difficult to express for many Pakistanis. The expression of masculinity in certain contexts substitutes for the lack of structural power of those who display it (Doane 2007). Many men who do manual labor associated with the extraction of natural resources in raw and difficult conditions see their circumstances and work as expressions of their masculinity and forms of male power. They contrast their prowess with the lack of masculinity of professionals in the conservation sector, who often hold structural power over these workers. In the same vein, some officials in Pakistan expressed Leo's potential services to me in overtly political terms, saying, for instance, how nice is it to have a Pakistani leopard screw American leopards, as if these acts serve as a kind of payback for all the harm America has done to Pakistan.

THE SNOW LEOPARD AND THE GOAT IN HISTORICAL PERSPECTIVE CASE TWO: THE POLITICAL ECONOMY OF SNOW LEOPARD CONSERVATION

In late October 2013, representatives of the snow leopard conservation community met in Bishkek, Kyrgyz Republic, at the Global Snow Leopard Forum (GSLF). The purpose of the meeting was to endorse a new global program to save the snow leopard and the mountain ecosystems of central and south Asia.

Hailed as a "New International Effort to Save the Snow Leopard and Conserve High-Mountain Ecosystem," the Global Snow Leopard and Ecosystem Protection Program (GSLEP) was launched with the assistance of the World Bank and the efforts of the Snow Leopard Trust as well as other partner organizations, such as the World Wildlife Fund, the Wildlife Conservation Society, and the Snow Leopard Conservancy. Linking the snow leopard and its ecosystem, the program articulates snow leopard conservation with climate change. Its website states that snow leopard ecosystems provide ecological services to a great number of people, and these ecosystems need protection because they are under threat from global climate change.

According to the Snow Leopard Network's website, the program is a "major outcome of the Global Snow Leopard Forum. It is a conservation strategy for the next 7 years approved by range country governments and consists of the 12 individual National Snow Leopard and Ecosystems Priorities." The Global Snow Leopard and Ecosystem Protection Program constructs the twelve home range countries as one single conservation management unit, thus creating new geographies of conservation. It creates opportunities for transboundary cooperation and new sources of funding. The themes of international and transboundary cooperation are prevalent in the GSLEP document that was produced by its secretariat in Bishkek.[15]

Some snow leopard conservation institutions saw the initiative as an opportunity to tap into much-needed funding for their work. But it was also clear from the very beginning that other organizations were not satisfied with the new initiative. They complained about lack of transparency in the proceedings and decision-making process that led to the establishment of the program and its subsequent activities.

GSLEP was conceived along the same lines as another World Bank–funded, international, transboundary conservation initiative targeted at saving global tiger populations. The Global Tiger Initiative had been launched in 2008 by World Bank president Robert Zorllick. Two years later, in November 2010, Prime Minister Vladimir Putin hosted a summit in Russia. Governments of thirteen tiger-range nations came together to form collective, international efforts to save the tiger. These countries committed resources and took measures to ensure that the tigers survive in the wild. The Global Tiger Initiative argued that current tiger conservation efforts were disjointed and confined to small protected areas under threat from encroachment. It recommended that tiger population conservation should be focused at a landscape level, on a much larger scale, through a series of strategies that would entail technical solutions, such as connecting habitats with "source" populations. The initiative identified forty-two source sites, places that harbored at least twenty-five breeding females around which landscape-level conservation management could be implemented. Landscape-level management planning, it was argued, was better suited than the strict protected-areas approach to the life cycle and ecological needs of large predators such as tigers (Snow Leopard Working Secretariat 2013, 2).

In order to understand why GSLEP was contentious, it is necessary to understand the conservation landscape of snow leopard professionals and institutions. There are three major NGOs in the snow leopard conservation world. The oldest of them is the Snow Leopard Trust, which also runs the Snow Leopard Network. This network represents almost all the snow leopard conservationists around the world. There is also Snow Leopard Conservancy, which is headed by Rodney Jackson and approaches conservation through the lens of both social and natural sciences.[16] Then there is Panthera, whose founder made his fortune in the mining industry and is therefore well-funded. Panthera is like the New York Yankees: because it is so well endowed it signs on the best scientists in the world. Panthera and the Wildlife Conservation Society work closely together, with many staff having worked for both organizations.

Opposition to GSLEP came from many national and international conservation institutions that were concerned it would create another cumbersome layer of bureaucracy that would slow down conservation efforts. These groups believed that the World Bank and state bureaucracies would seize control over major decisions regarding the direction of future research and action. They feared that rather than spending money on conservation action on the ground, money would be spent on making plans, conducting meetings and seminars, and supporting staff travel and visits. GSLEP thus appeared to some organization as being hijacked by handful of other organizations who would control potential funding.

Although hailed as a successful example of international political cooperation, GSLEP's success was undermined by a controversy over the population estimates and ultimately population status of the snow leopard according to the International Union for Conservation of Nature's Red List of Threatened Species.

IUCN Red Listing

The launch of GSLEP overlapped with another important process in snow leopard conservation, namely the assessment of the population for the IUCN Red List of Threatened Species. The assessment process brought under scrutiny one of the biggest questions that has plagued the snow leopard conservation community for years, namely, how many snow leopards remain in the world. In 2002 Rodney Jackson wrote, "There is now general agreement that population estimates of around 2,000 made in the early 1970s, when the endangered species regulations were enacted, are too low. Fox (1989) placed the total snow leopard range at 1.23 million km², with a world population of 3,350–4,050 animals. These figures were updated between 4,510 and 7,350 snow leopards within a total potential habitat area of 1,835,000 km² (Fox 1994)" (80–81).

By contrast with these earlier estimates of snow leopard habitat area, Jackson predicted the potential habitat to be three million square kilometers. He argued in his 2002 paper that if habitat is used as an index of density, there could be as many as six thousand to eight thousand snow leopards in the wild. He wrote,

> Drawing on the 1:1,000,000 World Digital Charts, and using GIS, Hunter and Jackson (1997) estimated potential habitat for snow leopard at about three million km², with some six percent falling within the existing or proposed network of *PAs*. . . . At a uniform density of one cat per 300 km² this would translate into a total population of about 10,000 individuals. Obviously, not all of this area is occupied by the species because of excessive hunting pressure, lack of sufficient prey, disturbance by livestock and attendant humans, presence of marginal habitat or other factors. However, on the basis of available habitat, there could easily be as many as 6,000 to 8,000 snow leopards, especially given densities in known "hotspots" of the order of 5–10 individuals per 100 km². Conversely, areas classified as offering good habitat may no longer support good numbers of snow leopard. This exemplifies the difficulty of making population estimates

without ground-truthing maps for their accuracy along with also verifying population extrapolations with data accruing from credible field status surveys. (81)

This long quote aptly sums up the challenges and the current state of knowledge about snow leopard populations.

The Numbers Game

Each snow leopard conservation organization uses a different set of numbers to count snow leopards living in the wild, depending upon its interpretation of the data from the field and perhaps its institutional philosophy. A brief look at the websites of major snow leopard conservation institutions shows that Snow Leopard Trust, the organization that led the campaign against delisting, gives the lowest figures. According to its website, "scientists estimate that there may only be between 3,920 and 6,390 snow leopards left in the wild."[17] The above figures are particularly important because they are lower than the IUCN's 2008 estimates, which were done for the Red List assessment and reflect a slight downward trend. The 2008 IUCN assessment (Jackson et al. 2008) mainly quotes figures from the Snow Leopard Survival Strategy (SLSS) 2003. The assessment states, "The Snow Leopard Survival Strategy (McCarthy et al., 2003, Table II) compiled national snow leopard population estimates, updating the work of Fox (1994). Many of the estimates are acknowledged to be rough and out of date, but the total estimated population is 4,080–6,590."[18]

Panthera's website gives a more optimistic number, stating, "Today, scientists believe that between 4,500 and 10,000 adult snow leopards remain in the wild; their exact number is relatively unknown given that they are extremely elusive and challenging to survey. The species is very rarely seen even by local people. However, new research, including camera trapping, is beginning to indicate there may be more snow leopards than previously thought."[19]

The World Wildlife Fund website basically gives the same numbers as reported in the 2008 Red List assessment report. It also states the following about the population trend: "Snow leopards are found in 12 countries—including China, Bhutan, Nepal, India, Pakistan, Afghanistan, Russia, and Mongolia—but their population is dropping."[20] So its overall conclusion is actually the opposite of Panthera's.

The Wildlife Conservation Society website gives almost the same figures as Panthera, which is not surprising, as scientists from both institutions published a joint paper in 2016 in which they argue that the snow leopard

TABLE 6.1. Snow leopard population estimates by major conservation organizations, 2017

	SUPPORTS DOWNLISTING	TOTAL ESTIMATED HABITAT, 2017	TOTAL ESTIMATED POPULATION, 2017	FUND-RAISING APPEAL, 2017
Snow Leopard Trust	No	2 million km²	3,920–6,390	"Save the Snow Leopard. Every day at least one snow leopard is killed. You can help stop this. Donate here."
Wildlife Conservation Society	Yes	3 million km²	4,000–10,000	"When you give to WCS you're helping ensure a future for the earth's most magnificent creatures and the habitats critical to their survival. Make your tax-deductible gift today!"
World Wildlife Fund	Not given	Not given	4,080–6,590	"Make a symbolic snow leopard adoption to help save some of the world's most endangered animals from extinction and support WWF's conservation efforts."
Panthera	Yes	2 million km²	4,500–10,000	"Donate for Wild Cats. Your gift today will help Panthera protect wild cats, the vast landscapes they roam, and the endless variety of life within them. These wild places are crucial to our planet's health and our own."
Snow Leopard Conservancy	Yes	1.2–1.6 million km²	4,500–7,500	There is no appeal message other than "Your Gifts at Work page highlights some of the projects your donations have supported over the past year!"

population was more than they thought. However, the society's website also emphasizes continued threats to the snow leopard: "Although the snow leopard recently had its status changed by IUCN from Endangered to Vulnerable, snow leopard populations may still be dwindling across parts of their range. Poaching, both for its skin and for traditional medicine, is a growing threat. So is the loss of its natural prey species (mostly large wild mountain goats and sheep), damage to its fragile, high-elevation habitat, and a lack of awareness amongst local communities and governments of the snow leopard's status and threats."[21]

The Global Snow Leopard and Ecosystem Protection Program website acknowledges the uncertainty behind these numbers. It gives the same figure reported by Jackson et al. in their 2008 assessment report and states, "There is, however, a great deal of uncertainty about the snow leopard's current distribution, as there is about the size of the total snow leopard population, which is roughly estimated at between 4,000 and 6,500 individuals."[22]

Downlisting the Snow Leopards

The critical number for Endangered status as defined by the Red List is that species must have "less than 2,500 mature animals *capable of breeding* and a decline of 20% over 16 years OR over the past two generations, whichever is greater." The IUCN carries out assessments of species on the Red List every five to ten years. The previous assessment for snow leopards was carried out in 2008 when its status remained unchanged as Endangered. The most recent assessment started in spring 2015 and concluded in the fall of 2017. A review team of four scientists—Rodney Jackson from Snow Leopard Conservancy, Tom McCarthy from Panthera, David Mallon from the London Zoological Society, and Charudutt Mishra from Snow Leopard Trust—assessed the current status of the snow leopard. Three of the four scientists reached the conclusion, after looking the data, that the snow leopard was not Endangered. Only Charudutt Mishra disagreed.

It is important to understand that IUCN revised its criteria for an Endangered status in 2015 before the assessment began. The main change is that the number that matters is not mature individuals but rather breeding individuals of a species. According to IUCN, the magic number here for snow leopards is 2,500 breeding (not mature) individuals; the number of breeding individuals is known as the "effective population" of a species. The effective population size is the ideal number of individuals of a species that are needed to ensure that a certain quantity and proportion of genetic variety is maintained, which is reflective of the total population of that species. In simple terms, it means how effectively a species is able to find a mate and spread its genome in the environment. Different species have adapted differently to this evolutionary instinct. Some males of a species randomly release their sperm in the environment hoping that they are able to find a mate; others do conscious selection. Despite their sparse population, low density, and vast habitat, snow leopards are very good at finding mates and spreading their genomes. The main reason is their marking behavior. Snow leopards are incessant markers. It is as if they trying to find someone to talk to in this empty and desolate landscape. The marking behavior of the snow leopards is an expression of its intentions to defend a territory but also to find mates. Even those young males without a territory, who are considered "floaters," are pretty efficient at dispersing their genes. This means that in the case of snow leopards, the population of breeding individuals is almost the same as its population of individuals overall, given that snow leopards start breeding at the age of two. Charudutt Mishra's main concern with the status of the snow leopard relates to disagreements about the mating age of snow leopards. He argues that while it may be biologically possible for snow leopards to breed in captivity at the age of two, even there it is very rare; and it is usually not until the age of three of four when they start mating in the wild. This disagreement has implications for the population size that could be considered breeding age and eventually the population size that could be considered endangered.

Under IUCN's new criteria, the number of snow leopards counted in population estimates has gone up (see below for detail of how the new criteria changed the way the population number was calculated). The current lowest estimate for snow leopard population is 4,080. If the 2008 IUCN criteria were used to calculate the effective population from this, there would only be about 2,000 (50 percent discount rate), which is less than 2,500 hence the Endangered status. However, using the 2015 criteria, the effective population is 3,200 (discount of 20 percent), which is more than 2,500 individuals, hence the snow leopard's status is no longer Endangered. One of the members of the IUCN assessment team with extensive knowledge of the Red List criteria wrote me about the explanation and rationale behind delisting: "Recent survey information indicated that snow leopard densities in several areas are higher than previously believed, implying that the overall population size is also likely to be larger than the minimum estimates."[23]

The three scientists from Panthera, Snow Leopard Conservancy, and London Zoological Society who concluded that the snow leopard did not merit an Endangered status defended their decision by referencing significant efforts made in assessing snow leopard populations in the last decade. The scientist from the Snow Leopard Trust disagreed, arguing that in addition to an unrealistic assumption of a mating age of two, the area from which the survey data was drawn was too small to make a global projection.

In an effort to promote their respective positions, Snow Leopard Trust and Panthera took to the print media to make their point. On November 13, 2015, SLT executive director Brad Rutherford cowrote an opinion piece for CNN in which he reiterated the standard conservation narrative and causes of declining snow leopard populations. He wrote, "As territories begin to overlap, snow leopards prey more and more on livestock, often a family's main source of income. The Snow Leopard Trust's ongoing studies in large parts of the Himalayan and Central Asian Mountains show intensifying killing of livestock by snow leopards as human pressures increase retaliatory killings of snow leopards to protect one's livelihood." The op-ed then arrives at the punchline by stating, "Adding to this are killings of snow leopards for the illegal wildlife trade, further chipping away at their overall population. As of today, there may be as few as 4,000 snow leopards remaining, and perhaps fewer than 2,500 breeding adults. And this number is falling."[24] The direct reference to "less than 2,500 breeding adults" is significant here because it is the threshold number that is used in the criteria for listing a species as Endangered. The use of this number was a direct intervention in the ongoing assessment process of snow leopard population estimates underway at IUCN at the time.

A couple months later, on January 16, 2016, the director of the Snow Leopard Program at Panthera, Tom McCarthy, published a rejoinder of a sort on the CNN website. The first noticeable difference between this and Rutherford's op-ed was the figure of global snow leopard populations. Whereas Rutherford has said that perhaps less than 4,000 snow leopards survive in the wild, McCarthy wrote, "Only 4,500 to 10,000 of the elusive cats roam roughly 800,000 square miles of precipitous terrain from southern Siberia in the north to India in the south, and east to west from Uzbekistan to Yunnan, China." McCarthy's op-ed ends on a hopeful but cautious note. He asks,

> Is the snow leopard now safe?
> Closer, but loss of native prey, poaching for hides and bones (valued in traditional Asian medicine), and the potentially serious impacts of climate change on their fragile high-elevation habitat still mean an uncertain future for snow leopards.
> We must fight on."[25]

Amid the contestation over whether the snow leopard is still endangered came the report from TRAFFIC, an organization that traces the global illegal trade in wildlife products. TRAFFIC's report claimed that one snow leopard a day is killed due to retaliation by angry farmers or poaching by unscrupulous traders (Nowell et al. 2016). This report seriously undermined the claims made by the three members of the IUCN assessment team that the snow leopard population is not as threatened as has been previously thought. The Snow Leopard Trust used the report to launch renewed efforts to publicize the plight of the snow leopard as under threat of extinction. In June 2016, SLT paid for a billboard in New York City's Times Square that repeated the claim made by TRAFFIC. Panthera, which regarded the threat to snow leopards from poaching as subsiding after the disintegration of the Soviet Union in the 1990s, raised doubts about the conclusion of the report. A month later, as the IUCN assessment process was underway, Tom McCarthy and colleagues (2016) of Panthera published a book titled *Snow Leopards*, in which they repeated that snow leopard populations may be more than what was previously thought, supporting the imminent revision of its status from Endangered to Vulnerable. In that same month, Snow Leopard Trust issued a statement of concern, questioning the research methodology of McCarthy's study and raised doubts over the procedure of inference, extrapolation, and interpretation used to arrive at new population numbers by Panthera and Wildlife Conservation Society scientists.

A key criticism of SLT and others who disagreed with the revision of status from Endangered to Vulnerable was that the higher numbers were based on surveys covering less than 2 percent of total snow leopard habitat and only conducted in the most suitable snow leopard habitats.[26] This means that there would be a bias toward a higher estimate because most suitable habitats harbor snow leopard populations at higher densities. McCarthy and coauthor Peter Zahler countered this criticism by pointing out that their surveys are conducted not just in prime snow leopard habitat but also in marginal areas and that there is consistent detection of snow leopards in areas where it was thought that the snow leopard did not occur (Gertz 2016). As McCarthy was quoted in an article on the topic, "I know some people that will argue that 'Well, we still do our camera trapping in only the best possible places, because we want to get good pictures of snow leopards.'" McCarthy continued, "That might have been the case 10 years ago. But what we're seeing now, particularly with Panthera—we've got five or six hundred cameras out in snow leopard range, and we don't just target high-level population areas. We target a number of places where we're not even sure snow leopards occur. So that argument doesn't hold a lot of water" (Gertz 2016). McCarthy does acknowledge that for an animal as difficult to observe as the snow leopard, informed guesses continue to play a big role in estimating the size of the population. "I would not say that what we have still goes much beyond a guesstimate," he said. "But the key takeaway here is [that] for once much more of the population figure was based on camera trapping, or genetic assessments, using fecal counts, sign surveys, rather than just more wild guessing" (Gertz 2016). It should be noted that SLT's own estimates of snow leopard numbers are taken from only one home-range country—Pakistan, which represents only 5 percent of total snow leopard habitat.

At a Global Snow Leopard and Ecosystem Protection meeting in Bishkek in August 2017, when it was certain that a Vulnerable ruling would be IUCN's final decision, the opposing group led by the Snow Leopard Trust, including all representatives of the twelve home range states, held a meeting to craft a joint statement of concern on behalf of the range states, in the face of imminent downlisting. The statement categorically rejected any change in the conservation status of snow leopards, using Pakistan as an example of globally declining population numbers.[27] This specter of declining Pakistani snow leopard population would play out on many different media platforms.

Prior to the IUCN decision, a report from Pakistan's Ministry of Climate Change appeared in the *Dawn* in June 2016 stating that rather than the prior estimate of three to four hundred snow leopards in Pakistan only two hundred were left.[28] Fifteen months later, on September 14, 2017, a day before IUCN's decision to down-list the snow leopard became public, SLT reported on its website that there were no more than a hundred snow leopards in Pakistan.[29] In March 2018, SLT scientists Mishra and Ale published a paper in *Science* in which they questioned IUCN's decision and again used the example of declining populations in Pakistan. But this time the population estimate was even lower. They claimed that the number of snow leopards left in Pakistan was only twenty-three.[30] What is most interesting about these data acrobatics is that they are all based on the same unpublished and non-peer-reviewed report![31]

On September 15, 2017, IUCN officially down-listed the snow leopard to Vulnerable. This decision sharply divided the snow leopard conservation community, and the news of the downlisting resulted in a flurry of statements from all major organizations. There was no official reaction from the home range countries, but SLT and its country offices issued statements of disagreements with the decision, while WCS, Panthera, and Snow Leopard Conservancy welcomed the decision with guarded optimism.

Two issues are central to the disagreements. The first is the issue of funding. From the perspective of the anti-delisting group, its timing was unhelpful, particularly in the context of the recently launched GSLEP which was promising considerable funding.[32] Generally speaking, megafauna with critical status defined by the authoritative IUCN Red List generate more funding than do species with lower levels of threat status. Moreover, there are certain sources of international funding that are earmarked for conservation of endangered species. There was a genuine concern that if snow leopards were down-listed, funding for their conservation would decline. This concern was openly stated by the groups advocating for Endangered status, including biologist Som Ale, who said, "This will have a tremendous (negative) impact on snow leopard conservation throughout its range.... I envisage that [the] snow leopard would be listed as low priority and [a] low-funding species while the opposite is what is necessary" (Gertz 2016).

The second issue is more complex and is related to the histories of different conservation organizations and their claims to having influence over snow leopard status. Each organization clearly wants to be seen as having had an impact on increasing snow leopard numbers, or at least arresting the decline. Some saw the GSLEP project as having been hijacked by SLT, which wanted to be seen as leading the snow leopard recovery effort out of endangered status and toward a hopeful goal of delisting by 2020. Clearly, when that status changed to Vulnerable before GSLEP was even implemented, it meant SLT would no longer be able to claim that GSLEP had made the difference.

CONCLUSION

The field of snow leopard conservation remains highly politicized. The struggle for scarce resources is at the same time a struggle to maintain the status quo in terms of whose voice is seen as the authority on the subject. Indeed, as social scientists, we see the whole process of scientific practice not simply as professionals applying objective analyses and making rational decisions but as individuals with bias and institutions defending their interests. We are scientists, but we are humans too.

A week after IUCN's decision, the Pakistani government, under advice from the country office of SLT, decided to challenge IUCN's decision by sending an official letter through the Ministry of Climate Change. A senior official from the ministry contacted me and asked my opinion on this proposed move. I replied that Pakistan would have to provide solid data to challenge this decision. The official also told me that he was thinking about calling a meeting to chart a course of action. I replied that "the ministry would have to ensure that this meeting does not turn into a 'vote' on snow leopard status. Science and democracy don't always go together." The downlisting was clearly seen by many of those involved primarily in terms of victory and defeat. This was perhaps inevitable given the acrimony that has developed over the years between the different players.

Conclusion

THE institutional representation of the snow leopard–farmer conflict at once privileges a scientific point of view and ignores the local point of view. In one of the seminal works on natural resource institutions and their representation of environmental problems and solutions, the anthropologist Michael Dove (1995) argued that in highlighting their own success and validation of their existence, institutions must obscure the role of local knowledge, practices, and interests. Local people and their institutions appear only as problems to be fixed. As the political ecologist Piers Blaikie's (1985) work reminds us, institutional responses to the plight of poor farmers in the face of deteriorating economic, political, and social conditions has been in the form of a steady dose of technical inputs. Blaikie pointed out three decades ago that conditions such as cultural ignorance and the sheer racism that prevailed during the colonial era still prevailed in the 1980s. The obscuring of local knowledge and experience and the emphasis on technical aspects by conservation organizations when dealing with snow leopard–farmer conflict is at the heart of the spectacle that sustains the political economy of conservation.

Conservation institutions have turned this conflict into one based on farmers' ignorance, without taking into account the agency of the snow leopard itself. The wild snow leopard that emerges in institutional literature is a highly disciplined species. The Baltis consider the snow leopard to be a companion species, but not necessarily a companion that they want to get stuck with. The ontology of the snow leopard for the Baltis is that it is a being in their midst, so they have to be careful in their dealings it. When a goat is killed by a snow leopard, the Baltis see in its death not necessarily the vanquishing of a life but rather the vanquishing of their labor. Goats are property in the sense that they are owned and claimed. Even when dead, their hides still have value.

The spectacle constructed by the conservation industry's obfuscation of the relationship between farmers and the snow leopard perpetuates the contradiction that those who sustain the snow leopards must be blamed for its demise. The image of snow leopard habitat that is presented is forever fraught with conflict in which predation of domestic livestock will always be an unnatural act. The spectacle brings this world-making project to fruition. It brings forth a world where the space for snow leopards is shrinking, despite the fact that the animal's historical range and habitat are pretty much intact. Through these spectacles, conservation organizations present their worldview as an actual view of the world. In this view, which rich consumers of developed countries consume, the snow leopards and the farmers are in direct opposition.

This situation has implications for the current debate on the Anthropocene and the accompanying awareness that the division between nature and culture is much more blurred than many have assumed in the past.[1] Yet as anthropologists Andreas Malm and Alf Hornborg (2014) remind us, the narrative of the Anthropocene is dominated by geologists who have naturalized its emergence as an inevitable evolutionary process. By contrast, Malm and Hornborg argue that the Anthropocene emerged due to agentive human decisions about modes of production. The fact that many in the conservation field are now calling for coexistence as an approach to protection of nature and society is somewhat cynical for the same reason. Now, when the activities and practices of Western and industrialized countries, which were at the forefront of the protected areas approach, are no longer compatible with this wilderness conservation ideology, as shown by climate change, we hear pronouncements of coexistence and doing away with the nature-culture boundary. These calls for more hybrid management regimes are of course welcomed, but they come without awareness of what was wrong with the wilderness approach in the first place.

Recent attention in anthropology to the world beyond humans is driven by the Latourian insight and the manifestation of this intellectual development.[2] When in the colonial and postcolonial eras, people from the rural areas of Third World countries protested against a conservation approach based on strict division of nature and culture because it affected their livelihoods, the advocates of protected areas used to say that local practices must confine themselves to non-wilderness areas. But when the practices of industrialized countries impact nature, as we now see with climate change, we no longer advocate a separation. Rather, we talk about coexistence. It would not be surprising if local people took a cynical view of the current proclamations by international conservation institutions and scientists that coexistence is the way forward in the Anthropocene.

A significant proportion of snow leopard food in terms of biomass consumed comes from domestic livestock, as found by multiple studies, including our 2011 study in Baltistan, showing that the proportion is as high as 70 percent. Local people, through their livestock, are subsidizing the region's snow leopard population, which causes substantial damage to the local economy (Anwar et al. 2011).

Are snow leopards responding to the Anthropocene? Is the high rate of livestock consumption something new? Perhaps, but perhaps not. Snow leopards have always been entangled with human society. Conservation institutions now see the fallacy of dividing nature from culture and ask us to think in terms of "novel" ecosystems. This understanding of ecosystems recognizes that nature everywhere has been shaped by humans, and that even though there may have been significant alterations, these ecosystems persist and function in a normal manner. Thus, although these ecosystems are not in their original state, they can nonetheless be considered normal. I do believe it is helpful to think of the central Karakoram ecosystem as novel (Corlett 2015). Humans have been in the region for at least two thousand years, but the human footprint has remained relatively low because of inaccessibility and lack of connectivity. Many species that were previously thought to have been made extinct seem to persist, albeit in low densities. There has always likely been some engagement between humans and snow leopards, and not much has changed to date.

In conservation biology literature, livestock are described as unnatural prey of the snow leopard. But let us look at the ecological context of this unnatural prey. The interactions between snow leopards and domestic livestock on a high-altitude pasture in the Pakistani Himalayas and Karakoram are as close to a "natural" system of a predator-prey relationship as it can get. Snow leopards and other wild predators have evolved a strategy to harvest this easy prey, but of course at some cost. The cost is the risk of being killed while attacking and eating domestic livestock. Having documented snow leopards' continued dependence on human-dominated landscapes, Alexander et al. (2016) conclude, "These findings suggest that snow leopards continue to use areas very close to such disturbances [by which they mean human activity], as long as there is sufficient prey. Improved knowledge about the effect of human activity on large carnivores, which require large areas and intact prey populations, is urgently needed for conservation planning at the local and global levels" (7). But such a finding can cut both ways.

Alexander and others may see this as justification for a more exclusionary approach to conservation with more protected areas, but we could come to an alternative conclusion. If snow leopards move around close to humans, then we should accept that as normal; that coexistence is the context for effective conservation.

Genuine adherence to a conservation model based on the idea of coexistence will require us to accept the fact that where there are snow leopards, there will be livestock predation. Creating boundaries between snow leopards and livestock—to separate them—has not worked in the past and will be unlikely to work in the future. Resolving the snow leopard–farmer conflict in Pakistan, and in other regions where snow leopard predation of livestock is a major problem, will require setting aside financial resources for compensating farmers for these losses. Of course any financial compensation mechanism has to be well thought out and executed, but it can be done. The benefits of such arrangements are ecological and social. As acknowledged by many ecologists, the availability of domestic livestock for snow leopards to eat takes pressure away from their "natural" prey thus reducing the chances of local extinction of that prey due to natural predation. But acceptance of this model would require shedding the ideological baggage that divides wild and domesticated nature. It would require accepting social responsibility for the costs of conservation and doing something about it.

FINANCIAL COMPENSATION AS A WAY FORWARD

It is worth asking how the presence of a compensation mechanism may have helped shape the attitudes of Balti farmers toward snow leopards. What impact has more than two decades of work by the Baltistan Wildlife Conservation and Development Organization had on local peoples' tolerance for snow leopards? The population trend data presented in chapter 5 suggests that the snow leopard population has been stable in the project area over the last twenty years. Ethnographic accounts presented in this book suggest that Balti farmers now claim to have adopted a proconservation stance toward the snow leopard in project areas; they actively talk about its protection and conservation, invoking Islamic code of ethics and human responsibility. One can question whether this is a "real" shift or merely a performance on the part of the Baltis to attract meager conservation and development resources toward them.

But this emphasis on a cultural shift is an unhelpful way of looking for a solution to this problem. The focus on the cultural shift is a result of an overwhelming interest in the sustainability of projects, which every conservation project has to think about. The solution to the question of sustainability is usually answered by presenting the cultural or institutional shift argument; once cultural norms or institutions have changed, it is assumed the flow of funding will be able to be shut off. I, however, see it somewhat differently. While I have argued that we have seen a shift in Balti attitudes toward snow leopards resulting from BWCDO's work, these changing attitudes are less the result of larger cultural changes resulting either from "awareness raising" activities or from changing broader economic and social structures, than from the changing transactional nature of the relationship between our project and local communities. Communities engage in protecting the snow leopard on a quid pro quo basis; their rationality for conserving the snow leopard is based on instrumentality. The farmers expect that in return for their proconservation behavior they will be compensated for their losses.

But many donors see compensation as a kind of dependency on outside resources and as antithesis to sustainability. This assessment is misleading because it constructs the relationship as a one-way exchange in which outside donors give money to the local people. The money transfer is seen as a real transfer of value in return for which the donors do not get anything. What this narrative obfuscates is the return in rural labor that is directed toward conservation. Conservation organizations impose an unnecessary and unjust burden on either the altruism of the local people (based on assumed traditional cultural beliefs) or on their civil responsibility when they demand that local people participate in conservation without direct compensation. In the absence of any fair compensation, the poor farmers, through their livestock losses and free labor, will continue subsidizing the institutions that claim to protect the snow leopard. The recently concluded IUCN assessment shows that snow leopards are no longer endangered. One of the reasons that they are no longer endangered is because of their consumption of farmers' livestock, but conservation institutions do not explicitly recognize this contribution to the snow leopard population.

The reluctance of snow leopard conservation institutions to accept financial compensation as a solution to the conflict comes at a time when environmentalists are actively promoting financial compensation as a tool and mechanism to achieve conservation and environmental goals in other arenas. The most common example is carbon offsets, which basically provide financial benefits for good behavior and practices to society, in this case reducing the emission of greenhouse gases either through reduced use of nonrenewable energy resources or through the adoption of cleaner technology. This mechanism is considered normal, and there are seemingly no questions about dependency and sustainability. It is clear in this trade-off that society trades its good behavior and practices for money. Why can't the same logic be applied to the snow leopard–farmer conflict?

At times, these demands for compensation of lost livestock have become vociferous with charges of moral corruption and dishonesty leveled against conservation organizations in Pakistan. Last year, farmers in Misgar, Hunza, trapped a snow leopard that had killed up to twenty livestock heads. The villagers refused to release the snow leopard and demanded compensation from the government wildlife department. Some villagers stated that rather than paying them the compensation they demanded, some state officials threatened them with a police case and imprisonment. When I was in Misgar last year, I heard one of the villagers say that many NGOs working for snow leopard conservation are "dollar wala NGOs," meaning that they spend money on strengthening their own organizations rather than on compensating farmers for their losses or building predator-proof corrals. The farmers in Baltistan are not country bumpkins who do not understand the political economy of international aid and conservation. In so many words they remind us that we, the NGOs, who are the bridge between society and state, must see conservation from their eyes.

Balti farmers see snow leopard predation as a natural phenomenon in their biophysical environment. They and other villagers across the region have come to feel threatened by another, newer, sense of predation: conservation projects and their long-term intentions. In this context, they see snow leopard predation not simply as a phenomenon of the natural world but increasingly as a phenomenon of the social world in which they have become the victims of unjust and unfair conservation policies. People in Hushe complain that snow leopards have become brave and unafraid of humans as a result of conservation initiatives: they now roam on the edges of the village in broad daylight. Because snow leopards have never been reported to attack humans, this situation is tolerated by villagers. They explain that snow leopards play a cat-and-mouse game with them; the moment they leave their animals unattended, the snow leopard pounces on them.

Snow leopard conservation is seen as yet another way in which outsiders impose regulations on their lands and curtail their independence. Often farmers have wondered aloud to me: if they are not compensated and cannot not kill snow leopards that kill their goats, what they are supposed to do. They say, "If the government and NGOs want us to let snow leopards hunt our goats, then it might as well hunt us down, too" (*Agar hakumat aur idaray chahtay hain key hum cheetay ko bukrion kaa shikar karnay dein tou phir hakumut humara shikar karay gee*).

This sense of vulnerability to (in this case, state-led) conservation was articulated in another way by a villager from Shimshal, in a region adjacent to Baltistan. Ali told me about a demand from the local wildlife department for a small piece of land to establish a checkpost to monitor illegal poaching in the area adjacent to Shimshal on which the government established national park in 1975. He said,

> How could we give them a place to establish their checkpost? Don't we know what happened to the Mughals when the British first came to India and asked them to grant them a piece of land the size of the hide of a horse? We all know what happened next: They cut up the skin of the horse in thin laces and made a long rope and encircled a large piece of land. Just like that, the government will trick us. They will start with just one foothold on our land but will eventually deprive us of all of it.

From Ali's perspective, the ecologist's checkpost carries the same potential for deception and dispossession as did the colonial government's horsehide. As mentioned earlier, even though the science of large predators is still inconclusive, scientists argue that we should nonetheless stress their importance as a keystone species as the basis for setting aside big chunks of territory. Just as the villagers fear, scientists see snow leopard conservation as a strategy to remove territory from the control of farmers. But the villagers recognize how dispossession can work through the agency of animal bodies; they have historical consciousness of it. To the local people, conservation is about control of territory by outsiders, and this perception of reality is the major source of conflict between farmers and conservationists vis-à-vis the snow leopard.

NOTES

PREFACE

1 There is a general perception among conservationists that because they can think in terms of nonlinear models of ecological science, they can figure out the complexity of social problems that arise as a result of a conservation intervention.

INTRODUCTION

1 See Oli, Taylor, and Rogers 1993; Anwar et al. 2011; Wegge, Shrestha, and Flagstad 2012; Lyngdoh 2014.This is also true for common leopards (*Panthera pardus*) across Pakistan (Shehzad et al. 2015).
2 According to the most commonly quoted figures since the 1980s, there are an estimated three to seven thousand snow leopards left in the wild worldwide, but as I will discuss later in this book, many conservationists consider this count unreliable. Most scientists I have talked to acknowledge that there has not been enough scientific rigor, or even any at all, behind previous projections of snow leopard populations.
3 Generally, conservation discourse blames this on irrational behavior of the local people. For example, the famous American naturalist George Schaller (1988, 147) wrote, "Villagers kill snow leopard merely because the animal presents a suitable target." This statement decontextualizes the conflict and represents people as inherently anti-animal and anti-conservation.
4 At the institutional level, there is acknowledgment of the burden of predation. For example, Johansson et al. (2015, 251) write that snow leopards mainly kill wild ungulates but also kill livestock opportunistically. A report by the FAO (2009,12) claims that "on a national level the losses

are hardly significant, but for the individual stock owner, they can be catastrophic. For a small-scale herder, losses to wildlife can mean the difference between economic independence and dire poverty."

5 For a discussion of these documents, see chapter 3.

6 Here I am using environmental historian William Cronon's (1992, 1350) formulation of narrative, according to which a narrative "cannot avoid a covert exercise of power: it inevitably sanctions some voices while silencing others. A powerful narrative reconstructs common sense to make the contingent seem determined, and the artificial seem natural." In this fashion, the narrative of snow leopard decline obfuscates, among other things, the cost that local villagers bear because of snow leopards' presence. This assumption, however, has received more scrutiny under SLSS 2014. See also chapter 3.

7 This policy has been successful, especially in the rich industrial countries of Europe and North Americ a, but an almost universal unintended consequence of this policy is the conflict with local people. Human-wildlife conflict is most intense on the boundaries of protected areas. Villages in Gilgit-Baltistan located on the edge suffer attacks frequently because parks provide a sanctuary where predators can find escape from angry farmers. The policy also does not take into account or obfuscates this two-way traffic between wild/nature and domestic/culture and the dependence of local people on it.

8 See William Cronon's famous article (1995) critiquing the idea of wilderness on the grounds that it could lead to unintentional denigration of non-wild parts of nature.

9 The response of Balti farmers and conservation organizations to snow leopard predation of farmers' livestock can be explained using Mary Douglas's (2005) conception of purity and danger. Like Douglas's conception of pollution, the snow leopard is seen by the local people as "matter out of place," so they try to put it back in its place. International and national conservationists, however, see humans, rather than the snow leopard, as "matter out of place," when they encroach on snow leopard habitat, so conservationists try to put humans in their place by creating protected areas.

10 Baltis use Islamic belief about how the biotic world is organized and how species are hierarchically arranged to serve those higher up in the chain. Like the Judeo-Christian belief that nature is created to serve humans, Baltis, too, see nature created to serve mankind; they see themselves as sitting atop the pyramid of biotic nature, not outside it. And when they see nature is behaving badly, they try to control it by eradicating it. But the similarity between the Baltis' Islamic beliefs and Western Judeo-Christian beliefs break down as the modes of production take effect. Despite the hierarchical view of nature, the kind of system imagined by

the Baltis requires holding a negotiated relationship with other members of the biotic community. It involves managing the resources exchanged across the boundaries of nature and culture.

11 About princely ecology, the perception of native Indian princes and their hunting practices in nineteenth-century British India, the historian Julie Hughes (2013, 5), states, "Within princely ecology, there was no popularly accepted and fundamental divide between people and wilderness of the sort famously identified and critiqued by William Cronon. This did not necessarily compromise the qualities that constituted wilderness."

12 Snow leopards often kill many more animals than they can actually eat. There are other predators, such as foxes and wolves, that do that as well, both to domestic and wild prey.

13 As the geographer Eric Swyngedouw (2007, 19–20) states, "All conceptions of the nature-culture divide involve designating boundaries, and constructing the relationship between humans and their environment. Instead of searching for nature and the natural, we should view these concepts as cultural and political construction, and analyze the implications of particular definitions and their applications."

14 I differentiate *meaning* from *value* in that the former is, simply, what is implied, while the latter is what is defended.

15 Jalais (2011, 9) writes, "By calling attention to two different representations of tigers in recent history, one colonial and the other national, the book highlights how representations, even of wild animals, are ultimately linked to power. Such images perpetuate the coercive and unequal relationship between those who partake of the 'global' tiger view versus those who live with 'wild tigers.'"

16 The states and international and national conservation institutions use reintroduction in variegated ways as a tool for alienating land for conservation from local people.

17 Anthropologist Michael Dove (1994, 2011), in his work on perception and reality of natural disasters, has shown that institutional facts emerge not from empirical observation of and objective reflection on reality but, from what those institutions want that reality to be. Dove argues that disagreement over what reality is, is settled through mobilizing self-serving narratives of it, backed by institutional power. My work on critiquing snow leopard conservation institutions is influenced by this line of thinking. In my work, I show that the question of the snow leopard's official status (according to the International Union for Conservation of Nature [IUCN] Red List of Threatened Species) is not settled through available scientific data, but rather the desired official status of the snow leopard becomes the means through which the scientific data is generated and interpreted. A very contentious and divisive process recently concluded at IUCN in which the snow leopard's official status was

down-listed from endangered to vulnerable. Clark, Rutherford, and Casey (2005, 7) make the same point when they write, "Carnivore management is a political process that is only partially scientific. It is a 'transscience' issue that involves science, but goes well beyond what science can offer."

18 It is true that improved methods have shown that there are more snow leopards than previously thought, but we do not know for sure what role domestic livestock may be playing in sustaining this population. In the following chapters I will show that it is possible that snow leopards rely significantly on domestic livestock from looking at the recent diet studies and historical accounts of snow leopards from the region. In field research and scientific papers many experts recognize this fact.

19 In November of 2017, I wrote an article for *Dawn*, an English-language newspaper in Pakistan, about the relationship between the snow leopard and conservation organizations. An extremely perceptive reader left the following comment on the article: "Excellent point about conservationists' dismay on the status change of snow leopards. No more dollars to spend on technical fees and advisory fees of so called experts. The snow leopard is an industry and keeping the growth rate of this industry requires continuing to portray poor villagers as the predators rather than the other way around" (Shoaib Akhtar, *Dawn*, November 1, 2017, https://www.dawn.com/news/1366847#comments).

20 More work could be done on the way that the specter of a world without snow leopards is used in images and media to create the spectacle that I discuss. This book focuses mainly on the discursive and technical elements that feed into creating this spectacle, rather than the visual material.

CHAPTER 1: THE SNOW LEOPARD AND THE GOAT IN HISTORICAL PERSPECTIVE

1 I modify Paul Greenough's Standard Environmental Narrative, which is a critique of scholarship that celebrates India as a region without environmental conflicts in the precolonial era. Greenough (2001) shows that conflict with predators and wildlife was an everyday reality for many rural folks.

2 Awareness about species extinction and general environmental degradation due to human action can be traced back to colonial interventions in the colonies (Grove 1990), but it was after the 1970s ecological awakening that a well-defined narrative appeared that still persists today.

3 There are some deviations from this narrative, such as Li et al. (2016), which states, "Based on occurrence records of snow leopards collected across all snow leopard range countries from 1983 to 2015, we built a snow leopard

habitat model using the maximum entropy algorithm (MaxEnt 3.3.3k). Then we projected this model into Late Glacial Maximum, mid-Holocene and 2070. Analysis of snow leopard habitat map from LGM to 2070 indicates that three large patches of stable habitat have persisted from the LGM to present in the Altai, Qilian, and Tian Shan-Pamir-Hindu Kush-Karakoram mountain ranges, and are projected to persist through the late 21st century" (188). They state that these three patches represent 35 percent of the snow leopard habitat, which is large enough to act as refugia. But Li et al. buttress this optimistic conclusion by stating that habitat fragmentation still remains a challenge.

4   There is a common belief in the standard environmental narrative that as human density has increased, predator population has decreased. One study, however, shows that there is no such relationship and a more robust factor to consider is the management regime (Linnell et al. 2009, 73).

5   Sibylle Noras, "Tibetan Snow Leopards Speak to Us from Centuries Past," *Saving Snow Leopards Report: The Global Guide to Conservation and Research* (blog), August 3, 2011. http://snowleopardblog.com/tibetan-snow-leopards-speak-to-us-from-centuries-past/.

6   Clouded leopard is considered a separate subgenus within the Panthera group.

7   The snow leopard is generally placed in the *Panthera* genus with the full name *Panthera uncia*, but others, such as the IUCN's Species Survival Commission's Cats Specialist Group, place it under a separate genus, *Uncia*, with the full name *Uncia uncia*.

8   Generally, wild animals in captivity live longer than those in the wild due to a secured food supply and less inter- and intraspecies hazards. They also breed for longer periods of time and produce larger litters (Blomqvist 1980).

9   China, which has the highest snow leopard population and the biggest habitats, did not have a specimen in a zoo until 1956 (Liao and Tan 1988, 33).

10 A few notable exceptions to this are Jackson (Hillard 1989) Fox and Chundawat (1988) and Schaller (1988).

11 One study shows that snow leopards do not prefer the steppe environment thus reinforcing the view that snow leopards mainly prefer broken and craggy mountain landscape (Johannson et al. 2016).

12 A telemetry study involves collection of data using remote technology. In this case snow leopards were fitted with radio transmitter collars, which transferred information, mainly about location and movement, through a radio signal to a receiver at a remote location.

13 An excessive reliance on technology means that very few ecologists actually go into the field to study the behavior of the snow leopard. This trend results in a professional bias toward a specific kind of method to study

the snow leopard. For example, the Snow Leopard Information Management System method, which relied on those techniques, is now being treated as completely useless—its results are often referred to as guestimate work. The new genetic techniques are considered accurate, but they are expensive and their handling is not that straightforward, with degradation and contamination of the DNA often occurring.

14   There is an emerging scholarship on the history of *shikar* (the hunt) from south Asia, which has broken away, and rightly so, from the traditional understanding of shikar as only a British cultural style. Historians and anthropologists are now paying attention to the hunting pursuits of indigenous rulers of India, while others are looking at the structure of the hunt (Allsen 2011) and the place of subalterns in it (Rashkow 2014).

15   As snow leopard populations increased in zoos, zoos changed their character. From being institutions that displayed animals for human curiosity and recreation in the early part of the twentieth century, zoos had become institutions that provided the public with information and education. Public interest in snow leopards changed as ecology, biodiversity, and endangered species became common topics in social discourse, especially as climate change became a public concern toward the end of the last century (Rothfels 2002).

16   Compared to the British attitudes toward large predators, a local Indian prince did not view tigers as a source of danger. But this was to change with the arrival of the British (Rangarajan 1999).

17   True, in recent years mining and other forms of industrial resource extraction activities have created new dangers for the snow leopard and its habitat, but the impact of such activities is miniscule compared to what would have been if agricultural expansion or urban settlement had happened.

18   George Schaller (1988) writes, "Hunting accounts written in the late nineteenth and early twentieth centuries rarely mention snow leopard because the authors seldom meet one of the cats, even after months and years in the mountains, which is not too surprising, for only those animals that remained elusive survive" (21).

19   Most authors have given accounts of their hunts in a matter-of-fact style, while few have used a romantic lens of the late nineteenth century to frame their narratives.

20   A rough estimate based on shooting licenses issued by Kashmir Game Department in 1903 suggested that each year up to twenty sportsmen came to Baltistan, Astor, and Gilgit for shooting.

21   Almost all officials on the Gilgit–Srinagar Road carried shotguns and rifles to replenish their pantries with game birds and wild goats. This is perhaps contrary to the popular belief that the British hunted only for sport and not meat (M. Pandian 1995).

22 According to environmental historian Harriet Ritvo (1987) it was only after science and technology tamed wilderness that nature began to be viewed with affection and nostalgia.
23 For the whole narrative of the encounter, see the wonderful description in Schaller's *Stones of Silence* on pages 22–28.

CHAPTER 2: PRODUCING WILDERNESS PREDATORS

1 Linnell, Sweneson, and Anderson et al. (2001, 348) write: "There is no doubt that the concept of hunting large carnivores as game species is far older in Europe than in North America and contributed greatly to their persistence."
2 This history of conservation and its critique is already available so I will not try to reproduce it here. For the critique of a conventional conservation approach based on establishment of national parks see Cronon (1995); Dowie (2009); Jacoby (2001); Neumann (2002); Robbins (2012); Spence (1999).
3 The Audubon Society was established in the United States in 1886 specifically to protect birds of economic value, such as those with feathers that were used in the millinery industry. The first federal wildlife act passed in the United States was the Lacey Act of 1900, which put penalties and sanctions on the illegal trade of wild flora and fauna, but predators and many other species of animals and plants that had no economic value were missing from that list.
4 Predators have been the focus of attention of the kings and political rulers throughout the world. Babar, the sixteenth-century Mughal emperor of India, had five hundred cheetahs in his hunting party. The British engaged in tiger hunting to emulate the previous kings and rulers of India and in the process appropriated their symbolic authority (A. Pandian 2001). Roosevelt thought that the American national animal should have been the grizzly bear rather than the eagle. And Ceausescu of Romania protected the largest population of wolves in Europe because he thought that he, like the wolf, was a great hunter (Quammen 2004, 214).
5 Wild predators have always been the focus of intense human discourse. Human society has created myths and legends about them as elements of danger, threat, power, and freedom. They are rare in nature so they invoke a sense of mystery and awe (Steneck and Sala 2005). The nature writer David Quammen argues that while there have been many wild animals that invoke fear in humans, there has always been something different about the top, what he calls the "alpha predator," in the ways in which humans react to it (2004 6). Large predators in some ways remind us of the perfection of nature and its power. They represent the spectacle of raw power in its most natural form; the power to rule and to kill (A. Pandian 2001; Jalais 2011; Boomgaard, 2001). Yet their wildness and

predatory nature make them an ideal other who have learned to exercise restraint and show cultured behavior (Ritvo 1987).

6   Worster (1994) argues that in the first half of the twentieth century, mostly game animals were managed, and there was a tendency to manage wildlife as trees. Trees were seen as an economic resource so wildlife, especially game species, could be managed like them. This misguided approach, said Worster, led to the fiasco of Kaibab deer when the main predator of the ecosystem was eradicated, which resulted in a crash in the population of the deer. This alerted wildlife managers about the role of predators in maintaining a community of species.

7   A study on the famous Chipko movement in northern India shows the popularity of certain environmental fads in the theory of Himalayan environmental degradation. One is the concept of ecosystem (Rangan 2000). Social scientists have argued that it is impossible to grasp the complexity of the natural environment using scientific models because the data, information, and level of analysis required is beyond the means and capacity of any institution (Blaikie 1985). They also maintain that the ecosystem model commands a privileged status in the policy arena because of its association with scientific practice. Lowe (2006) argues that scientific facts however are not neutral, rather they are set in motion to serve particular interests and points of view and are inherently political in nature.

8   For more discussion on this topic see, Lowe 2006; Lewis 2003; and Orlove and Brush 1996.

9   Lynx and other fur-bearing predators, or carnivores, were protected from poachers for their economic value.

10 Seidensticker described a mix of indigenous methods and modern techniques to capture a tiger. First, a tiger is encircled by beaters with a white muslin cloth four feet high and then driven into a gully where the blow or dart gun is used to shoot it in the rump, not at the heart or face. This technique was most likely learned from old shikaris, who used it to kill and trap tigers in Nepal.

11 My argument is that if conservation programs consider humans to be part of a predator ecosystem, they are most likely to accept conflict as an inherent management issue that is likely to be addressed. But accepting human presence goes against the basic tenets of the modern conservation movement.

12 The method came under intense criticism during the debate among snow leopard conservationists over designation of status under IUCN's Red List of Threatened Species, which will be discussed in chapter 6.

13 For details see Jackson et al. (2006); McCarthy et al. (2008); Xu et al. (2008); Stevens et al. (2011).

14 The only published article in which the snow leopard is clearly declared as controlling the ecosystem through trophic cascade appeared in *National*

Geographic in 2008. The author, Doug Chadwick, interviewed many snow leopard ecologists and wrote, "As the top carnivore of the alpine and sub-alpine zones, the snow leopard strongly influences the numbers and whereabouts of hoofed herds overtime. That in turn affects plant communities, and thus shapes the niches of many smaller organisms down the food chain" (117). But this statement is not based on any scientific study of the snow leopard's ecosystem; rather it is a kind of "academic reflex," that is, it is used because it is almost a convention to repeat this claim because others have done so as well.

15 Conservation institutions rationalize a particular decision despite having insufficient data and information by using the familiar tropes of urgency. For example, in the 1980s, when the International Union for Conservation of Nature introduced the idea of biogeographical scale conservation, it anticipated the problem of defining the boundaries of these regions but argued, "The academic ramification of defining and revising biogeographical lines are endless, but park planners have an urgent practical job to do and simply cannot wait for a perfect method or data. As pressure for land increases, land use options are irrevocably closed. The next decade may be the last chance for conservationists to add large new protected areas to the existing system" (MacKinnon and MacKinnon 1986, 12). That this was the last chance, however, hardly turned out to be true because the expansion of the protected area system kept pace in the 2000s with the trend of the 1980s and 1990s. In 2009 Dowie writes that the "total area of land now under conservation protection worldwide has doubled since 1990, when the World Parks Commission set a goal of protecting 10 percent of the planet's surface" (ix).

16 By the 1970s both Pakistan and India had passed laws for the conservation of large predators, including snow leopards. Throughout the world in the 1970s, states and private institutions started formulating laws for the protection of wild predators and their habitats in natural conditions. These interventions came at the heels of a new international regime of wildlife management as enshrined in some landmark treaties and regulation, such as the 1973 Endangered Species Act in the United States and the 1971 Convention on International Trade in Endangered Species (CITES). New national parks were established not just for protection of landscape and scenery but also for wild predators and national pride. Ecology had finally intersected with the modernity of scientific objectivity.

CHAPTER 3: HUMAN-WILDLIFE CONFLICT

1 Alexander et al. (2015) defined human-wildlife conflict "as those occurring when an action by either humans or wildlife has an adverse effect on the other, often occur when human activities and wildlife overlap spatially

and compete for resources" (1). They then give a typology of the conflict that includes "many forms including crop or property damage, livestock predation, and animal attacks on people.... Direct economic costs of conflict include market-price for victims' crops and livestock losses or medical expenses incurred as a result of attack. Indirect costs include opportunity costs associated with conflict mitigation and protection activities, transaction costs associated with pursuing compensation, and 'hidden' social costs such as diminished states of psychological or physical well-being" (1).

2 Alexander et al. (2015) state, "Although perceptions underpinning HWCs are complex and tend to be context-specific, it is helpful to deconstruct them along several dimensions. Here we identified, on the basis of previous HWC research, 4 domains related to threats and costs to humans: fear of carnivores; perceived risk posed to humans; perceived risk posed to livestock; attitudes towards carnivore control; and two domains related to attitudes and beliefs: willingness to conserve the species; and beliefs on the role the species plays in the wider environment/ecosystem. In a given context, perceptions of wildlife species, which form the basis for potential persecution or protection of a given species, are shaped by the interactions between these domains" (2). Here it is clear that perception of local people about conservation and conservationists is not even part of the equation. It is assumed that villagers see conservation as a neutral activity.

3 For various debates about the economic and social cost of conservation, see Neumann (2002), Adams and Hutton (2007), and Agrawal and Redford (2009).

4 The first study that looked at the prey remains in the snow leopard's diet using next-generation DNA techniques was conducted in the Gobi region of Mongolia, where about 20 percent of snow leopard scat was shown to have livestock remains (Shehzad et al. 2012).

5 The difference between the wildlife biologist and the conservation biologist is that the latter has a normative position, in addition to a scientific mind. That is, the conservationist is interested in saving animals as much as studying them. Thus scientific knowledge is produced with one eye on the missionary disposition in which saving animals becomes an ethical practice. I call them scientists, and those I come across most often have a doctorate degree in wildlife or conservation biology, with fieldwork in either snow leopards or other big cats and predators.

6 I was one of them. The participants were divided into various working groups and the division among the Western scientists and participants from the home range was obvious. I had just started graduate school in anthropology and was learning critical insights into the politics of scientific knowledge production in a conservation institution. I was

participating both as a participant snow leopard expert and a participant observer anthropologist. The conference was dominated by natural scientists, such as wildlife biologists, ecologists, and conservation biologists, who represented mostly the United States and Europe. The second-tier scientists were from the home range countries. They did not have degrees in modern ecological studies; rather, they were trained in mostly colonial-era sciences, such as forestry and veterinary medicines. Participants from India, Nepal, Bhutan, Pakistan, and, to a certain extent, China were trained in this way.

7 The specific goals of Snow Leopard Survival Strategy are to "assess and prioritize threats to snow leopard across their range; define and prioritize appropriate conservation, education, and policy measures to alleviate threats; and prioritize topics for snow leopard research and identify viable and preferred research methods" (Snow Leopard Network 2014, 5).

8 Other processes of habitat degradation and encroachment include large-scale infrastructure development, such as road, railway, and dam construction, in snow leopard home range.

9 In chapter 1, I discussed the issue of snow leopard habitat in comparison to other big cats and argued that the narrative of habitat degradation is less convincing in the case of snow leopards.

10 In some regions, particularly in former socialist states, introduction of a market-led economy has contributed to an increase in commercialization of livestock, hence increased livestock numbers in snow leopard habitat. But this trend cannot be generalized.

11 About the Naltar Valley in Hunza, Naqvi and Fatima (2012) write, "About 20% of population depends on the agriculture and very few on livestock for their livelihood" (69). Then there is the problem with locally produced data on number of livestock. This data is seldom collected with seriousness and precision. For example, a group of Pakistani researchers (Khan et al., 2013) reported the following from Shimshal: "In 2010 it was being used for grazing for 5,000 yaks, 2,000 goats, 1,900 sheep, and 500 cows, along with a few hundred wild herbivores such as Himalayan ibex and blue sheep, whereas the 10,429-ha area is only just enough to feed 715 yaks for a maximum of six months" (74). I know this figure to be inflated because I did my fieldwork on Shimshali pastoralism (Hussain 2015). The figure of 5,000 yaks in Shimshal is about three times higher than what I observed. Also, as a matter of fact, Shimshalis do not have cows!

12 It is for this reason some conservation biologists suggest that when predicting snow leopard density, its wild prey population is not enough, the presence of domestic livestock must also be taken into account.

13 Hushe is noted to have close to a thousand ibex in an area of about five hundred square kilometers. If it is that only young, old, or injured and unhealthy snow leopards attack livestock, then it seems that availability

of domestic prey is an integral part of the overall life cycle of snow leopard populations. After all, if there are no humans or their livestock, where will these subadult or old snow leopards get their food?

14 Predators are often equated with cruel and inconsiderate rulers who impose economic hardship on society. For example, in Baltistan, the snow leopard metaphor has been used to describe rulers who imposed heavy taxes on the local peasantry (Emerson 1983).

15 Balti farmers also have a myth about the snow leopard that is tied to its ecological role. I will discuss this aspect in the local response to conservation.

16 See Radhika Govindrajan's beautiful ethnography *Animal Intimacies* (2018), where she describes the behavior of the goats in Uttarkhand, India, that makes them so hard to look after.

17 During the 1970s state wildlife officials in Montana, Wyoming, and Idaho refused to believe that what people were seeing were wolves. Rather they claimed that these were cases of mistaken identity, and these animals were actually coyotes (Urbigkit 2008, 59).

18 Our data show that farmers also exaggerate the numbers of snow leopards they have killed due to concern for the safety of their animals.

19 Real assessment of damage can only be done when organizations actually start recording it themselves. This can be done by instituting compensation programs like the one I was involved with, in which claims become an important source of recording data on predation.

20 The exaggeration by farmers of the snow leopard's predation of domestic livestock is equally matched with the exaggeration by conservationists of the snow leopard's role as the apex predator. Both require proof.

21 Sometimes even the institutional literature coming out of these conservation organizations can explain this issue in a sophisticated manner. A report by the Wildlife Conservation Society on the same topic put the matter even more clearly. The authors of the report state, "Recording absolute levels of crop losses by individual farmers or communities will not necessarily adequately explain what those losses really mean to individual farmers. Where individual researchers have probed more deeply it has become apparent that the issue of crop raiding is sometimes conceived as part of a wider issue that people are concerned about, such as their loss of 'ownership' of wildlife to the State" (Hill, Osborn, and Plumptre 2002, 23).

22 Our study provides two main insights into human-wildlife conflicts. First, human perceptions can be at considerable odds with the actual patterns of livestock depredation, and, second, livestock depredation by snow leopards and wolves show rather different patterns in prey selectivity and ecological determinants. This suggests that while interviews of local people, which have been commonly employed to study livestock-depredation conflicts, could yield accurate information on peoples' perception of a

conflict situation, the reality of livestock depredation must be measured additionally and independently (Suryawanshi et al. 2013).

23 Villagers in Delhi took out licenses to shoot macaque monkeys, despite their having religious status in India, because the monkeys were attacking children and stealing food from peoples' kitchens. Even religious tolerance can wane in the face of economic conditions (Gandhi, 2012).

24 Rajaratnam, Vernes, and Sangay (2016) write, "Despite large predators like the tiger and leopard being culturally revered amidst a Buddhist population respecting the sanctity of life, there is growing resentment to livestock predators and a reported increase in retaliatory killing" (143).

25 I have noted elsewhere that despite the fact national laws allow farmers to kill a problem animal, they seldom do so openly because they don't want to get entangled with the state and its power. Most villagers consider the killing of a snow leopard a very rationale response and almost a right, which they frankly have. Ibraheem, a farmer from Hushe, was narrating a story about how he lost fifteen goats to a snow leopard a few years back. He said that he was very mad and wanted to kill a snow leopard, a natural and bold reaction. Other times a respondent would replace the *I* with *the people* often saying, "what choice do people have other than kill a predator?"

26 Alex Kohler (2000, 70–71) states, "Current biodiversity conservation discourse and practice are still largely based on conventional paradigms of metropolitan science and are dominated by Northern capitalists interest . . . the decisive campaigns to implement a world-wide ban on ivory were all run outside the African continent, mainly by Western conservation agencies in the USA and the UK. These agencies greatly profited from their campaigns in terms of increased membership and funding, but when it came to pay for anti-poaching programs, the promises of the United States and the European Community to make good on lost ivory revenues were not fulfilled, and the burden to sponsor the conservation of this 'part of the world heritage' was placed on Africans."

27 There are, however, examples from North America that suggest that the economic burden of conservation cannot be discounted. Nyhus et al. (2005) diverge from the conclusions of Clark, Rutherford, and Casey (2005) and Treves and Bruskotter (2014) about the effectiveness of compensation near Yellowstone National Park. "When implemented under ideal conditions—i.e., in a timely, transparent, and equitable manner—economic compensation can go far in promoting positive people-park relationships and support increased levels of tolerance toward 'offending' wildlife. For example, in the United States, compensation for losses incurred by cattle ranchers living near Yellowstone National Park due to the reintroduction of the gray wolf has facilitated increased tolerance for wolves by members of the public" (Nyhus et al. 2005).

28 Naho Ikeda (2004), reporting from Kanchenjunga National Park in Nepal, stated that the villagers, too, are aware of such problems: "Furthermore, one herder pointed to the possibility that the level of damage from livestock depredation may increase in the future as a result of conservation success" (329).
29 Webber, Hill, and Reynolds (2007, 177) state that when conservation organizations fail to acknowledge the intensity of the conflict, there is local resistance to environmental initiatives that can lead to reduced support for conservation.

CHAPTER 4: DOMESTICATING LANDSCAPES

1 For more detail, see Lobsang (1997).
2 Regionally specific cultural beliefs about snow leopards exist in the home-range countries. Most of these myths highlight the secret and elusive natures of gods through the elusive nature of the snow leopard. Som Ale (2012) writes of a widespread local belief, in Everest (Nepal), that sees the snow leopard as the dog of the mountain god Taubuche. The act of appeasing the snow leopard in ceremonies is a social norm. Ale goes on to state, "A thousand of years ago in the foothills of the Himalayas, Guru Rimpoche (also known as Padma Sambhava in Tibet and Nepal), the Indian yogi who brought the teachings of Buddhism from India to Tibet, plowed a series of valleys out of the mountains to serve as *beyul* (Shangri-La or fabled Shambala) in Nepal, Tibet and Sikkim. The refuges there were to remain hidden in a time of unprecedented religious crisis, protect the dharma until the misfortune passed. These valleys are protected from the world by the mountain Gods. Only the true followers, the ones who really practice Buddhist teachings, can find beyul. If people with ill intentions try to follow beyul, it is believed, snow leopards will attack them at the mountain passes and drive them away" (125–26).
3 The discourse of a socially responsible community that fulfills its moral and divine duties has become quite common in the region, which is the result of three decades of community mobilization in Baltistan that has mainly been carried out by the Aga Khan Rural Support Program, a rural development organization that will be discussed in chapter 5.
4 *Mahoul* is the Urdu word for "environment." Like the word *environment* in English, mahoul, too, can be used metaphorically to imply "company," as in "bad company."
5 I don't want to give an impression that Islamic beliefs about animals are similar to that in Bonism. The major difference is that in Bonism talking and shape-shifting animals are an everyday occurrence, but in Islam, animals speak under the miraculous power of Allah or a religious figure.

6 Compared to the Balti belief system in which landscapes and species are not strictly demarcated as belonging to nature or culture, conservation discourse and practice is all about making those boundaries explicit and real.
7 Generally, I observed that local knowledge about the snow leopard had been, by and large, accurate. When I first starting doing surveys, using a now discarded method of line transect, I always consulted the local people, mostly a hunter or a herder, about where to look for snow leopard signs. They knew the travel routes of the snow leopard and would point to the *daar* (a Balti word for "mountain ridge") that the snow leopard took. When I graduated from line transect to camera traps, I used the same method: asking people where snow leopards travel and how they ambush their herd. This helped me fix cameras at spots that always yielded success. Even later when we started collecting scat samples to ascertain the population number, we relied on local people to collect them for us.
8 If using the definition of domestication as provided by Bradshaw (2006) "that breeding, care, and feeding are totally controlled by humans, producing a reproductively isolated population" (1928S), then the domestic goats of the Baltis are not strictly domesticated.
9 Afforestation schemes under the Aga Khan Rural Support Program have resulted in tree plantations on land surrounding the villages, which are also referred to as jungle by the Baltis.
10 I have not heard this myth outside Baltistan and not many people have talked about it in academic scholarship. The myth has a limited geographical range and is usually confined to the Balti-speaking population; it is not even recognized in Gilgit, Hunza, Gojal, or Chitral. In Gojal there are other myths, of mergich realm (a Wakhi word for the area of permanent snow where, according to local mythology, mountain fairies live), but not about the otter. My quick cursory survey among many social scientists at a conference on the Himalayas at Yale in the winter of 2013 also yielded no parallels. A quick email to colleagues in Nepal, Tajikistan, India, and Mongolia also resulted in no one hearing of this myth. The origins of the myth are not clear at all. No reference has been found in the local texts or even the colonial texts, which started recording the cultures of some local societies in the nineteenth century.
11 There are eight folk songs in Baltistan that show empathy toward animals as conscious beings.
12 This point perhaps resonates with MacDonald's (2004) analysis about trophy hunting and its effects on local cultural power dynamics in which the older generation was losing control over ibex as a resource.
13 Studies from tiger conservation in India (Jalais 2011), elephant conservation in China (Hathaway 2013), and wolf conservation in Norway (Breitenmoser 1998) show that local people think that as a result of conservation these wild animals had become bolder and deadlier than before.

CHAPTER 5: MODERNIZATION AND THE
TRANSACTIONAL MODE OF CONSERVATION

1. It is important to note that the equity issue, which is emphasized in the "official" objectives of the Aga Khan Rural Support Program, is not addressed in practice. Rather, the issue is blatantly obfuscated in reports and documents of the program. By keeping the criteria for Village Organization formation at a minimum of 75 percent participation rate by the village households, the program systematically creates the boundary between those who are in the Village Organization and those outside it. The people outside the Village Organization, the other 25 percent or less of the villagers, are invariably those who are poor and do not have common economic interests with the rest of the village. Regarding the selection of Productive Physical Infrastructure projects of the Village Organization, Ahmed and Khan (1998) write "almost, invariably, [villagers] are able to agree on a project of overriding importance to *all* the villagers" (6; emphasis added). Such a statement glosses over the reality that not all villagers are in the Village Organization.
2. In the last few years the program's savings and credit activities have evolved into a formal financial institution, the First Microfinance Bank, which has branches all over Gilgit-Baltistan and also the rest of Pakistan.
3. This was the model that Steve Edwards from International Union for Conservation of Nature-US brought to Pakistan from South Africa. There was also quite an overlap of staff from the Aga Khan Rural Support Program to IUCN, including myself and a few other colleagues, who went to work on important positions in the IUCN. This was the reason that more than wildlife biologists, it was the social scientists who spearheaded the effort to implement the Mountain Areas Conservancy Project in the way they did at AKRSP.
4. Despite its overwhelming success, trophy hunting has been opposed by those who regard indigenous hunting with nostalgia. Hunting by local people is now illegal; it is poaching (Jacoby 2001). Our camera trapping surveys, however, show that "illegal" subsistence hunting still goes on in some participating villages, as we caught images of local hunters with guns. We are not sure about the severity of this violation.
5. The collective labor that is spent on guarding ibex against outsiders has solidified the existing social institution of cooperative labor.
6. I would like to thank Usman Ifikhar for helping me out in designing and implementing the program.
7. George Schaller spent about two weeks in the upper Gojal and Braldu Valleys. He did not interview any local herder about snow leopard presence or sightings, and he made extremely pessimistic judgment about the fate of the snow leopard on surveys based only on sign density. My

surveys included extensive interviews with local hunters, herders, trekkers, and mountaineers.

8   More than 50 percent of the scat samples collected belonged to the snow leopards, which we considered to be a very good identification ratio. Usually, the success rate varies from 20 to 60 percent. For example, Weiskopf, Kachel, and McCarthy (2016) state, "Field identification success varied across study sites, ranging from 21% to 64% genetically confirmed snow leopard scats" (233).

9   Literature shows that about 25 percent of the snow leopard diet globally consists of domestic livestock (Lyngdoh et al. 2014).

10 The composition of small-bodied prey in the snow leopard diet varies according to the season. Pikas show up in the winter, while marmots show up in summertime diets.

11 A snow leopard requires approximately 1.5 to 2.5 kilograms of meat per day, or 40 to 45 grams of food per kilogram of its body weight daily (Fox 1989). Because about 30 percent of ungulate prey consists of unusable items such as bone, skin, or stomach contents, an adult snow leopard would be expected to consume between 700 and 1,200 kilograms of prey annually. Jackson and Hunter (1996) estimated that a population of 150 to 230 blue sheep is required to sustain a single snow leopard without depleting the prey base, but this number could be lower in areas where livestock, marmot, and other small prey are also taken (Oli et al. 1993).

CHAPTER 6: THE POLITICAL ECONOMY OF THE SNOW LEOPARD

1   The Ministry of Environment later changed its name to Ministry of Climate Change.

2   This is an important point because there remained confusion among the various parties as to what was WCS's responsibility with regards to constructing a rehabilitation facility in Pakistan.

3   "Pakistan: Insurance Scheme against Snow Leopard Attacks Planned," *Big Cat Rescue* (blog), November 7, 2006, http://bigcatrescue.blogspot.com/2006/11/pakistan-insurance-scheme-against-snow.html.

4   Ryan C. Crocker, "Snow Leopard Send Off," US Department of State Archive, August 8, 2006, https://2001-2009.state.gov/g/oes/rls/rm/2006/70090.htm.

5   Ryan C. Crocker, "Snow Leopard Send Off," US Department of State Archive, August 8, 2006, https://2001-2009.state.gov/g/oes/rls/rm/2006/70090.htm.

6   This did not turn out to be true. As of January 2019, Leo, who is now thirteen, is still at the Bronx Zoo.

7   Claudia McMurray, "Hope for Leo the Snow Leopard," September 25, 2006, US Department of State Archive, https://2001-2009.state.gov/g/oes/rls/rm/2006/73246.htm.

8. Judy Aita, staff writer for Washington File, a product of the Bureau of International Information Programs of the US State Department, wrote, "Sehba Musharraf, the first lady of Pakistan, said Leo marks 'the beginning of a new dimension' in the multifaceted U.S.-Pakistani relationship. 'Leo will return to Pakistan,' the first lady said. 'But before he returns, Pakistan will develop a snow leopard conservation center for rehabilitation and breeding facilities for snow leopards with the support of the United Nations and in cooperation with the Bronx Zoo.'" "Snow Leopard Cub Settles into Bronx Zoo," September 25, 2006, https://bigcatrescue.org/snow-leopard-cub-settles-into-bronx-zoo.

9. Associated Press, "Pakistan Snow Leopard Cub Heads to Bronx: Cub to Become Part of Breeding Program for Snow Leopards at Zoo," Science on NBCNews.com, August 8, 2006, http://www.nbcnews.com/id/14252884/ns/technology_and_science-science/t/pakistan-snow-leopard-cub-heads-bronx/#.XLtXbehKjIV.

10. US Fish and Wildlife Service, Endangered Species, "Permits: Frequently Asked Questions: Loans and Gifts," last updated December 11, 2018, www.fws.gov/endangered/permits/faq.html.

11. Paula J. Dobriansky, "Conservation as Diplomacy," May 19, 2008, US Department of State Archive, https://2001-2009.state.gov/g/rls/rm/105158.htm.

12. Rhett A. Butler, "Pakistani Snow Leopard Settles in at Bronx Zoo," *Mongabay*, February 26, 2007, https://news.mongabay.com/2007/02/pakistani-snow-leopard-settles-in-at-bronx-zoo.

13. "Orphaned Snow Leopard Unlikely to Return to Natural Habitat," *Dawn*, January 9, 2011, https://www.dawn.com/news/597247.

14. In 2015 another article appeared in the *Dawn* in which a demand was made to bring Leo back to Pakistan. Jamal Shahid, "Pakistan Seeks Return of Snow Leopard from US," *Dawn*, June 1, 2015, https://www.dawn.com/news/1185473.

15. Wild snow leopards are not only a means of reproduction for conservation institutions they also engender international diplomatic relations and get entangled in politics that seem far afield from nature conservation. As mentioned earlier, the case of the Global Snow Leopard and Ecosystem Protection Program shows that snow leopards transcend national boundaries to produce new "regions" of cooperation. Currently all twelve home range countries are on board, with Kyrgyztan acting as the headquarters of the program. The collaborative work involved represents an impressive effort to protect snow leopards at an international level. While GSLEP has unified countries at official levels, it has the effect of alienating a significant proportion of the snow leopard conservation institutions on the ground.

16 Full disclosure: Baltistan Wildlife Conservation and Development Organization has been working with the conservancy since 2004 and receiving funding and technical assistance.
17 Snow Leopard Trust, "Key Snow Leopard Facts, accessed November 10, 2018, https://www.snowleopard.org/snow-leopard-facts.
18 IUCN Red List, "Snow Leopard," accessed January 10, 2017, www.iucnredlist.org/details/22732/0.
19 Panthera, "Snow Leopard: The State of the Snow Leopard," accessed January 10, 2017, https://www.panthera.org/cat/snow-leopard.
20 World Wildlife Fund, "Snow Leopard: Facts," accessed January 10, 2017, www.worldwildlife.org/species/snow-leopard.
21 Wildlife Conservation Society, "Snow Leopards: Challenges," accessed November 30, 2018, https://www.wcs.org/our-work/species/snow-leopards.
22 Global Snow Leopard and Ecosystem Protection Program, "Snow Leopard Habitat," accessed January 10, 2017, www.globalsnowleopard.org/the-snowleopard/cat-facts/snow-leopard-habitat.
23 A member of the IUCN review team. Pers. comm.
24 Barney Long and Brad Rutherford, "Why Snow Leopards Are in Trouble," November 13, 2015, http://edition.cnn.com/2015/11/13/opinions/long-rutherford-snow-leopards.
25 Tom McCarthy, "Big Cats on the Roof of the World: Protecting Asia's Elusive Snow Leopards," January 26, 2016, http://edition.cnn.com/2016/01/24/asia/asia-snow-leopards.
26 Emily Gertz (2016) writes, "Gustaf Samelius, assistant scientific director of Snow Leopard Trust, lauded *Snow Leopards* as 'a fantastic source of information put together' but said that the authors of the book's population estimate chapter 'have been a little uncritical at how they arrived at the numbers.' While some of the data were gathered via tracking, camera trapping, or genetic sampling of snow leopard fecal samples, the studies are being conducted across too small an extent of the cat's range to justify the higher population estimate, he said. The rest is still guesswork, even if it comes from people working on the ground in snow leopard range states. 'I teach a wildlife biology conservation class,' Samelius said. 'We talk about estimating abundance a lot. I tell them, 'We can land on the moon, but we have a very hard time estimating abundance of animals.'"
27 "Statement of Concern Regarding the Status of the Snow Leopard on the IUCN Red List," August 24–25, 2017, www.globalsnowleopard.org/blog/2017/09/26/statement-of-concern-regarding-the-status-of-the-snow-leopard-on-the-iucn-red-list.
28 Ikram Junaidi, "Only 200 Snow Leopards Left in Pakistan," *Dawn*, updated June 22, 2016, https://www.dawn.com/news/1266413.

29 Snow Leopard Trust, "Statement on IUCN Red List Status Change of the Snow Leopard," September 14, 2017, https://www.snowleopard.org/statement-iucn-red-list-status-change-snow-leopard.

30 They however later made an amendment to their claim by saying that this was the population detected in the best snow leopard habitat in the country.

31 The author of this unpublished report has also claimed to have conducted a survey of nine thousand households in Giglit-Baltistan. Just for the sake of comparison, when the government of Pakistan conducts its House Income Expenditure survey of all of Pakistan, it interviewed close to eighteen thousand households.

32 The GSLEP is viewed as bringing much-needed funds for snow leopard conservation. According to the report, "The Snow Leopard Trust estimates that NGOs and multilaterals contribute less than US$8 million per year directly to snow leopard conservation" (GSLEP 2013, x). GSLEP is likely to raise that amount, and it is estimated that about US$200 million will be spent for snow leopard conservation, directly or indirectly over the next seven years.

CONCLUSION

1 The Anthropocene discussed as a geological epoch calls for a coexistence approach (Corlett 2015).

2 The protected areas, or wilderness, approach is already doomed because not only do people disobey geographical and ecological boundaries but animals do not adhere to them either. This is the point made by Bruno Latour in his famous proposition that we have never been modern. He argues that if success at keeping nature and culture apart is the marker of the modern era, then we have never been modern because we have not able to keep them separate (Latour 2012).

REFERENCES

Adams, William, and Jon Hutton. 2007. "People, Parks and Poverty: Political Ecology and Biodiversity Conservation." *Conservation and Society* 5 (2): 147–83.

Aflalo, Frederick George, ed. 1904. *The Sportsman's Book for India*. London: Horace Marshall & Son.

African Wildlife Foundation. 2005. "Human Wildlife Conflict: Lessons Learned from AWF's African Heartlands." AWF Working Paper.

Agrawal, Arun, and Kent Redford. 2009. "Conservation and Displacement: An Overview." *Conservation and Society* 7 (1): 1. https://doi.org/10.4103/0972-4923.54790.

Ahmed, Javed, and Shoaib Sultan Khan. 1998. "Investment in People—A Key to Enhance Sustainability: Lessons from Northern Pakistan." *Enhancing Sustainability: Resources for Our Future*. Sustainable Use Initiative Technical Series, vol. 1. Edited by Hendrik A. Van Der Linde and Melissa H. Danskin. Gland, Switzerland: International Union of Conservation of Nature.

AKRSP (Aga Khan Rural Support Program). 1993. Eleventh Annual Review. Gilgit. Aga Khan Rural Support Programme.

———. 1996. Fourteenth Annual Review. Gilgit. Aga Khan Rural Support Programme.

Ale, Som. 2012. "Pangje." In *Snow Leopard: Stories from the Roof of the World*, edited by Don Hunter, 121–28. Boulder: University Press of Colorado.

Ale, S. B., and C. Mishra. 2018. "The Snow Leopard's Questionable Comeback." *Science* 359, no. 6380 (March 9, 2018):110. doi: 10.1126/science.aas9893.

Alexander, Justine S., Arjun M. Gopalaswamy, Kun Shi, and Philip Riordan. 2015. "Face Value: Towards Robust Estimates of Snow Leopard Densities." Edited by Antoni Margalida. *PLoS ONE* 10 (8): e0134815. https://doi.org/10.1371/journal.pone.0134815.

Alexander, Justine Shanti, Arjun M. Gopalaswamy, Kun Shi, Joelene Hughes, and Philip Riordan. 2016. "Patterns of Snow Leopard Site Use in an Increasingly Human-Dominated Landscape." Edited by Elissa Z. Cameron. *PLoS ONE* 11 (5): e0155309. https://doi.org/10.1371/journal.pone.0155309.

Allsen, Thomas T. 2006. *The Royal Hunt in Eurasian History*. Philadelphia: University of Pennsylvania Press.

Anwar, Muhammad Bilal, Rodney Jackson, Muhammad Sajid Nadeem, Jan E. Janečka, Shafqat Hussain, Mirza Azhar Beg, Ghulam Muhammad, and Mazhar Qayyum. 2011. "Food Habits of the Snow Leopard Panthera Uncia (Schreber, 1775) in Baltistan, Northern Pakistan." *European Journal of Wildlife Research* 57 (5): 1077–83. https://doi.org/10.1007/s10344-011-0521-2.

Bagchi, Sumanta, and Charudutt Mishra. 2006. "Living with Large Carnivores: Predation on Livestock by the Snow Leopard (*Uncia Uncia*)." *Journal of Zoology* 268 (3): 217–24. https://doi.org/10.1111/j.1469-7998.2005.00030.x.

Bairnsfather, Peter Robert. 1914. *Sport and Nature in the Himalayas*. London: Harrison & Sons.

Barua, Maan, Shonil A. Bhagwat, and Sushrut Jadhav. 2013. "The Hidden Dimensions of Human-Wildlife Conflict: Health Impacts, Opportunity and Transaction Costs." *Biological Conservation* 157 (January): 309–16. https://doi.org/10.1016/j.biocon.2012.07.014.

Benson, Etienne. 2010. *Wired Wilderness: Technologies of Tracking and the Making of Modern Wildlife*. Baltimore: Johns Hopkins University Press.

Beschta, Robert L., and William J. Ripple. 2009. "Large Predators and Trophic Cascades in Terrestrial Ecosystems of the Western United States." *Biological Conservation* 142 (11): 2401–14. https://doi.org/10.1016/j.biocon.2009.06.015.

Bininda-Emonds, Olaf R. P., Denise M. Decker-Flum, John L. Gittleman. 2001. "The Utility of Chemical Signals as Phylogenetic Characters: An Example from the Felidae." *Biological Journal of the Linnean Society* 72 (1): 1–15. https://doi.org/10.1006/bijl.2000.0492.

Bird-David, Nurit. 1990. "The Giving Environment: Another Perspective on the Economic System of Gatherer-Hunters." *Current Anthropology* 31 (2): 189–96.

Blaikie, Piers M. 1985. *The Political Economy of Soil Erosion in Developing Countries*. New York: Longman.

Bloch, Maurice. 1995. "People into Places: Zafimaniry Concepts of Clarity." In *The Anthropology of Landscape: Perspectives on Place and Space*, edited by Eric Hirsch and Michael O'Hanlon. Oxford Studies in Social and Cultural Anthropology. New York: Oxford University Press.

Blomqvist, Leif. 1980. "Population and a Review of the Breeding Results During the 1970s." In *The Annual Report of the Captive Snow Leopard (Panthera Uncia)*, edited by Leif Blomqvist, 32–50. Helsinki, Finland: Helsinki Zoo.

———, ed. 1998. *International Pedigree Book of Snow Leopards 5, Panthera uncia*. Helsinki, Finland: Helsinki Zoo.

Bocci, Anna, Sandro Lovari, Muhammad Zafar Khan, and Emiliano Mori. 2017. "Sympatric Snow Leopards and Tibetan Wolves: Coexistence of Large Carnivores with Human-Driven Potential Competition." *European Journal of Wildlife Research* 63 (6). https://doi.org/10.1007/s10344-017-1151-0.

Boitani, Luigi. 1992. "Wolf Research and Conservation in Italy." *Biological Conservation* 61 (2): 125–32. https://doi.org/10.1016/0006-3207(92)91102-X.

Boomgaard, P. 2001. *Frontiers of Fear: Tigers and People in the Malay World, 1600–1950*. Yale Agrarian Studies Series. New Haven, CT: Yale University Press.

Bradshaw, John W. S. 2006. "The Evolutionary Basis for the Feeding Behavior of Domestic Dogs (*Canis familiaris*) and Cats (*Felis catus*)." *Journal of Nutrition* 136 (7): 1927S–1931S. https://doi.org/10.1093/jn/136.7.1927S.

Breitenmoser, Urs. 1998. "Large Predators in the Alps: The Fall and Rise of Man's Competitors." *Biological Conservation* 83 (3): 279–89. https://doi.org/10.1016/S0006-3207(97)00084-0.

Brockington, Dan. 2002. *Fortress Conservation: The Preservation of the Mkomazi Game Reserve, Tanzania*. Bloomington: Indiana University Press.

Brockington, Dan, Rosaleen Duffy, and Jim Igoe. 2008. *Nature Unbound: Conservation, Capitalism and the Future of Protected Areas*. Sterling, VA: Earthscan.

Bruce, Charles Granville. 1910. *Twenty Years in the Himalayas*. London: Edward Arnold.

Bruner, A. G. 2001. "Effectiveness of Parks in Protecting Tropical Biodiversity." *Science* 291 (5501): 125–28. https://doi.org/10.1126/science.291.5501.125.

Burrard, Gerald. 1925. *Big Game Hunting in the Himalayas and Tibet*. London: H. Jenkins Ltd.

Chadwick, Doug. 2008. "Out of the Shadows: The Elusive Central Asian Snow Leopard Steps into a Risk-Filled Future." *National Geographic*, June 2008, 107–29.

Chatterjee, Partha. 2004. *The Politics of the Governed: Reflections on Popular Politics in Most of the World*. Leonard Hastings Schoff Memorial Lectures. New York: Columbia University Press.

Chen, Pengju, Yufang Gao, Andy T. L. Lee, Lhaba Cering, Kun Shi, and Susan G. Clark. 2016. "Human-Carnivore Coexistence in Qomolangma (Mt. Everest)

Nature Reserve, China: Patterns and Compensation." *Biological Conservation* 197 (May): 18–26. https://doi.org/10.1016/j.biocon.2016.02.026.

Chetri, Madhu, Morten Odden, and Per Wegge. 2017. "Snow Leopard and Himalayan Wolf: Food Habits and Prey Selection in the Central Himalayas, Nepal." Edited by Marco Festa-Bianchet. *PLoS ONE* 12 (2): e0170549. https://doi.org/10.1371/journal.pone.0170549.

Chundawat, Raghu S., and G. S. Rawat. 1994. "Food Habits of the Snow Leopard in Ladakh, India." In *Proceedings of the Seventh International Snow Leopard Symposium Trust and Northwest Plateau Institute of Biology*, edited by J. L. Fox and D. Jizeng, 127–32. Seattle: International Snow Leopard Trust.

Clark, Susan G., Murray B. Rutherford, and Denise Casey, eds. 2005. *Coexisting with Large Carnivores: Lessons from Greater Yellowstone*. Washington, DC: Island Press.

Coleman, Jon T. 2004. *Vicious: Wolves and Men in America*. New Haven, CT: Yale University Press.

Collet, John. 1884. *A Guide for Visitors to Kashmir: With a Route Map of Kashmir*. Calcutta: W. Newmann & Co.

Corlett, Richard T. 2015. "The Anthropocene Concept in Ecology and Conservation." *Trends in Ecology and Evolution* 30 (1): 36–41. https://doi.org/10.1016/j.tree.2014.10.007.

Craighead, John, J., and Frank C. Craighead Jr. 1971. "Grizzly Bear–Man Relationships in Yellowstone National Park." *BioScience* 21 (6):845–57.

Cronon, William. 1992. "A Place for Stories: Nature, History, and Narrative." *Journal of American History* 78 (4): 1347–76. https://doi.org/10.2307/2079346.

———. 1995. "The Trouble with Wilderness: Or, Getting Back to the Wrong Nature." In *Uncommon Ground: Toward Reinventing Nature*, edited by William Cronon, 1st ed. New York: W. W. Norton & Co.

Cunha, F. S. 1997. "Hunting of Rare and Endangered Fauna in the Mountains of Post-Soviet Central Asia." In *Proceedings of the Eighth International Snow Leopard Symposium, November 12–16, 1995*, 110–20. Seattle: International Snow Leopard Trust.

Dani, Ahmad Hasan. 1989. *History of Northern Areas of Pakistan*. Islamabad: National Institute of Historical and Cultural Research.

Darrah, Henry. 1898. *Sport in the Highlands of Kashmir: Being a Narrative of an Eight Months' Trip in Baltistan and Ladak, and a Lady's Experiences in the Latter Country; Together with Hints for the Guidance of Sportsmen*. London: Rowland Ward.

Davis, Brian W., Gang Li, and William J. Murphy. 2010. "Supermatrix and Species Tree Methods Resolve Phylogenetic Relationships within the Big

Cats, Panthera (Carnivora: Felidae)." *Molecular Phylogenetics and Evolution* 56 (1): 64–76. https://doi.org/10.1016/j.ympev.2010.01.036.

Dickman, A. J., E. A. Macdonald, and D. W. Macdonald. 2011. "A Review of Financial Instruments to Pay for Predator Conservation and Encourage Human-Carnivore Coexistence." *Proceedings of the National Academy of Sciences* 108 (34): 13937–44. https://doi.org/10.1073/pnas.1012972108.

Divyabhanusinh. 2002. *The End of a Trail: The Cheetah in India.* Oxford India Paperbacks. New Delhi: Oxford University Press. First published 1995.

———. *The Story of Asia's Lions.* Delhi: Marg, 2008.

Doane, Molly. 2007. "The Political Economy of the Ecological Native." *American Anthropologist* 109 (3): 452–62. https://doi.org/10.1525/aa.2007.109.3.452.

Douglas, Mary. 2005. *Purity and Danger: An Analysis of the Concepts of Pollution and Taboo.* London: Routledge. First published 1966.

Dove, Michael. 2011. *The Banana Tree at the Gate: A History of Marginal Peoples and Global Markets in Borneo.* Yale Agrarian Studies Series. New Haven, CT: Yale University Press.

Dove, Michael R. 1994. "The Existential Status of the Pakistani Farmer: Studying Official Constructions of Social Reality." *Ethnology* 33 (4): 331–51. https://doi.org/10.2307/3773903.

Dove, Michael R., and Mahmudul Huq Khan. 1995. "Competing Constructions of Calamity: The April 1991 Bangladesh Cyclone." *Population and Environment* 16 (5): 445–71. https://doi.org/10.1007/BF02209425.

Dowie, Mark. 2009. *Conservation Refugees: The Hundred-Year Conflict between Global Conservation and Native Peoples.* Cambridge, MA: MIT Press.

Eckholm, Erik. 1976. "Losing Ground." *Environment: Science and Policy for Sustainable Development* 18, no. 3 (1976): 6-11.

Elton, Charles S. 1927. *Animal Ecology.* New York: Macmillan.

Emerson, Richard M. 1983. "Charismatic Kingship: A Study of State-Formation and Authority in Baltistan." *Politics and Society* 12 (4): 413–44. https://doi.org/10.1177/003232928301200401.

Ferretti, Francesco, Sandro Lovari, Isabelle Minder, and Bernardo Pellizzi. 2014. "Recovery of the Snow Leopard in Sagarmatha (Mt. Everest) National Park: Effects on Main Prey." *European Journal of Wildlife Research* 60: 559–62.

Filippi, F. de. 1915. "Expedition to the Karakoram and Central Asia, 1913–1914." *Geographical Journal* 46 (2): 85–99.

Foucault, Michel. 2008. *The Birth of Biopolitics.* Edited by Michael Senellart. Translated by Graham Burchell. New York: Palgrave.

Fox, Joseph L. 1989. "A Review of the Status and Ecology of the Snow Leopard." (Unpublished report.) Seattle: International Snow Leopard Trust.

———. 1994. "Snow Leopard Conservation in the Wild: A Comprehensive Perspective on a Low Density and Highly Fragmented Population." In *Proceedings of the Seventh International Snow Leopard Symposium: Held in Xining, Qinghai, People's Republic of China, July 25–30, 1992*, edited by Joseph L. Fox and Du Jizeng, 3–15. Seattle: International Snow Leopard Trust in Cooperation with the Chicago Zoological Society.

Fox, Joseph L., and Raghunandan S. Chundawat. 1988. "Observations of Snow Leopard Stalking, Killing and Feeding Behavior." *Mammalia* 52 (1): 137–40.

Fox, Joseph L., Satya P. Sinha, Raghunandan S. Chundawat, and Pallav K. Das. 1991. "Status of the Snow Leopard Panthera Uncia in Northwest India." *Biological Conservation* 55 (3): 283–98. https://doi.org/10.1016/0006-3207(91)90033-6.

Francke, August Hermann. 1901. "The Spring Myth of the Kesar-Saga." *Indian Antiquary* 30, 329–41.

Freeman, Helen. 1982. "Characteristics of the Social Behaviour in the Snow Leopard." In *International Pedigree Book of Snow Leopards* 3, edited by Leif Blomqvist, 117–20. Helsinki, Finland: Helsinki Zoo.

———. 1983. "Behavior in Adult Pairs of Captive Snow Leopards (*Panthera Uncia*)." *Zoo Biology* 2 (1): 1–22. https://doi.org/10.1002/zoo.1430020102.

Fretwell, Stephen D. 1987. "Food Chain Dynamics: The Central Theory of Ecology?" *Oikos* 50 (3): 291. https://doi.org/10.2307/3565489.

Gandhi, Ajay. 2012. "Catch Me If You Can: Monkey Capture in Delhi." *Ethnography* 13, no. 1, 43–56.

Gannon, J. R. C. 1932. "A Frontier Tour (Being Extracts from a Diary Written during a Journey Made with H. E. Lord Rawlinson, C.-in-G. in India, through Dir, Chitral, and the Gilgit Agency, in 1923)." *Himalayan Journal* 4.

Geptner, V. G., A. A. Nasimovich, A. G. Bannikov, and Robert S. Hoffmann. 1989. *Mammals of the Soviet Union*. New York: Brill.

Gertz, Emily J. 2016. "A New Snow Leopard Population Estimate Has Scientists on Edge." *TakePart*, July 12, 2016. www.takepart.com/article/2016/07/12/new-snow-leopard-population-estimate-has-scientists-on-edge.

Govindrajan, Radhika. 2018. *Animal Intimacies: Interspecies Relatedness in India's Central Himalayas*. Animal Lives. Chicago: University of Chicago Press.

Greenough, Paul. 2001. "Naturae Ferae: Wild Animals in South Asia and the Standard Environmental Narrative." In *Agrarian Studies: Synthetic Work at the Cutting Edge*, edited by James C. Scott and Nina Bhatt, 141–85. New Haven, CT: Yale University Press.

Grove, Richard. 1990. "The Origins of Environmentalism." *Nature* 345 (6270): 11–14. https://doi.org/10.1038/345011a0.

Guha, Ramachandra. 2003. "The Authoritarian Biologist and the Arrogance of Anti-humanism: Wildlife Conservation in the Third World." In *Battles over Nature: Science and the Politics of Conservation*, edited by Vasant K. Saberwal and Mahesh Rangarajan, 139–57. Delhi: Permanent Black.

Guthman, Julie. 1997. "Representing Crisis: The Theory of Himalayan Environmental Degradation and the Project of Development in Post-Rana Nepal." *Development and Change* 28 (1): 45–69. https://doi.org/10.1111/1467-7660.00034.

Haila, Yrjö, and Peter Taylor. 2001. "The Philosophical Dullness of Classical Ecology, and a Levinsian Alternative." *Biology and Philosophy* 16 (1): 93–102. https://doi.org/10.1023/A:1006632817807.

Hairston, Nelson G., Frederick E. Smith, and Lawrence B. Slobodkin. 1960. "Community Structure, Population Control, and Competition." *American Naturalist* 94 (879): 421–25.

Hathaway, Michael J. 2013. *Environmental Winds: Making the Global in Southwest China*. Berkeley: University of California Press.

Hatkoff, Julianna, Isabella Hatkoff, and Craig Hatkoff. 2010. *Leo the Snow Leopard: The True Story of an Amazing Rescue*. New York: Scholastic Press.

Hayward, Matt, and Michael J. Somers, eds. 2009. *Reintroduction of Top-Order Predators*. Conservation Science and Practice Series, no. 5. Hoboken, NJ: Wiley-Blackwell.

Heptner, V. G., and A. A. Sludskii. 1992. *Mammals of the Soviet Union: Volume 2, Part 2, Carnivora (Hyenas and Cats)*. New York: Brill.

Herda-Rapp, Ann, and Theresa L. Goedeke, eds. 2005. *Mad about Wildlife: Looking at Social Conflict over Wildlife*. Human-Animal Studies, vol. 2. Boston: Brill.

Hill, C., F. Osborn, and A. J. Plumptre. 2002. "Human-Wildlife Conflict: Identifying the Problem and Possible Solutions." 1. Albertine Rift Technical Report Series. New York. Wildlife Conservation Society.

Hillard, Darla. 1989. *Vanishing Tracks: Four Years among the Snow Leopards of Nepal*. New York: William Morrow.

Holling, Crawford S. 1959. "Some Characteristics of Simple Types of Predation and Parasitism." *The Canadian Entomologist* 91, no. 7, 385–98.

Holmern, Tomas, Julius Nyahongo, and Eivin Røskaft. 2007. "Livestock Loss Caused by Predators Outside the Serengeti National Park, Tanzania." *Biological Conservation* 135 (4): 518–26. https://doi.org/10.1016/j.biocon.2006.10.049.

Houghton, H. L. 1913. *Sport and Folklore in the Himalayas*. London: Edward Arnold.

Hughes, Julie E. 2013. *Animal Kingdoms: Hunting, the Environment, and Power in the Indian Princely States*. First Harvard University Press edition. Cambridge, MA: Harvard University Press.

Hunter, Luke. 2011. *Carnivores of the World*. Princeton Field Guides. Princeton, NJ: Princeton University Press.

Hussain, Shafqat. 2000. "Protecting the Snow Leopard and Enhancing Farmers' Livelihoods: A Pilot Insurance Scheme in Baltistan." *Mountain Research and Development* 20 (3): 226–31. https://doi.org/10.1659/0276-4741(2000)020[0226:PTSLAE]2.0.CO;2.

———. 2003. "The Status of the Snow Leopard in Pakistan and Its Conflict with Local Farmers." *Oryx* 37 (1). https://doi.org/10.1017/S0030605303000085.

———. 2012. "Forms of Predation: Tiger and Markhor Hunting in Colonial Governance." *Modern Asian Studies* 46 (5): 1212–38.

———. 2015. *Remoteness and Modernity: Transformation and Continuity in Northern Pakistan*. Yale Agrarian Studies Series. New Haven, CT: Yale University Press.

Igoe, Jim. 2010. "The Spectacle of Nature in the Global Economy of Appearances: Anthropological Engagements with the Spectacular Mediations of Transnational Conservation." *Critique of Anthropology* 30 (4): 375–97. https://doi.org/10.1177/0308275X10372468.

Igoe, Jim, and Dan Brockington. 2007. "Neoliberal Conservation: A Brief Introduction." *Conservation and Society* 5 (4): 432–49.

Ikeda, Naho. 2004. "Economic Impacts of Livestock Depredation by Snow Leopard *Uncia uncia* in the Kanchenjunga Conservation Area, Nepal Himalaya." *Environmental Conservation* 31 (4): 322–30. https://doi.org/10.1017/S0376892904001778.

Jackson, R., D. Mallon, T. McCarthy, R. A. Chundaway, and B. Habib. 2008. "*Panthera Uncia*." In *IUCN Red List of Threatened Species. Version*. e.T22732A9381126. http://dx.doi.org/10.2305/IUCN.UK.2008.RLTS.T22732A9381126.en.

Jackson, Rodney, comp. 2002. "Snow Leopard Status, Distribution and Protected Areas Coverage: A Report." In *Contributed Papers to the Snow Leopard Survival Strategy Summit*, 79–103. Los Gatos: International Snow Leopard Trust.

Jackson, Rodney, and Gary Ahlborn. 1989. "Snow Leopards (*Panthera Uncia*) in Nepal: Home Range and Movements." *National Geographic Research* 5 (2): 161–75.

Jackson, Rodney, Gary Ahlborn, Gurung Mahesh, and Ale Som. 1996. "Reducing Livestock Depredation Losses in the Nepalese Himalaya." In *Proceedings of the Seventeenth Vertebrate Pest Conference 1996*. 30. Edited by Robert M. Timm, and A. Charles Crabb. Davis: University of California. http://digitalcommons.unl.edu/vpc17/30.

Jackson, Rodney, and Don O. Hunter. 1996. "Snow Leopard Survey and Conservation Handbook." Seattle, Washington, and Fort Collins Science Center, Colorado: International Snow Leopard Trust and U.S. Geological Survey. http://snowleopardconservancy.org/pdf/SL_Survey_Cons_Hand book_Part_1.pdf.

Jackson, Rodney M., Jerry D. Roe, Rinchen Wangchuk, and Don O. Hunter. 2006. "Estimating Snow Leopard Population Abundance Using Photography and Capture-Recapture Techniques." *Wildlife Society Bulletin* 34 (3): 772–81. https://doi.org/10.2193/0091-7648(2006)34[772:ESLPAU]2.0.CO;2.

Jacoby, Karl. 2001. *Crimes against Nature: Squatters, Poachers, Thieves, and the Hidden History*. Berkeley: University of California Press.

Jalais, Annu. 2011. *Forest of Tigers: People, Politics and Environment in the Sundarbans*. New Delhi: Routledge.

Janečka, Jan E., R. Jackson, Z. Yuquang, L. Diqiang, B. Munkhtsog, V. Buckley-Beason, and W. J. Murphy. 2008. "Population Monitoring of Snow Leopards Using Noninvasive Collection of Scat Samples: A Pilot Study." *Animal Conservation* 11 (5): 401–11. https://doi.org/10.1111/j.1469-1795.2008.00195.x.

Janečka, Jan E., Yuguang Zhang, Diqiang Li, Bariushaa Munkhtsog, Munkhtsog Bayaraa, Naranbaatar Galsandorj, Tshewang R. Wangchuk, et al. 2017. "Range-Wide Snow Leopard Phylogeography Supports Three Subspecies." *Journal of Heredity* 108 (6): 597–607. https://doi.org/10.1093/jhered/esx044.

Jettmar, Karl. 2002. *Beyond the Gorges of the Indus: Archaeology before Excavation*. Oxford University Press.

Johansson, Örjan, Tom McCarthy, Gustaf Samelius, Henrik Andrén, Lkhagvasumberel Tumursukh, and Charudutt Mishra. 2015. "Snow Leopard Predation in a Livestock Dominated Landscape in Mongolia." *Biological Conservation* 184 (April): 251–58. https://doi.org/10.1016/j.biocon.2015.02.003.

Johansson, Örjan, Geir Rune Rauset, Gustaf Samelius, Tom McCarthy, Henrik Andrén, Lkhagvasumberel Tumursukh, and Charudutt Mishra. 2016. "Land Sharing Is Essential for Snow Leopard Conservation." *Biological Conservation* 203 (November): 1–7. https://doi.org/10.1016/j.biocon.2016.08.034.

Johansson, Tino. 2009. *Beasts on Fields: Human-Wildlife Conflicts in Nature-Culture Borderlands*. Saarbrucken: VDM Verlag.

Kellert, Stephen R., Matthew Black, Colleen Reid Rush, and Alistair J. Bath. 1996. "Human Culture and Large Carnivore Conservation in North America." *Conservation Biology* 10 (4): 977–90. https://doi.org/10.1046/j.1523-1739.1996.10040977.x.

Kennion, R. L. 1910. *Sport and Life in the Further Himalayas*. London: William Blackwood.

Khalaf, Norman Ali B. 1988. "Activity Patterns and Reproductive Behaviour of Snow Leopards, *Panthera Uncia* (Schreber, 1775) at Jersey Wildlife Preservation Trust, Jersey Island." In *International Pedigree Book of Snow Leopards 5, Panthera uncia*, edited by Leif Blomqvist, 61–71. Helsinki, Finland: Helsinki Zoo.

Khan, Muhammad Zafar, Babar Khan, Saeed Awan, Garee Khan, and Rehmat Ali. 2013. "High-Altitude Rangelands and Their Interfaces in Gilgit-Baltistan, Pakistan: Current Status and Management Strategies." In *High-Altitude Rangelands and Their Interfaces in the Hindu Kush*, edited by Wu Ning, Gopal S. Rawat, Srijana Joshi, Muhammad Ismail, Eklabya Sharma, 66–77. Kathmandu: International Centre for Integrated Mountain Development.

Khatiwada, Janak Raj, Mukesh Chalise, and Randall Kyes. 2007. "Survey of Snow Leopard (*Uncia uncia*) and Blue Sheep (*Pseudois nayaur*) Populations in the Kangchenjunga Conservation Area (KCA), Nepal." Seattle: Snow Leopard Trust. http://snowleopardnetwork.org/bibliography/KhatiwadaFinal07.pdf.

Kinloch, Brig-General Alexander A. A. 1892. *Large Game Shooting in Thibet, the Himalayas, Northern and Central India*. Calcutta: Thacker, Spink and Co.

Kitchener, S. L., D. A. Meritt, and M. A. Rosenthal. 1975. "Observations on the Breeding and Husbandry of Snow leopards at Lincoln Park Zoo, Chicago." *International Zoo Yearbook* 15, no. 1, 212–17.

Knight, John. 1999. "Monkeys on the Move: The Natural Symbolism of People-Macaque Conflict in Japan." *Journal of Asian Studies* 58 (3): 622–47. https://doi.org/10.2307/2659114.

———. 2000. Introduction to *Natural Enemies: People-Wildlife Conflicts in Anthropological Perspective*, edited by John Knight, 1–35. London: Routledge.

Koenigsmarck, Count Hans Von. 1910. *The Markhor: Sport in Cashmere*. London: Kegan Paul, Trench, Trubner & Co Ltd.

Kohler, Alex. 2000. "Half-Man, Half-Elephant: Shapeshifting among the Baka of Congo." In *Natural Enemies: People-Wildlife Conflicts in Anthropological Perspective*, edited by John Knight, 50–77. London: Routledge.

Koshkarev, E. P. 1990. "The Environment-Related Stability of Snow Leopard (*Uncia uncia*) Populations in Connection with Its Location in the Natural Habitats and Chances for Spread within the USSR." In *International Pedigree Book of Snow Leopards 6*, edited by Leif Blomqvist, 37–50. Helsinki, Finland: Helsinki Zoo.

———. 1994. "Poaching in the Former USSR." *Snow Line, Bulletin of International Snow Leopard Trust* 12 (2): 6–7.

Lamarque, F., J. Anderson, R. Fergusson, M. Lagrange, Y. Ose-Owusu, L. Bakker. 2009. "Human-Wildlife Conflict in Africa Causes, Consequences and Management Strategies." FAO Forestry Paper 157. Rome: Food and Agriculture Organization of the United Nations.

Latour, Bruno. 2012. *We Have Never Been Modern*. Translated by Catherine Porter. N.p.: Crypt Publishing. First published 1993.

Lawrence, Walter. 1895. *The Valley of Kashmir*. London: Henry Frowde.

Leopold, Aldo. (1949) 1990. *A Sand County Almanac: With Essays on Conservation from Round River*. New York: Ballentine Books.

Lewis, Michael L. 2004. *Inventing Global Ecology: Tracking the Biodiversity Ideal in India, 1947-1997*. Ohio University Press Series in Ecology and History. Athens: Ohio University Press.

Lhagvasuren, B., and B. Munkhtsog. 2000. "The Yak Population in Mongolia and Its Relation with Snow Leopards as a Prey Species." In *Yak Production in Central Asian Highlands: Proceedings of the Third International Congress on Yak Held in Lhasa, P. R. China, 4–9 September*, edited by H. Jianlin, C. Richard, O. Hanotte, C. McVeigh, and J. E. O. Rege, 69–75. Nairobi, Kenya: International Livestock Research Institute.

Li, Juan, Thomas M. McCarthy, Hao Wang, Byron V. Weckworth, George B. Schaller, Charudutt Mishra, Zhi Lu, and Steven R. Beissinger. 2016. "Climate Refugia of Snow Leopards in High Asia." *Biological Conservation* 203 (November): 188–96. https://doi.org/10.1016/j.biocon.2016.09.026.

Liao, Y, and B. Tan. 1988. "A Preliminary Study of the Geographic Distribution of Snow Leopards in China." In *Proceedings of the Fifth International Snow Leopard Symposium*, edited by H. Freeman, 32–40. Seattle: International Snow Leopard Trust and Wildlife Institute of India.

Linnell, John D. C., Urs Breitenmoser, Christine Breitenmoser-Würsten, John Odden, and Manuela von Arx. 2009. "Recovery of Eurasian Lynx in Europe: What Part Has Reintroduction Played?" In *Reintroduction of Top-Order Predators*, edited by Matt W. Hayward and Michael J. Somers, 72–91. Oxford, UK: Wiley-Blackwell. https://doi.org/10.1002/9781444312034.ch4.

Linnell, John D. C., Jon E. Swenson, and Reidar Anderson. 2001. "Predators and People: Conservation of Large Carnivores Is Possible at High Human

Densities If Management Policy Is Favourable." In *Animal Conservation Forum* 4, no. 4, 345–49.

Lobsang, Ghulam Hussain. 1997. *Tarik-e-Bon Falsafa Aur Baltistan, Ladakh Aur Tibet Ka Fikri Khulasa*. Lahore: Vanguard Books.

Locher, Fabien, and Grégory Quenet. 2009. "L'histoire environnementale: origines, enjeux et perspectives d'un nouveau chantier." *Revue d'histoire moderne et contemporaine* 4, no. 56–4, 7–38. https://doi.org/10.3917/rhmc.564.0007.

Lopez, Barry Holstun. (1978) 2004. *Of Wolves and Men*. New York: Scribner Classics.

Lorimer, D. L. R. 1931. "An Oral Version of the Kesar Saga from Hunza." *Folklore* 42 (2): 105–40. https://doi.org/10.1080/0015587X.1931.9718395.

Lovari, S., R. Boesi, I. Minder, N. Mucci, E. Randi, A. Dematteis, and S. B. Ale. 2009. "Restoring a Keystone Predator May Endanger a Prey Species in a Human-Altered Ecosystem: The Return of the Snow Leopard to Sagarmatha National Park." *Animal Conservation* 12 (6): 559–70. https://doi.org/10.1111/j.1469-1795.2009.00285.x.

Lowe, Celia. 2006. *Wild Profusion: Biodiversity Conservation in an Indonesian Archipelago*. Information Series. Princeton, NJ: Princeton University Press.

Lydekker, Richard. 1896. *A Hand Book to the Carnivora. Part 1. Cats, Civets, and Mongooses*. London: Edward Lloyd, Ltd.

Lyngdoh, Salvador, Shivam Shrotriya, Surendra P. Goyal, Hayley Clements, Matthew W. Hayward, and Bilal Habib. 2014. "Prey Preferences of the Snow Leopard (*Panthera Uncia*): Regional Diet Specificity Holds Global Significance for Conservation." Edited by Cédric Sueur. *PLoS ONE* 9 (2): e88349. https://doi.org/10.1371/journal.pone.0088349.

MacArthur, Robert H., and Edward O. Wilson. 1967. *The Theory of Island Biogeography*. Princeton, NJ: Princeton University Press.

MacDonald, Kenneth. 2004. "Developing 'Nature': Global Ecology and the Politics of Conservation in Northern Pakistan." In *Confronting Environments: Local Environmental Understanding in a Globalizing World*, edited by J. G. Carrier, 71–96. Walnut Creek, CA: Alta Mira Press.

Macintyre, Donald. 1889. *Hindu-Koh: Wanderings and Wild Sports on and Beyond the Himalayas*. London: William Blackwood and Sons.

MacKenzie, John M. 1988. *The Empire of Nature: Hunting, Conservation, and British Imperialism*. Studies in Imperialism. Manchester, UK: Manchester University Press. Distributed exclusively in the USA by St. Martin's Press.

MacKinnon, John Ramsay, and Kathy MacKinnon. 1986. *Review of the Protected Areas System in the Indo-Malayan Realm*. Gland, Switzerland: IUCN.

Madhusudan, M. D. 2003. "Living Amidst Large Wildlife: Livestock and Crop Depredation by Large Mammals in the Interior Villages of Bhadra Tiger Reserve, South India." *Environmental Management* 31 (4): 466–75. https://doi.org/10.1007/s00267-002-2790-8.

Mallon, David. 1984. "The Snow Leopard, *Panthera Uncia*, in Mongolia." In *International Pedigree Book of Snow Leopards 4*, edited by Leif Blomqvist, 3–9. Helsinki, Finland: Helsinki Zoo.

Malm, Andreas, and Alf Hornborg. 2014. "The Geology of Mankind? A Critique of the Anthropocene Narrative." *Anthropocene Review* 1 (1): 62–69. https://doi.org/10.1177/2053019613516291.

Mangan, J. A. 1986. *The Games Ethic and Imperialism: Aspects of the Diffusion of an Ideal*. Sport in the Global Society 2. Portland, OR: F. Cass.

Markham, Frederick. 1854. *Shooting in the Himalayas: A Journal of Sporting Adventures and Travel in Chinese Tartary, Ladac, Thibet, Cashmere, &c.* London: R. Bentley.

Matthiessen, Peter. (1978) 2008. *The Snow Leopard*. Penguin Classics. New York: Penguin.

Mauss, Marcel. 2011. *The Gift: Forms and Functions of Exchange in Archaic Societies*. Mansfield Centre, CT: Martino Publishing. First published 1925.

McCarthy, Kyle P., Todd K. Fuller, Ma Ming, Thomas M. McCarthy, Lisette Waits, and Kubanych Jumabaev. 2008. "Assessing Estimators of Snow Leopard Abundance." *Journal of Wildlife Management* 72 (8): 1826–33. https://doi.org/10.2193/2008-040.

McCarthy, Thomas M. 1999. "Snow Leopard Conservation Plan for the Republic of Mongolia." www.snowleopardnetwork.org/bibliography/McCarthy_1999.pdf.

McCarthy, Thomas M., and Guillame Chapron. 2003. "Snow Leopard Survival Strategy." Seattle: ISLT and SLN.

McCarthy, Thomas, David Mallon, Eric Sanderson, Peter Zahler, and K. Fisher. 2016. "What Is a Snow Leopard? Biogeography and Status Overview." In *Snow Leopards: Biodiversity of the World: Conservation from Genes to Landscape*, edited by Thomas McCarthy and David Mallon, 23–42. San Diego: Academic Press. https://doi.org/10.1016/B978-0-12-802213-9.00003-1.

McLaren, B. E., and R. O. Peterson. 1994. "Wolves, Moose, and Tree Rings on Isle Royale." *Science* 266 (5190): 1555–58. https://doi.org/10.1126/science.266.5190.1555.

Medina, Laurie Kroshus. 2015. "Governing through the Market: Neoliberal Environmental Government in Belize." *American Anthropologist* 117 (2): 272–84. https://doi.org/10.1111/aman.12228.

Mikhail, Alan. 2013. "Unleashing the Beast: Animals, Energy, and the Economy of Labor in Ottoman Egypt." *The American Historical Review* 118, no. 2, 317–48.

———. 2016. *The Animal in Ottoman Egypt.* Oxford: Oxford University Press.

Milton, Kay. 2000. "Ducks out of Water: Nature Conservation as Boundary Maintenance." In *Natural Enemies: People-Wildlife Conflicts in Anthropological Perspective*, edited by John Knight, 229–46. London: Routledge.

Mock, John. 2018. "Khandut Revisited: Monuments, Shrines, and Newly Discovered Rock Art in Wakhan District." *Afghanistan* 1 (2): 282–301. https://doi.org/10.3366/afg.2018.0018.

Namgail, Tsewang, Joseph L. Fox, and Yash Veer Bhatnagar. 2007. "Carnivore-Caused Livestock Mortality in Trans-Himalaya." *Environmental Management* 39 (4): 490–96. https://doi.org/10.1007/s00267-005-0178-2.

Naqvi, A. N., and K. Fatima. 2012. "Incidence of Livestock Diseases in Nomal and Naltar Valleys Gilgit, Pakistan." *Pakistan Journal of Agricultural Research* 25 (1): 69–75.

Nash, Roderick, and Char Miller. 2014. *Wilderness and the American Mind*, 5th ed. New Haven, CT: Yale University Press.

Neumann, Roderick P. 2002. *Imposing Wilderness: Struggles over Livelihood and Nature Preservation in Africa*. California Studies in Critical Human Geography 4. Berkeley: University of California Press.

Nowell, Kristin, Peter Jackson, and IUCN/SSC Cat Specialist Group, comp. and eds. 1996. *Wild Cats: Status Survey and Conservation Action Plan.* IUCN/SSC Action Plans for the Conservation of Biological Diversity. Gland, Switzerland: IUCN.

Nowell, Kristin, Juan Li, Mikhail Paltsyn, and Rishi Kumar Sharma. 2016. *An Ounce of Prevention: Snow Leopard Crime Revisited.* Cambridge, UK: TRAFFIC.

Nyhus, Philip J., Steve A. Osofsky, Paul Ferraro, H. Fischer, and Francine Madden. 2005. "Bearing the Costs of Human-Wildlife Conflict: The Challenges of Compensation Schemes." *Faculty Scholarship* 15. http://digitalcommons.colby.edu/faculty_scholarship/15.

Nyhus, Philip J., and Ronald Tilson. 2004. "Characterizing Human-Tiger Conflict in Sumatra, Indonesia: Implications for Conservation." *Oryx* 38 (1): 68–74. https://doi.org/10.1017/S0030605304000110.

Odden, J, M. E. Smith, R. Aanes, and J. E. Swenson. 1999. "Large Carnivores That Kill Livestock: Do 'Problem Individuals' Really Exist?" *Wildlife Society Bulletin (1973-2006)* 27 (3): 698–705.

Oelschlaeger, Max. 1991. *The Idea of Wilderness: From Prehistory to the Age of Ecology.* New Haven, CT: Yale University Press.

Ogada, Mordecai O., Rosie Woodroffe, Nicholas O. Oguge, and Laurence G. Frank. 2003. "Limiting Depredation by African Carnivores: The Role of Livestock Husbandry." *Conservation Biology* 17 (6): 1521–30. https://doi.org /10.1111/j.1523-1739.2003.00061.x.

Ogra, Monica, and Ruchi Badola. 2008. "Compensating Human–Wildlife Conflict in Protected Area Communities: Ground-Level Perspectives from Uttarakhand, India." *Human Ecology* 36 (5): 717–29. https://doi.org/10.1007 /s10745-008-9189-y.

Oli, Madan K., Iain R. Taylor, and D. M. E. Rogers. 1993. "Diet of the Snow Leopard (*Panthera Uncia*) in the Annapurna Conservation Area, Nepal." *Journal of Zoology* 231 (3): 365–70. https://doi.org/10.1111/j.1469-7998.1993 .tb01924.x.

Oli, Madan K., Iain R. Taylor, and M. Elizabeth Rogers. 1994. "Snow Leopard *Panthera uncia* Predation of Livestock: An Assessment of Local Perceptions in the Annapurna Conservation Area, Nepal." *Biological Conservation* 68 (1): 63–68. https://doi.org/10.1016/0006-3207(94)90547-9.

Orlove, Benjamin S., and Stephen B. Brush. 1996. "Anthropology and the Conservation of Biodiversity." *Annual Review of Anthropology* 25 (1): 329–52. https://doi.org/10.1146/annurev.anthro.25.1.329.

Pandian, Anand S. 2001. "Predatory Care: The Imperial Hunt in Mughal and British India." *Journal of Historical Sociology* 14 (1): 79–107. https://doi.org /10.1111/1467-6443.00135.

Pandian, M. S. S. 1995. "Gendered Negotiations: Hunting and Colonialism in the Late 19th Century Nilgiris." *Contributions to Indian Sociology* 29 (1–2): 239–63. https://doi.org/10.1177/006996679502900101 2.

Peterson, M. Nils, Jessie L. Birckhead, Kirsten Leong, Markus J. Peterson, and Tarla Rai Peterson. 2010. "Rearticulating the Myth of Human-Wildlife Conflict." *Conservation Letters* 3 (2): 74–82. https://doi.org/10.1111/j.1755-263X .2010.00099.x.

Pluskowski, Aleks. 2010. "The Zooarchaeology of Medieval 'Christendom': Ideology, the Treatment of Animals and the Making of Medieval Europe." *World Archaeology* 42 (2): 201–14. https://doi.org/10.1080/004382410036 72815.

Quammen, David. 2003. *Monster of God: The Man-Eating Predator in the Jungles of History and the Mind*. New York: W. W. Norton.

Rajaratnam, Rajanathan, Karl Vernes, and Tiger Sangay. 2016. "A Review of Livestock Predation by Large Carnivores in the Himalayan Kingdom of Bhutan." In *Problematic Wildlife: A Cross-Disciplinary Approach*, edited by Francesco M. Angelici, 143–71. New York: Springer International Publishing.

Rangan, Haripriya. 2000. *Of Myths and Movements: Rewriting Chipko into Himalayan History*. New York: Verso.

Rangarajan, Mahesh. 1999. *Fencing the Forest: Conservation and Ecological Change in India's Central Provinces, 1860–1914*. Studies in Social Ecology and Environmental History. Delhi: Oxford University Press.

———. 2004. "The Raj and the Natural World: The War against Dangerous Beasts in Colonial India." In *Wildlife in Asia: Cultural Perspectives*, edited by John Knight, 207–32. New York: Routledge.

Rashkow, Ezra D. 2014. "Making Subaltern *Shikaris*: Histories of the Hunted in Colonial Central India." *South Asian History and Culture* 5 (3): 292–313. https://doi.org/10.1080/19472498.2014.905324.

Ray, Justina C. 2005. "Large Carnivorous Animals as Tools for Conserving Biodiversity: Assumptions and Uncertainties." In *Large Carnivores and the Conservation of Biodiversity*, edited by Justina C. Ray, Kent Redford, Robert Steneck, and Joel Berger, 34–56. Washington, DC: Island Press.

Ripple, W. J., J. A. Estes, R. L. Beschta, C. C. Wilmers, E. G. Ritchie, M. Hebblewhite, J. Berger, et al. 2014. "Status and Ecological Effects of the World's Largest Carnivores." *Science* 343 (6167). https://doi.org/10.1126/science.1241484.

Ritvo, Harriet. 1987. *The Animal Estate: The English and Other Creatures in the Victorian Age*. Cambridge, MA: Harvard University Press.

Robbins, Paul. 2012. *Political Ecology: A Critical Introduction*. 2nd ed. Critical Introductions to Geography. Malden, MA: J. Wiley & Sons. First published 2004.

Roberts, Tom J. 1997. *The Mammals of Pakistan*. Rev. ed. Karachi: Oxford University Press.

Rosen, Tatjana, Shafqat Hussain, Ghulam Mohammad, Rodney Jackson, Jan E. Janečka, and Stefan Michel. 2012. "Reconciling Sustainable Development of Mountain Communities with Large Carnivore Conservation: Lessons from Pakistan." *Mountain Research and Development* 32 (3): 286–93. https://doi.org/10.1659/MRD-JOURNAL-D-12-00008.1.

Røskaft, Eivin, Angela Mwakatobe, and Julius Nyahongo. 2013. "Livestock Depredation by Carnivores in the Serengeti Ecosystem, Tanzania." *Environment and Natural Resources Research* 3 (4). https://doi.org/10.5539/enrr.v3n4p46.

Rothfels, Nigel. 2002. *Savages and Beasts: The Birth of the Modern Zoo*. Baltimore: Johns Hopkins University Press.

Rundall, Lieut. Lionel Bickerseth. 1915. *The Ibex of Sha-Ping and Other Himalayan Studies*. London: Macmillian.

Saberwal, Vasant K., James P. Gibbs, Ravi Chellam, and A. J. T. Johnsingh. 1994. "Lion-Human Conflict in the Gir Forest, India." *Conservation Biology* 8 (2): 501–7. https://doi.org/10.1046/j.1523-1739.1994.08020501.x.

Sanderson, Eric, Jessica Forrest, Colby Loucks, Joshua Ginsberg, Eric Dinerstein, John Seidensticker, and Peter Leimgruber et al. 2010. "Setting Priorities for Tiger Conservation: 2005–2015." In *Tigers of the World: The Science Politics, and Conservation of Panthera tigris*, 2nd ed., edited by Ronald Tilson and Philip J. Nyhus, 143–61. Norwich, NY: William Andrew Publishing.

Schadt, Stephanie, Eloy Revilla, Thorsten Wiegand, Felix Knauer, Petra Kaczensky, Urs Breitenmoser, Luděk Bufka, et al. 2002. "Assessing the Suitability of Central European Landscapes for the Reintroduction of Eurasian Lynx: Lynx Habitat Suitability." *Journal of Applied Ecology* 39 (2): 189–203. https://doi.org/10.1046/j.1365-2664.2002.00700.x.

Schaller, George B. 1988. *Stones of Silence: Journeys in the Himalaya*. Chicago: University of Chicago Press.

Schaller, George B., Ren Junrang, and Qiu Mingjiang. 1988. "Status of the Snow Leopard *Panthera uncia* in Qinghai and Gansu Provinces, China." *Biological Conservation* 45 (3): 179–94. https://doi.org/10.1016/0006-3207(88)90138-3.

Seidensticker, John. 1976. "On the Ecological Separation between Tigers and Leopards." *Biotropica* 8 (4): 225–34. https://doi.org/10.2307/2989714.

Sharma, Sandeep, Kamal Thapa, Mukesh Chalise, Trishna Dutta, Yash Veer Bhatnagar, and Thomas McCarthy. 2006. "The Snow Leopard in Himalaya: A Step towards Their Conservation by Studying Their Distribution, Marking Habitat Selection, Co-Existence with Other Predators, and Wild Prey-Livestock-Predator Interaction." In *Conservation Biology in Asia*, edited by J. A. McNeely, T. M. McCarthy, A. Smith, L. Ollsvig-Whittaker, and E. D. Wikramanayake, 184–96. Kathmandu, Nepal: Society for Conservation Biology Asia Section and Resources Himalaya.

Shehzad, Wasim, Thomas Michael McCarthy, Francois Pompanon, Lkhagvajav Purevjav, Eric Coissac, Tiayyba Riaz, and Pierre Taberlet. 2012. "Prey Preference of Snow Leopard (*Panthera uncia*) in South Gobi, Mongolia." Edited by Robert DeSalle. *PLoS ONE* 7 (2): e32104. https://doi.org/10.1371/journal.pone.0032104.

Shehzad, Wasim, Muhammad Ali Nawaz, François Pompanon, Eric Coissac, Tiayyba Riaz, Safdar Ali Shah, and Pierre Taberlet. 2015. "Forest without Prey: Livestock Sustain a Leopard *Panthera pardus* Population in Pakistan." *Oryx* 49 (2): 248–53. https://doi.org/10.1017/S0030605313001026.

Sittert, Lance van. 1998. "'Keeping the Enemy at Bay': The Extermination of Wild Carnivora in the Cape Colony, 1889–1910." *Environmental History* 3 (3): 333–56. https://doi.org/10.2307/3985183.

SLN (Snow Leopard Network). 2014. "Snow Leopard Survival Strategy. Revised 2014 Version." Seattle: Snow Leopard Network. http://snowleopardconservancy.org/wp-content/uploads/2014/10/Snow_Leopard_Survival_Strategy_2014.1-reduced-size.pdf.

Smirnov, M. N., G. A. Sokolov, and N. Zyryanov. 1990. "The Snow Leopard in Siberia." In *International Pedigree Book of Snow Leopards 6*, edited by Leif Blomqvist, 9–15. Helsinki, Finland: Helsinki Zoo.

Snow Leopard Working Secretariat. 2013. Global Snow Leopard and Ecosystem Protection Program. "Bishkek Declaration," Bishkek, Kyrgyz Republic. www.globalsnowleopard.org/who-we-are/bishkek-declaration.

Spence, Mark David. 1999. *Dispossessing the Wilderness: Indian Removal and the Making of the National Parks*. New York: Oxford University Press.

Stebbing, Edward Percy. 1912. *Stalks in the Himalaya: Jottings of a Sportsman-Naturalist*. London: John Lane.

Steneck, R., and E. A. Sala. 2005. "Large Marine Carnivores: Trophic Cascades and Top-down Controls in Coastal Ecosystems Past and Present." In *Large Carnivores and the Conservation of Biodiversity*, edited by J. Ray, K. Redford, R. Steneck, and J. Berger, 110–37. Washington, DC: Island Press.

Stevens, Kara, Alex Dehgan, Maria Karlstetter, Farid Rawan, Muhammad Ismail Tawhid, Stephane Ostrowski, Jan Mohammad Ali, and Rita Ali. 2011. "Large Mammals Surviving Conflict in the Eastern Forests of Afghanistan." *Oryx* 45 (2): 265–71. https://doi.org/10.1017/S0030605310000517.

Sukumar, Raman. *The Story of Asia's Elephants*. Delhi: Marg, 2011.

Suryawanshi, Kulbhushansingh R., Yash Veer Bhatnagar, Stephen Redpath, and Charudutt Mishra. 2013. "People, Predators and Perceptions: Patterns of Livestock Depredation by Snow Leopards and Wolves." Edited by Nathalie Pettorelli. *Journal of Applied Ecology* 50 (3): 550–60. https://doi.org/10.1111/1365-2664.12061.

Swyngedouw, Eric. 2007. "Impossible 'Sustainability' and the Postpolitical Condition." In *The Sustainable Development Paradox: Urban Political Economy in the United States and Europe*, edited by Rob Krueger and David Gibbs, 13–40. New York: Guilford Press.

Taylor, Neville. 1903. *Ibex Shooting on the Himalayas*. London: Sampson Low, Martson & Co.

Trevelyan, Raleigh. 2007. *Golden Oriole: Childhood, Family and Friends in India*. Np.: Long Riders' Guild Press. First published 1987.

Treves, A., and J. Bruskotter. 2014. "Tolerance for Predatory Wildlife." *Science* 344 (6183): 476–77. https://doi.org/10.1126/science.1252690.
Tropp, Jacob. 2002. "Dogs, Poison and the Meaning of Colonial Intervention in the Transkei, South Africa." *Journal of African History* 43 (3): 451–72. https://doi.org/10.1017/S0021853702008186.
Urbigkit, Cat. 2008. *Yellowstone Wolves: A Chronicle of the Animal, the People, and the Politics.* Blacksburg, VA: McDonald & Woodward Pub. Co.
Verdade, Luciano M., and Cláudia B. Campos. 2004. "How Much Is a Puma Worth?: Economic Compensation as an Alternative for the Conflict between Wildlife Conservation and Livestock Production in Brazil." *Biota Neotropica* 4 (2): 1–4. https://doi.org/10.1590/S1676-06032004000200014.
Wang, S. W., and D. W. Macdonald. 2006. "Livestock Predation by Carnivores in Jigme Singye Wangchuck National Park, Bhutan." *Biological Conservation* 129 (4): 558–65. https://doi.org/10.1016/j.biocon.2005.11.024.
Ward, A. E. 1887. The Sportsman's Guide to Kashmir and Ladakh. Calcutta: Calcutta Central Press Co.
Webber, A. D., C. M. Hill, and V. Reynolds. 2007. "Assessing the Failure of a Community-Based Human-Wildlife Conflict Mitigation Project in Budongo Forest Reserve, Uganda." *Oryx* 41 (2): 177–84. https://doi.org/10.1017/S0030605307001792.
Wegge, Per, Rinjan Shrestha, and Øystein Flagstad. 2012. "Snow Leopard *Panthera uncia* Predation on Livestock and Wild Prey in a Mountain Valley in Northern Nepal: Implications for Conservation Management." *Wildlife Biology* 18 (2): 131–41. https://doi.org/10.2981/11-049.
Weiskopf, Sarah R., Shannon M. Kachel, and Kyle P. McCarthy. 2016. "What Are Snow Leopards Really Eating? Identifying Bias in Food-Habit." *Wildlife Society Bulletin* 40 (2): 233–40. https://doi.org/10.1002/wsb.640.
Wescoat, James L. 1995. "The 'Right of Thirst' for Animals in Islamic Law: A Comparative Approach." *Environment and Planning D: Society and Space* 13 (6): 637–54. https://doi.org/10.1068/d130637.
West, Paige. *Conservation Is Our Government Now: The Politics of Ecology in Papua New Guinea.* Durham, NC: Duke University Press, 2006.
West, Paige, James Igoe, and Dan Brockington. 2006. "Parks and Peoples: The Social Impact of Protected Areas." *Annual Review of Anthropology* 35 (1): 251–77. https://doi.org/10.1146/annurev.anthro.35.081705.123308.
Whistler, Hugh. 1924. *In the Himalayas: Sport and Travel in the Rhotang and Baralacha, with Some Notes on the Natural History of That Area.* London: H. F. & G. Witherby.

Worster, Donald. 1994. *Nature's Economy: A History of Ecological Ideas.* 2nd ed. Studies in Environment and History. Cambridge: Cambridge University Press.

Xu, Aichun, Zhigang Jiang, Chunwang Li, Jixun Guo, Shenglin Da, Qinghu Cui, Shuangying Yu, and Guosheng Wu. 2008. "Status and Conservation of the Snow Leopard *Panthera uncia* in the Gouli Region, Kunlun Mountains, China." *Oryx* 42 (3): 460–63. https://doi.org/10.1017/S0030605308000252.

Yu, Li, and Ya-ping Zhang. 2005. "Phylogenetic Studies of Pantherine Cats (Felidae) Based on Multiple Genes, with Novel Application of Nuclear β-Fibrinogen Intron 7 to Carnivores." *Molecular Phylogenetics and Evolution* 35 (2): 483–95. https://doi.org/10.1016/j.ympev.2005.01.017.

INDEX

A

ACAP (Annapurna Conservation Area Project), 68
Aflalo, Frederick George, *Sportsman's Book for India, The*, 33–34
Africa, 40, 42, 45, 100, 173n26
Africa Wildlife Foundation (AWF), 74–75, 76
Aga Khan Foundation, 108
Aga Khan Rural Support Program (AKRSP), 96, 108–10, 113–14, 117, 174n3, 175n9, 176n1
agricultural expansion, 25–26, 40, 166n17
Aita, Judy, 178n8
AKRSP (Aga Khan Rural Support Program), 96, 108–10, 113–14, 117, 174n3, 175n9, 176n1
Ale, Som, 150, 151, 174n2
Ali (Balti assistant), 3
Ali (Shimshal villager), 159
Ali, Afzal, 101
Ali, Ghulam, 98–99, 101
Allah, 95–96, 97, 100, 174n5
Altai Mountains, 16, 24, 165n3
Amboseli National Park, 75–76
America, 40, 41. *See also* United States
American Naturalist, 44

Anchan, Ali Sher, 12
Animal Ecology (Elton), 43
animals, domestic: attitudes toward, 175n11; definition of, 175n8; going wild, 7, 98–99; grazing by, 90; herders and, 100; as prey, 37; religious views toward, 93, 95, 97, 174n5; wild animals and, 97–99, 103, 104–5. *See also* cows; dzo; goats, domestic; sheep, domestic; yaks
animals, mythical, 17–18, 93–94, 103–5, 167n5, 174n2, 175n10
animals, trophy, 14, 26, 31, 32–34, 126
animals, wild: attitudes toward, 167–68n5, 175n11; in captivity, 165n8, 166n15; domestic animals and, 97–99, 104–5, 106; as game animals, 28, 168n6; immobilization of, 46–47, 168n10; religious views toward, 93–97, 174n5; relocation of, 47; small-bodied, 19, 177nn10,11; snow leopards as, 6–7, 66; status of, 15. *See also* cheetahs; goats, wild; ibex; lynx; markhor; tahr; tigers; wolves
Annapurna Conservation Area Project (ACAP), 68

Anthropocene Epoch, 154–55, 180n1
anthropology and anthropologists, 13, 58, 74, 83–84, 100, 104, 154, 166n14, 170–71n6
Astor, Pakistan, 27, 28, 36, 166n20
Audubon Society, 167n3
AWF (Africa Wildlife Foundation), 74–75, 76

B

Bairnsfather, Peter Robert, 29, 34
Baltis: broqs and, 99–100; as ethnic group, 92; views of, 93–96, 97–98, 100–101, 105, 153, 162–63n10, 175n6. *See also* farmers; herders; hunters; snow leopard–farmer conflict; snow leopard–farmer contact
Baltistan: commodification of nature in, 113–14; community organization in, 108–10, 174n3; domestication and wildness in, 99; economic situation of, 89–91; geography of, 13, 89; history of, 12; hunting in, 14, 27–28, 32, 37, 57, 110–13, 166n20; insurance programs in, 116–21; Islamic influence in, 95–97; modernization in, 26–27; people of, 91–92; political situation of, 92–93; research in, 65, 70, 155; as snow leopard habitat, 4, 30, 48; snow leopards as metaphor in, 172n14; surveys in, 121–27; transactional relationships in, 108, 115, 117, 127–28, 157
Baltistan Wildlife Conservation and Development Organization (BWCDO), 60, 83, 107, 119–20, 156–57, 179n16
Barthian transactional order, 115

begaar (forced labor tax), 101
beyul (valleys for refuge), 174n2
Bhutan, 22, 68, 73
Bhutto, Zulfiqar Ali, 92
biodiversity, 45, 56, 73, 77, 80–81, 173n26
biogeographical scale conservation, 169n15
biology and biologists: evolutionary, 18–19; field, 56, 60; molecular, 51; technology and, 21; wildlife, 21, 46–47, 72, 140, 170n5, 171n6, 176n3. *See also* conservation biology and biologists
biotic communities, 43, 162–63n10
birds, 3, 19, 102, 166n21, 167n3
Blaikie, Piers, 153
blue sheep, 4, 80, 82, 171n11
Bonism, 12, 91, 93–95, 96, 100–101, 104, 114, 174n5
bounty payments, 25, 33–34, 40
breeding, interspecies, 90, 99, 104–5
breeding programs, 24, 132, 135, 139, 178nn8,9
British Empire, 24–25
British Raj, 13, 27, 28, 30
Bronx Zoo, 130, 133, 134–36, 140, 177n6, 178n8
broq, 90, 92, 99–102, 100*fig.*, 116
broq-pa (ethnic group), 92
Bruce, Granville, 28
Buddhism, 12, 73, 91, 94, 173n24, 174n2
buffer zones, 55, 56
Burrard, Gerald, 30, 32, 33, 36
Bush, Laura, 135
BWCDO (Baltistan Wildlife Conservation and Development Organization), 60, 83, 107, 119–20, 156–57, 179n16

C

camera traps, 19, 20, 51–52, 103, 144, 149–50, 175n7, 176n4, 179n26
capitalism, 84, 173n26
Carnivora (order), 18
carnivores: agriculture benefiting, 25; conservation of, 53, 79, 168n9; humans and, 6, 15, 155–56; in human-wildlife conflicts, 170n2; hunting of, 167n1; Islamic view of, 95; management of, 164n17; in trophic cascade, 43, 52. *See also* predators
carrying capacity, 126–27
cattle, 90, 91*fig.*, 102, 105, 171n11
cattle ranchers, 173n27
Ceausescu, Nicolae, 167n4
ceremonies, 101, 133–34, 174n2
Chadwick, Doug, 169n14
Chandwat, Raghu, 50
cheetahs, 24, 25–26, 167n4
China, 12, 14, 23, 49, 59, 72, 74, 165n9, 175n13
Chipko movement, 168n7
Chitral Gol National Park, 38, 48, 59
Chundawat, Raghu S., 73, 80
CITES (Convention on International Trade in Endangered Species), 38, 169n16
classification systems, 21–22, 53–54
climate change, 26, 61, 141, 154, 166n15
clouded leopards, 167n6
CNN, 148
coexistence approach to conservation, 79, 154–56, 180n1
Coleman, Jon, 38
Collet, John, 29
colonialism, 13, 15, 25, 40, 42–43, 153, 154, 159, 163n15, 164n2

commodification of nature, 10, 108, 111, 113–14
common leopards, 18, 161n1
compensation programs: benefits of, 172n19, 173n27; effects of, 127, 156–57; ethics and, 79–80; funding for, 75–77; objections to, 74–79, 80–85, 87–88; transactional approach and, 107. *See also* insurance programs
conservation: animal behavior changed by, 106, 175n13; biodiversity, 173n26; community-based, 84, 108–10, 113–14; economic situation of farmers and, 79, 84, 107–8, 173n27; human factor in, 51, 80–81, 107; issues in, 79–80; of natural resources, 42; of nature, 106, 133; political economy of, 8–12, 106, 153; predation aided by, 82, 174n28
conservation approach. *See* landscape-level approach to conservation
conservation biology and biologists: compensation programs and, 77, 83–85, 88; conference participation by, 171n6; farmers and, 12, 57, 66–67, 70, 73, 159, 169n9, 172n20; on human-wildlife conflict, 58, 72; NGOs and, 142; normative positive of, 45–46, 170n5; on predation, 70; research by, 21, 50, 121, 171n12; snow leopard status and, 36; views of, 8
conservation discourse, 41, 52, 55, 104, 161n3, 175n6
conservation institutions, 86*table*; attitudes toward, 106, 154–55; compensation programs and, 79, 83–85, 88, 157; cultural factors used by, 73; data interpretation by, 144–46; disagreements among, 129–31, 139, 142;

INDEX   203

conservation institutions (*continued*) farmers helped by, 13; farmers misunderstood by, 47, 60–61, 64, 66–67, 68, 69, 70–71, 153–54; funding for, 9–11, 83, 87, 141; goals of, 41, 53; human-wildlife conflict and, 57; international influence of, 178n15; landscape-level approach and, 55–56; narratives of, 163n17; policies advocated by, 5–6; protected areas and, 169n15; role of, 58; on snow leopard population, 15–16; as snow leopard protection leaders, 4; transactional approach and, 127–28; wildlife reintroduction and, 163n16

conservation narrative, 14–16, 26–27, 35–36, 37, 58–59, 64, 106

conservation organizations: compensation programs and, 78, 83, 157–58, 172n19, 174n29; cultural factors and, 73; data used by, 144–46; disagreements among, 129–30, 141–43; donors and, 8, 10, 87; farmers helped by, 13; on farmers' losses, 172n21; farmers misunderstood by, 4–6, 76, 153–54, 164n19; funding for, 117, 120–21, 150–51, 164n19, 173n26, 174n29; goals of, 151; insurance and, 117; narrative of, 9–10, 65; population estimates by, 145*table*; protected areas and, 162n9; religious beliefs used by, 95–96; snow leopards and, 164n19; transactional approach and, 107–10, 128

conservation policy, 52–53, 54

conservation scientists, 51, 59, 86–87, 121

Convention on International Trade in Endangered Species (CITES), 38, 169n16

cooperation, 129, 139, 141, 176n5, 178n15
Corbett National Park, 79
core zones, 55, 56
corrals, predator-proof, 107, 120, 121
corridors of connectivity, 54, 55, 56
cows, 90, 91*fig.*, 102, 105, 171n11
Craighead, Frank, 47
Craighead, John, 47
Critically Endangered (status), 15, 151
Crocker, Ryan, 134
Cronon, William, 162n6, 163n11
crops, 58, 77, 90, 170n1, 172n21
Curzon, Lord, 42

D

Darrah, Henry, 32
dart guns, 46–47, 168n10
Dawn (newspaper), 136–37, 138, 150, 164n19, 178n14
deer, 168n6
delisting, 144, 147, 151
development, equitable, 108, 176n1
development institutions and organizations, 13, 108, 110
development projects, 84, 95, 108, 116–18, 128
Dickman, Amy, 79
diet of snow leopards: domestic livestock in, 49, 52, 59–60, 70, 72, 80–82, 124, 155, 164n18, 170n4, 177nn9,11; meat requirement for, 177n11; research lacking on, 86; small-bodied prey in, 177nn10,11
Divyabhanusinh (historian), 24
Dixon, Mary, 136
DNA, 125*table*; in classification, 18; in diet analysis, 52, 60, 81, 170n4; disadvantages of using, 166n13; in population estimation, 121, 124,

126–27; in species identification, 51–52, 60, 124
donors: AKRSP and, 108, 109; Baltistan and, 128; compensation programs and, 157; conservation organizations and, 8, 10, 87; donor countries, 115; influences on, 15, 74, 87; insurance programs and, 119–20, 121; limited funding from, 77; perception of, 11–12, 59
Douglas, Mary, 162n9
Dove, Michael, 130, 153, 163n17
Dowie, Mark, 169n15
downlisting, 9, 146–51, 163–64n17
dzo, 90, 102, 115*fig.*

E

ecological science. *See* ecology
ecology: emergence of science of, 41, 164n2; evolution of science of, 45–46, 169n16; humans excluded from, 46, 47; landscape-level approach and, 54–56; moral, 114; myths and, 105; political, 58, 74; of predators, 39, 44, 46, 47, 52; presentism in, 16; of prey animals, 44–45, 155–56; princely, 163n11; scope of, 43; of snow leopards, 14, 16–21, 37, 41, 49, 57–58, 67–68, 85–86, 123; social, 74
ecosystems: Balti view of, 96–97, 105; in Himalayan environmental degradation theory, 168n7; humans excluded from, 41, 47; humans included in, 155, 168n11; ignorance of, 66–68; importance of, 45–46; livestock depredation and, 72; predators in, 41, 43–44, 52–53, 168n6; snow leopards in, 43, 57, 64, 66–68,

141, 168–69n14; trophic levels and cascades in, 43–44
ecotourism, 113, 117–18, 119
Edwards, Steve, 176n3
elephants, 42, 175n13
Elton, Charles, *Animal Ecology*, 43
Endangered (status), 9, 15, 146–49
Endangered Species Act (1973), 135, 169n16
Endangered Species Program, 38
environment: attitudes toward, 8; awareness of, 14, 164n2; humans and, 90–91, 163n13; knowledge of, 47; Mahoul, compared to, 174n4; species in, 170n2; theories of, 15
environmental conflicts, 8, 164n1
environmental degradation, 14, 164n2, 168n7
ethics, 13, 43, 75–76, 79–80, 84, 95, 108–15, 156, 170n5
Europe, 21–24, 40, 41, 42, 162n7
European Community, 173n26
exchange relationships, 10, 11, 15, 83–84, 104, 111, 157, 164n2
extraction activities, 166n17

F

fairies, 175n10
farmers: average situation of, 90–91; compensation programs and, 74, 75, 76–78, 78–79, 83, 127, 156–57; conservation efforts and, 13, 56, 66–69, 82, 84, 88, 106, 158–59, 162n9; cultural connection to snow leopards, 73–74; economic connection to snow leopards, 9, 11–12, 60; economic situation of, 84; exaggeration by, 70–72, 172nn18,20; as hunters, 5–6, 64, 77, 158; as information source,

farmers (*continued*)
59; insurance programs and, 117–21; livestock loss and, 124, 173n25; organizational packages supplied to, 109; stresses on, 71, 77, 172n21; as threat to snow leopards, 4–5, 6–7, 41, 57–59; transactional relationships and, 117–18; trophy animals and, 114–15; wildlife and, 78. *See also* snow leopard–farmer conflict; snow leopard–farmer contact
fecal specimens. *See* scat
Felidae subfamily, 18
First Microfinance Bank, 176n2
Flagstad, Øystein, 81–83
folks songs, Balti, 175n11
Food and Agriculture Organization, 74, 75
food chains, 43–44, 169n14
food web, 43, 45
forestry, 90, 109, 175n9
Fossey, Dian, 45
Fothergill, Rupert, 47
Foucault, Michel, 113, 114
Fox, Joseph L., 73
Freeman, Helen, 5, 20
Friends of Nairobi National Park, 75–76
Full Moon Night Trekking, 117–18, 119

G

game species, 37, 42, 166n21, 167n1, 168n6
Gannon, J. R. C., 32–33
genetic research. *See* DNA
Gertz, Emily, 179n26
Gilgit, Pakistan (city), 37, 133
Gilgit, Pakistan (province), 12–13, 27–28, 89, 130, 166n20
Gilgit Agency, 37
Gilgit-Baltistan, Pakistan: finance in, 176n2; human-wildlife conflict in, 162n7; hunting in, 27–28, 110; Leo (snow leopard) and, 132–34, 137, 138–39; neoliberal ethic in, 113; political status of, 92; religion in, 96; as snow leopard habitat, 27–28; surveys in, 180n31
Gilgit-Baltistan Forest and Wildlife Department, 130, 133, 158
Gilgit-Srinagar Road, 166n21
Global Environment Facility, 110
Global Snow Leopard and Ecosystem Protection Program (GSLEP). *See* GSLEP (Global Snow Leopard and Ecosystem Protection Program)
Global Snow Leopard Forum (GSLF), 141
Global Tiger Initiative, 142
goats, domestic, 70*fig.*; as commodity, 84; going wild, 7, 98–99; humans and, 69, 90, 102; insurance programs and, 116, 118–19; as partially domesticated, 175n8; as property, 153; snow leopards killing, 3–4, 7, 11–12, 19, 59, 65–66, 73, 173n25; wild animals and, 106
goats, wild, 4, 20, 52, 80–81, 166n21. *See also* ibex; markhor
Gobi region, 170n4
government, aversion to, 78, 105, 159
Greenough, Paul, 164n1
Green World Hypothesis, 44
grizzly bear, 47, 167n4
GSLEP (Global Snow Leopard and Ecosystem Protection Program): budget problems, 86*table*; controversy on, 141–43; expectations for, 129; funding by, 180n32; landscape-level approach

of, 54–55; launching of, 9, 61, 141; results of, 178n15; scope of, 4–5; on snow leopard population, 146; snow leopard status and, 150, 151; on threats to snow leopard, 61, 62–63*table*, 87

GSLF (Global Snow Leopard Forum), 141

guns, 3, 29, 32, 166n21, 176n4

Guthman, Julie, 47

H

habitat of snow leopards, 17*map*, 86*table*; in China, 165n9; degradation of, 61, 171n8, 171n9; description of, 26; disagreements over, 64–65, 68; encroachment on, 5, 15, 27, 171n8; inaccessibility of, 20–21; livestock increase in, 171n10; misconceptions about, 154; in Pakistan, 150, 180n30; population density and, 126, 143–44, 149; range of, 29–30; research on, 49, 53, 85, 87, 164–65n3, 165n11; size of, 50; suitability of, 20, 36–37, 56; threats to, 166n17

Haider Tughalt, Mirza, *Tārīkh-e-Rāshidī*, 12

Haila, Yrjö, 45

Haji (Hushe person), 101, 106

halal and haram, 105

Helsinki Zoo, 22

Hemis National Park, 50

herbivores, 43–44, 52, 95, 171n11. *See also* prey animals

herders, 91*fig*.; attitudes toward, 5, 68–69; broqs and, 99–100; Chinese, 23; cultural influences on, 6–7; economic situation of, 161–62n4; as information source, 122, 175n7, 176–77n7; insurance programs and, 116–18; snow leopards and, 101–3. *See also* farmers

Hillard, Darla, *Vanishing Tracks*, 50

Himalaya Mountains, 13, 15, 49, 78, 107, 155, 168n7

Himalayan environmental degradation theory, 15, 168n7

Hindu Kush, 49, 165n3

Hla and Hlu (Bon deities), 93–94

Holocene epoch, 27

Hornberg, Alf, 154

Hughes, Julie, 163n11

human-human conflict, 12, 56–58

human populations, 4, 25, 54–55, 64–65, 67

humans and environment, 90–91, 163n13

humans in Islamic view, 95

human-wildlife conflict, 86*table*; characteristics of, 8; compensation programs and, 107; definition of, 169–70n1; domains of, 170n2; ecosystem in, 65–68; funding for management of, 87; habitat in, 64–65; human-human conflict and, 12, 56–58; in India, 164n1; as inherent issue, 168n11; livestock loss and, 59–61, 68–72, 81–82, 172–73n22; location of, 162n7; snow leopards threatened in, 61; sociological issues in, 77–79; solutions to, 72–77, 79; tigers in, 25; unanticipated, 47. *See also* snow leopard–farmer conflict

human-wildlife contact, 6, 15, 16–18, 34–36, 52, 54, 56, 162n9, 165n4

Hunter, Luke, 53

hunters: of big game, 13, 37; as information source, 122, 175n7, 177n7; in myth, 94, 104; pelts taken by, 22–23,

hunters (*continued*)
29–30; status of, 101; written accounts by, 19, 27–29, 30–33, 166nn18,19

hunting: by British officials for food, 166n21; by farmers, 5–6, 64, 77, 158; of game species, 167n1; in India, 163n11, 166n14; licenses for, 33–34, 110, 112, 166n20; of predators, 24–25, 26, 41; restrictions on, 24, 53, 77, 105, 110, 176n4; rulers associated with, 167n4. *See also* trophy hunting

Hunza area, Pakistan, 13, 104, 111, 114, 127, 158, 171n11

Huq Khan, Mahmudul, 130

Hushe Valley, 120*table*, 122*fig.*, 125*table*, 127*fig.*; domestic animals in, 98–99; livestock predation in, 65, 121, 122; prey animals in, 171–72n13; snow leopard population in, 124, 126, 127; trophy hunting in, 111

Hushe village, Pakistan, 106, 158

Hussain, Shafqat, 170–71n5, 171n11

Huxley, Julian, 45

I

ibex: as commodity, 111, 115; cultural dynamics and, 175n12, 176n5; domestic animals joining, 7, 98–99; ethics and, 114; in myth, 94–95, 104; population of, 126, 171nn11,13; as prey, 4, 30–31, 35, 106; as trophy animal, 13, 14, 28, 110, 112, 115; villagers' perception of, 67

Ibraheem (Hushe farmer), 173n25

Ifikhar, Usman, 176n6

India: attitudes toward predators in, 166n16, 167n4, 169n16; compensation programs in, 78–79; environmental conflicts in, 164n1; environmental movements in, 168n7; hunting in, 25, 28, 33, 40–41, 166n14, 167n4, 173n23; livestock predation in, 66; Pakistan and, 13, 92–93; princely ecology in, 163n11; research in, 50; wildlife conservation in, 42, 53, 169n16, 175n13

Indus River and area, 13, 26, 89, 116, 126

industrialization, 26–27, 38, 154, 166n17

infrastructure, 108–10, 118, 171n8

instrumentality, 108, 111, 114–15, 157

Insurance Committees, 118–19, 120–21

insurance programs, 81, 83, 107, 116–21, 127–28. *See also* compensation programs

International Pedigree Book of Snow Leopards, 22

International Union for Conservation of Nature (IUCN). *See* IUCN (International Union for Conservation of Nature); Red List of Threatened Species

interviews with local people, 59, 121–23, 172n22, 176–77n7

irrigation channels, 89–90, 109, 112–13

Islam: on animals, 95–97, 101, 156, 162n10, 174n5; Bonism and, 93, 114, 174n5; fundamentalist perception of, 139; government policy and, 105; myths and, 104; in Pakistan, 12, 91–92

island biogeography (theory), 44, 45

Isle Royale National Park, 44

IUCN (International Union for Conservation of Nature): classification by, 165n7; Leo (snow leopard) and, 130, 132–34; population estimates by, 144, 148, 149; programs of, 110; rationalizations by, 169n15; staff of, 176n3; status assessments by, 9, 146–

47, 150–52, 157, 163–64n17. *See also* Red List of Threatened Species
ivory, 173nn26,27

J

Jackson, Rodney, 21, 49–50, 142, 143–44, 146
Jalais, Annu, 8, 163n15
Judeo-Christian beliefs, 162–63n10
"jungle," 99, 175n9

K

Kanchenjunga National Park, 174n28
Karakoram Highway, 130
Karakoram Mountains and area, 13, 28, 49, 78, 97–98, 107, 155, 165n3
Kashmir Game Preservation Department, 33–34, 166n20
Kashmir region, 27–28, 29, 91–92
Kaufmann, General, 22
Kennion, Roger Lloyd, 28, 31–32
Kesar (cultural hero), 94, 104
Khunjerab National Park, 130
Khyber-Pukhtunkhwa (KPK) province, 132, 133–34, 137, 139
killing by snow leopards, surplus, 7, 35, 163n11
killing of snow leopards: retaliatory, 7, 72–73, 87, 108, 148–49, 173nn24,25; traditional, 61
kings, 167n4
Kinloch, Alexander, 36
Knight, John, 58
knowledge production, 9, 45, 47
KPK (Khyber-Pukhtunkhwa) province, 132, 133–34, 137, 139
Krabathang, Pakistan, and area, 97–98, 126

Krabathang Village Conservation Committee, 97
Kyrgyzstan, 129, 178n15

L

Lacey Act (1900), 167n3
Ladakh, India, 12–13, 50, 59–60, 73
landscape as habitat, 68, 80, 93, 97, 105, 106, 155
landscape-level approach to conservation, 10, 54–56, 71, 142
Langu Gorge, Nepal, 49, 59
Late Glacial Maximum (LGM), 165n3
Latour, Bruno, and Latourian insight, 154, 180n2
Lawrence, Walter, 29, 35
Leipzig Zoo, 22
Leo (snow leopard): in Bronx Zoo, 177n6; ceremony for hand-over of, 133; children's book about, 140; decisions about, 132–35; publicity about, 135–37; transfer of, to United States, 129; transnational relationships and, 130–32, 137–39, 140–41, 178nn8,14
leopards, clouded, 167n6
leopards, common, 18, 161n1
leopards, snow. *See* snow leopards
Leopold, Aldo, *Sand County Almanac, A*, 43
LGM (Late Glacial Maximum), 165n3
Line of Control, 13, 93
line transect, 175n7
Linnaeus, Carl, 21–22
lions, 18, 42, 45, 66
livestock: commercialization of, 171n10; compensation for loss of, 157–58; grazing by, 90; population of, 64–65, 126, 171n11; risk to, 170n2; in snow

INDEX 209

livestock (*continued*)
  leopard density prediction, 171n12; in tiger diet, 79; as unnatural prey, 66, 81–82, 88, 154, 155–56
livestock in snow leopard diet: historical views on, 34–36; of old and disabled animals, 65–66, 171–72n13; percentage of, 59–60, 124, 155, 170n4, 177n9; as "subsidy," 12, 80–83; sufficient numbers of, 126; as supplement to wild prey, 177n11
livestock predation, 120*table*; causes of, 5, 68–69, 82; compensation for, 74–77; conservationists' view of, 5, 88, 161–62n4, 162n9; disagreements over, 64, 65–66, 68–69, 70–72; economic damage of, 70–71; farmers' view of, 6–7, 72–73, 162n9; funding helped by, 9; high level areas of, 4, 121; insurance for, 116; level of, 59–61, 122–23; measurement of, 172–73n22; as natural act, 156, 158; research on, 46
Li Yu (Chinese scholar), 18
Lolly (snow leopard), 139
Lorimer, David, 104
Lydekker, Richard, 22, 35
lynx, 46, 72, 168n9

M

Maasai, 75
macaque monkeys, 173n23
Macdonald, D. W., 68
MacDonald, Ken, 111, 114
Madagascar, 100
Mahoul (environment), 96, 174n4
Mallon, David, 146
Malm, Andreas, 154
Mammals of Pakistan, The (Roberts), 38–39

market rationality, 113–14, 117
Markham, Fred, 33, 35, 36, 37
markhor: in conservation programs, 110; hunting of, 14, 28, 110, 112, 115; population of, 126; as prey, 4, 30–31, 35, 67, 106, 115–16; sharing habitat with snow leopards, 36
marmots, 19, 177nn10,11
masculinity and power, 140–41
Matthiessen, Peter, *Snow Leopard, The*, 38–39
maximum entropy algorithm, 165n3
McCarthy, Tom, 50, 146, 148; *Snow Leopards*, 149, 179n26
meaning, 8, 114–15, 163n14
Medina, Laurie, 113
megafauna, 151
Mehdi (farmer), 98
Memorandum of Understanding, 131, 136–37, 138, 139
mergich realm (myth), 175n10
microscopes, 60
Mishra, Charudutt, 146–47, 150
molecular analysis, 18, 21, 51
Mongolia, 23, 49, 50, 59, 72–73, 101, 170n4
monkeys, 173n23
moose, 44
Moscow Zoological Garden, 22
Mountain Areas Conservancy Project, 110, 113–14, 176n3
mountain fairies, 175n10
mountain lions, 47
Mount Everest National Park, 52
Murdoch, Colin, 46
Musharraf, Pervaiz, 135
Musharraf, Sehba, 134–35, 178n8
myths, 17–18, 93–94, 103–5, 167n5, 174n2, 175n10

N

Nairobi National Park, 75–76
Naltar Valley and area, 130, 139, 171n11
National Geographic, 49, 168–69n14
national parks, 42, 46, 65, 78, 169n16. *See also names of specific national parks*
natural disasters, 130, 163n17
Natural History Museum, 37
nature, views of, 41–42, 93–96, 104–5
nature and culture: boundaries between, 61, 83, 163n13, 175n6; coexistence of, 154–56; as fluid, 97–99; human-wildlife conflict in, 81–82; in modern era, 180n2; predators disturbing, 61; *rashore* animals and, 7; resource flow between, 83, 163n10; as separate, 6, 175n6
NBC news, 135
neoliberalism, 84, 108–10, 110–15
Nepal, 15, 47, 49, 59, 68, 82–83, 101, 174n28
NGOs: compensation programs and, 74–76, 78–79; funding by, 180n32; governmental views toward, 133–34; local views toward, 105–6, 108, 116–17, 128, 158; religious views toward, 96, 105; spectacular accumulation by, 10; transactional relationships and, 114–15
9/11 attacks, 119, 134
North America, 38, 162n7, 173n27
Northern Areas Wildlife Preservation Act (1975), 38
Norway, 175n13

O

Operation Noah, 47
otters, 103–5
ounces. *See* snow leopards

P

packages (subsidized supplies), 109
Paine, Robert, 44
Pakistan: Baltistan and, 92–93; conservation movements in, 6, 55, 107–8, 169n16, 176n3; finance in, 176n2; Food, Agriculture and Forests of Northern Areas, 137; India and, 13, 92–93; Kashmir and, 92; Ministry of Climate Change, 150, 151–52, 177n1; Ministry of Environment, 130–31, 132, 133, 136–37, 177n1; political instability of, 119; self-image of, 132–33, 139; snow leopards in, 48–49, 123, 150; surveys in, 180n31; trophy hunting in, 110; United States and, 129, 131–33, 134–36, 139–41, 178n8; wildlife in, 26; wildlife rehabilitation facility for, 135–39, 177n2, 178n8; world image of, 134
Pamir Mountains, 165n3
Panthera (genus), 18, 53, 165n6
Panthera (organization), 4, 53, 142, 144–45, 145*table*, 148, 149, 150
Panthera uncia. See snow leopards
Panther tigiris. See tigers
Partition (1947), 13
pastoralism, 26–27, 65
pasturage, 67–68, 70*fig.*
pasture settlements. *See* broq
paw prints, 7, 121
PAWS (Population Assessment of World Snow Leopards), 11
pelts of snow leopards: in ceremonies, 101; as collector's items, 14, 32, 33, 37; sources of, 22–23, 29–30, 59; as tax payments, 17; trade of, 24
pikas, 19, 177n10

poaching, 86*table*; control of, 24, 87, 168n9, 173n26; hunting by locals as, 176n4; snow leopard–farmer conflicts and, 59; as threat to snow leopards, 146, 148–49

poisons, 57, 101

policy lack as threat to snow leopards, 61

politics and science, 168n7

Population Assessment of World Snow Leopards (PAWS), 11

population of snow leopards, 62–63*table*, 85*table*, 125*table*, 145*table*; artificially high, 4; assessment of, 51–52, 121–24, 126–28, 143–44; conflicting reports on, 15–16, 23–24, 38, 147–50, 180n30; as difficult to assess, 11, 36–37, 144, 146, 161n2, 179n26; naturally low, 27; protection for, 4–5, 83; stable, 156; threats to, 4, 23, 59–61

power, 8, 9, 13, 47, 140–41, 162n6

PPIs (Productive Physical Infrastructures), 108, 109–10, 176n1

predator-prey theory, 44–45, 155

predators: alpha, 167n5; apex, 57, 172n20; attitudes toward, 37–39, 41, 43–45, 57, 78, 166n16, 167n4, 167–68n5, 172n14, 173n24; conservation of, 66, 169n16; economic value of fur-bearing, 168n9; environmental movements and, 42–43; eradication of, 25, 40, 78, 168n6; human culture and, 167–68n5; keystone, 52, 57, 72, 105; in predator-prey theory, 44–45, 155; religious views toward, 96, 173n24; research on, 21, 45–47, 52–53; role of, 43–44, 67, 168n6; views of, 8, 24–25, 72–73. *See also* carnivores; snow leopards; species, keystone

prey animals, 86*table*; carrying capacity and, 126–27; density of, 50, 121, 123; depletion of, 64, 146; domestic, 171–72n13; "natural" and "unnatural," 155–56; predators and, 44–45, 52, 67, 105; small-bodied, 177n10; snow leopards and, 126–27, 171n12; sufficient numbers of, 61, 177n11; wild and domestic ratio of, 4–6, 16, 35, 59, 65–66, 81

production modes, 154, 162n10

Productive Physical Infrastructures (PPIs), 108, 109–10, 176n1

Project Snow Leopard. *See* BWCDO (Baltistan Wildlife Conservation and Development Organization)

Project Tiger, 41

protected areas approach to conservation: background of, 6; disagreements and, 64; as doomed, 180n2; expansion of, 169n15; funding of, 76–77; humans excluded from, 162n9; human-wildlife conflict and, 162n7; landscape-level conservation and, 142; predator conservation and, 47; rationalization for, 53, 156; research and, 51; as solution, 82; theories of, 45; wilderness approach and, 154

Putin, Vladimir, 142

Q

Qatal gah (mosque), 94

Qazi (Pakistani man), 97

Qilian Mountains, 165n3

Quammen, David, 167n5

Quran, 97

R

radio collars, 20, 21, 46–47, 48, 49, 50–51, 165n12
Rajatarangini (Sanscrit chronicle), 12
rashore goats, 7, 98–99
Rasool, Ghulam, 100*fig.*, 102
Rawat, G. S., 80
reciprocity, 10, 15, 83–84, 111, 157
Red List of Threatened Species, 9, 15, 143–44, 146, 151, 163n17, 168n12. *See also* IUCN (International Union for Conservation of Nature)
Rhodesia, 47
rifles. *See* guns
Rimpoche (Indian guru), 174n2
Ritvo, Harriet, 167n22
robdar animals, 101
Roberts, Rom, *Mammals of Pakistan, The*, 38
rock drawings, 16–17
romanticism, 166n19
Rondu Valley, 89, 97, 116, 120*table*, 122, 125*table*, 126, 127*fig.*
Roosevelt, Theodore, 167n4
rulers, 42–43, 167n4, 172n14
Rundall, Lionel B., 31
Russia, 14, 20, 22, 23, 46, 142
Rutherford, Brad, 148

S

Sadpara Lake, Pakistan, and area, 3, 73, 103
Sagarmatha National Park, 60, 80–81
Samelius, Gustav, 179n26
Sand County Almanac, A (Leopold), 43
scat, 125*table*; collection of, 175n7; diet and, 4, 49, 51, 59–61, 81, 121, 124, 170n4; in snow leopard density estimation, 56; in snow leopard population estimation, 48, 121, 126, 150, 179n26; species identification from, 177n8; visual analysis of, 59–60
Schaller, George: on hunting, 34; research methods of, 176n7; on snow leopard sightings, 21; snow leopard studies by, 48–50, 123; *Stones of Silence*, 48; on villagers, 161n3; writings of, 38, 45, 166n18
Schreber, Johann Christian Daniel von, 21–22
Science, 150
science, metropolitan, 173n26
science and politics, 168n7
scientists, 122*fig.*, 170–71n6
Seidensticker, John, 47, 168n10
September 11, 2001 attacks, 119, 134
Serengeti Research Project, 44
settlements, summer. *See* broq
Shakoor (native guide), 67, 103–4, 105
shamans, 93, 101
Shayok River, 89
sheep, domestic, 19, 69, 90, 98–99, 102
sheep, wild, 4, 16, 19, 80, 82, 171n11
Shigar River and Valley, 89
shikar (the hunt), 166n14
shikaris (local hunting guides), 23, 30, 168n10
Shimshal, Pakistan, 65, 159, 171n11
Shin (ethnic group), 92
Shrestha, Rinjan, 81–83
Siberia, 16–17, 20, 21
signs (sign density), 121–22, 124, 126, 176n7
Singh, Ranjeet, 12–13
sink populations, 55

Skardu, Pakistan (district), 12–13

Skardu, Pakistan (town and area), 3, 89, 91, 94, 103

Skoyo area, Pakistan, 107, 115–17, 118

Skoyo broq, 100*fig.*, 102

SLC (Snow Leopard Conservancy), 4, 141, 142, 145*table*, 150, 179n16

SLIMS (Snow Leopard Information Management System), 11, 51, 125*table*, 166n13, 168n12

SLSS (Snow Leopard Survival Strategy): on conservation efforts, 76–77; on farming, 4–5, 64, 66; goals of, 171n7; scope of, 61, 162n6; snow leopard population estimates by, 144; on threats to snow leopard, 61, 62–63*table*

SLT (Snow Leopard Trust), 4, 10, 20, 51, 61, 141, 142, 144–45, 145*table*, 148, 149–51

Smithsonian Museum, 44

Snow Leopard, The (Matthiessen), 38–39

Snow Leopard Conservancy (SLC), 4, 141, 142, 145*table*, 150, 176n16

snow leopard–farmer conflict, 16, 34–35, 59, 64, 74, 153–54

snow leopard–farmer contact, 5, 11, 66, 87, 101, 107, 128, 153, 155–56, 158

Snow Leopard Information Management System (SLIMS), 11, 51, 166n13, 168n12

Snow Leopard Network, 142

snow leopards, 7*fig.*, 62–63*table*, 86*table*; attacks by, 102, 103; attitudes toward, 6–7, 56–57, 72–73, 115; behavior of, 3–4, 6, 19–20, 56, 106, 147; breeding by, 18–19, 55, 146–47, 147–48, 178n15; breeding programs for, 24, 132, 139, 178nn8,9;

in captivity, 19–20, 22–23, 30, 139, 165n9, 166n15; in China, 74; classification of, 18, 22, 123, 143, 146–51, 165n7; commodification of, 10–11; compared to human rulers, 6; conservation of, 4, 8–12, 169n16; conservation organizations and, 164n19; density of, 56, 82, 171n12; distribution of, 16–21, 29–30, 85–86; ecosystem of, 65–68; elusiveness of, 4, 14, 16, 27, 34, 36–38, 101–3, 166n18; as Endangered species, 15, 16; home range countries of, 16; home range of, 20, 48, 49, 50, 53, 61, 141, 150, 178n15; hunting of, 28–29; identification of, 177n8; in international relations, 178n15; killed by farmers, 172n18; livestock depredation by, 34–36; longevity of, 18–19; in myth, 103–5, 174n2; narrative of, 162n6; ontology of, 27, 64, 65–68, 153; perception of, 4, 7, 14, 17–18, 24, 30–32, 38–39, 156–57; physical description of, 18, 20, 48; political economy of, 129–30; potential eradication of, 41; as predators of livestock, 6–7, 49, 52, 87–88, 116, 120*table*, 148, 155–56, 158, 162n9, 171–72n13, 172–73n22; as predators of wild animals, 30–32, 36–38, 48–52, 52–53, 168–69n14; range of, 89; religious views toward, 94, 96–97; research on, 85–87, 85*chart*, 123*map*, 175n7; role of, 67; scat of, 59–61, 170n4; status of, 9–10, 16–21, 38–39, 52–53, 129–30, 163–64n17; tame, 17; territoriality of, 48, 56; as threatened species, 27; threats to, 61, 166n17; as trophy animals, 32–34; trophy animals and, 84–85;

in Western Europe, 21–24; in zoos, 14. *See also* diet of snow leopards; habitat of snow leopards; Leo (snow leopard); population of snow leopards

Snow Leopards (McCarthy et al.), 149, 179n26

Snow Leopard Summit (2002), 61

Snow Leopard Survival Strategy (SLSS). *See* SLSS (Snow Leopard Survival Strategy)

Snow Leopard Trust (SLT), 4, 10, 20, 51, 61, 141, 142, 144–45, 145*table*, 148, 149–51

social sciences and scientists, 8, 58, 74, 84, 87–88, 142, 151, 168n7, 176n3

source populations, 55

South Africa, 176n3

Soviet Union, 16, 22–24, 149, 171n10

spang (grassy meadow), 98

species, economic, 42, 167n3, 168nn6,9

species, keystone, 4, 39, 44, 52, 57, 159. *See also* predators, keystone

species, prey. *See* prey animals

species, wild, 15, 43, 45, 53–54

spectacular accumulation, 10, 87

specters and spectacles, 10, 11, 164n20

Sportsman's Book for India, The (Aflalo), 33–34

Sportsman's Guide to Kashmir and Ladak, The (Ward), 30

Srinigar, Kashmir, 23

Stebbing, Edward Percy, 19, 30, 33, 36

Stones of Silence (Schaller), 48

sub-alpine zones, 169n14

subsidies: compensation as, 79; for farmers, 76, 84, 90, 109; for insurance programs, 117, 119; livestock depredation as, 12, 60, 76, 80–83, 155, 157

surveys, 123*map*; controversy over, 149; damage assessment, 70, 71, 172n19; emphasis on, 87; of households, 180n31; insurance and, 116–21; methodology for, 11, 51, 176–77n7; results of, 59, 176n4; semiotics and, 121–27; technology for, 51

sustainability of conservation programs, 74, 156–57

Swyngedouw, Eric, 163n13

T

tahr, 52, 80–81

Takht-e-Sulieman (Throne of Soloman), 102

Taqi (Basho Valley man), 105

Tārīkh-e-Rāshidī (Haider Tughalt), 12

Taubuche (mountain god), 174n2

taxes, 17, 30–31, 101, 172n14

Taylor, Peter, 45

technology, 57, 153, 165–66n13

telemetry, 21, 50, 165n12

Tensley, Arthur, 43

terrorism, 119, 129, 131, 132, 134, 139

Theory of Himalayan Degradation, 15, 168n7

Thomas, Patrick, 135

Throne of Solomon (Takht-e-Sulieman), 102

Tian Shan Mountains, 165n3

Tibet and Tibetan influence, 12, 91–92, 94

tigers: capturing of, 168n10; in conservation programs, 53, 141–42, 175n13; habitat of, 25, 26; hunting of, 25, 40, 167n4; perceptions of, 163n15, 166n16; as predators, 79, 173n25; research on, 47; taxonomy of, 18–19; in tiger-human conflict, 25

totemism, 42, 104
trade, illegal, 148–49, 167n3
trade bans, 38
traditional and modern, 84
TRAFFIC, 148–49
transactional approach, 107–8, 115, 117, 127–28, 157
transcendental perspective on nature, 41–42
transhumance, 89, 90
transscience, 164n17
trapping, 22–23, 29–30, 37, 101, 127, 158, 168n10
trekking, 29, 117–18, 177n7
Trevelyan, Raleigh, 37
trophic cascade, 43–45, 52–53, 67, 95, 168–69n14
trophic levels, 43–44, 52
trophy animals, 14, 26, 28–29, 31, 32–34, 126
trophy hunting, 13, 27–28, 84–85, 110, 111–15, 116–17, 126, 175n12, 176n4

U

Uncia uncia. See snow leopards
ungulates, domestic, 52, 60, 105
ungulates, wild: in Balti view, 105; foraging preference of, 52; as prey, 44–45, 60, 81, 161n4, 177n11; snow leopard population and, 5, 124; as trophy animals, 85
United Nations, 110, 135, 178n8
United States: conservation movements in, 6, 167n3, 169n16; ivory trade and, 173n26; Pakistan and, 129, 131–33, 134–36, 139–41, 178n8; predators in, 42, 78
urban settlement, 38, 166n17
US Department of State, 178n8

US Fish and Wildlife Services, 38
USSR, 16, 22–23, 149, 171n10
utilitarian perspective on nature, 41–42

V

Vanishing Tracks (Hillard), 50
vegetation, 20, 25, 52, 169n14
vermin, predators as, 4, 14, 25, 33–34, 41, 107
village insurance committees, 118–19, 120–21
Village Organizations, 108–10, 176nn1,2
Vulnerable (status), 9, 15, 149–50, 151

W

Wang, S. W., 68
war as threat to snow leopard, 61
Ward, A. E., 34; *Sportsman's Guide to Kashmir and Ladak, The*, 30
warming period (Holocene), 27
water supply, 89–90, 108–9
WCS (Wildlife Conservation Society): as conservation leader, 4; farmer losses and, 172n21; Leo (snow leopard) and, 130–31, 132, 133, 135–36, 138–39; misrepresentations of, 140; Pakistan and, 134, 139, 177n2; Panthera (organization) and, 142; on snow leopard population, 144–46, 145*fig.*, 149; on snow leopard status, 150
Wegge, Per, 81–83
Whistler, Hugh, 31
wild and domesticated, 7, 81–82, 83, 88, 93–94, 97–99, 156, 174n29. *See also* nature and culture
wilderness, 38, 40, 42, 53, 68, 163n11, 167n22

wilderness approach to conservation, 154, 180n2
Wildlife Conservation Society (WCS). *See* WCS (Wildlife Conservation Society)
wildlife rehabilitation facility, 131, 134, 135–39, 177n2, 178n8
wildlife reintroduction, 8, 46, 80–81, 163n16
wolves: confused with other animals, 172n17; in conservation programs, 175n13; ecosystem role of, 44; European, 40; as predators, 116, 163n12, 172n22; reintroduction of, 8, 173n27; research on, 46; as symbol, 38, 167n4
Woodland Park Zoo, 61
World Bank, 9, 61, 129, 141–42
World Parks Commission, 169n15
World Wildlife Fund (WWF), 4, 45, 79, 130, 132, 133–34, 141, 144–45, 145*table*
Wyoming, 78

Y

yaks, 56, 65, 90, 105, 171n11
Ya-ping Zhang (Chinese scholar), 18
Yellowstone National Park, 47, 173n27

Z

Zafiminary (African ethnic group), 100
Zambezi River and dam, 47
Zoological Society (England), 22
zoos, 14, 22, 24, 61, 165n9, 166n15. *See also* Bronx Zoo
Zorllick, Robert, 142

CULTURE, PLACE, AND NATURE
Studies in Anthropology and Environment

The Kuhls of Kangra: Community-Managed Irrigation in the Western Himalaya, by Mark Baker

The Earth's Blanket: Traditional Teachings for Sustainable Living, by Nancy Turner

Property and Politics in Sabah, Malaysia: Native Struggles over Land Rights, by Amity A. Doolittle

Border Landscapes: The Politics of Akha Land Use in China and Thailand, by Janet C. Sturgeon

From Enslavement to Environmentalism: Politics on a Southern African Frontier, by David McDermott Hughes

Ecological Nationalisms: Nature, Livelihood, and Identities in South Asia, edited by Gunnel Cederlöf and K. Sivaramakrishnan

Tropics and the Traveling Gaze: India, Landscape, and Science, 1800–1856, by David Arnold

Being and Place among the Tlingit, by Thomas F. Thornton

Forest Guardians, Forest Destroyers: The Politics of Environmental Knowledge in Northern Thailand, by Tim Forsyth and Andrew Walker

Nature Protests: The End of Ecology in Slovakia, by Edward Snajdr

Wild Sardinia: Indigeneity and the Global Dreamtimes of Environmentalism, by Tracey Heatherington

Tahiti Beyond the Postcard: Power, Place, and Everyday Life, by Miriam Kahn

Forests of Identity: Society, Ethnicity, and Stereotypes in the Congo River Basin, by Stephanie Rupp

Enclosed: Conservation, Cattle, and Commerce among the Q'eqchi' Maya Lowlanders, by Liza Grandia

Puer Tea: Ancient Caravans and Urban Chic, by Jinghong Zhang

Andean Waterways: Resource Politics in Highland Peru, by Mattias Borg Rasmussen

Conjuring Property: Speculation and Environmental Futures in the Brazilian Amazon, by Jeremy M. Campbell

Forests Are Gold: Trees, People, and Environmental Rule in Vietnam, by Pamela D. McElwee

The Nature of Whiteness: Race, Animals, and Nation in Zimbabwe, by Yuka Suzuki

Organic Sovereignties: Struggles over Farming in an Age of Free Trade, by Guntra A. Aistara

Caring for Glaciers: Land, Animals, and Humanity in the Himalayas, by Karine Gagné

Living with Oil and Coal: Resource Politics and Militarization in Northeast India, by Dolly Kikon

Working with the Ancestors: Mana *and Place in the Marquesas Islands,* by Emily C. Donaldson

Roses from Kenya: Labor, Environment, and the Global Trade in Cut Flowers, by Megan A. Styles

The Snow Leopard and the Goat: Politics of Conservation in the Western Himalayas, by Shafqat Hussain

Printed by Libri Plureos GmbH in Hamburg, Germany